Social constructionist
psychology

Social constructionist psychology

**A critical analysis of theory
and practice**

**EDITED BY
DAVID J. NIGHTINGALE AND
JOHN CROMBY**

Open University Press
Buckingham · Philadelphia

Open University Press
Celtic Court
22 Ballmoor
Buckingham
MK18 1XW

email: enquiries@openup.co.uk
world wide web: http://www.openup.co.uk

and
325 Chestnut Street
Philadelphia, PA 19106, USA

First Published 1999

A catalogue record of this book is available from the British Library

ISBN 0 335 20192 X (pb)   0 335 20193 8 (hb)

Library of Congress Cataloging-in-Publication Data
Social constructionist psychology : a critical analysis of theory and
   practice / edited by David J. Nightingale and John Cromby.
        p.   cm.
     Includes bibliographical references and index.
     ISBN 0–335–20193–8 (hbk)   ISBN 0–335–20192–X (pbk)
     1. Social psychology. 2. Social perception. 3. Cultural
relativism. 4. Subjectivity. 5. Discourse analysis.
6. Psychology—Philosophy. I. Nighingale, David J., 1963– .
II. Cromby, John, 1961– .
HM1033.S63   1999
302—dc21   99–25217
                                                        CIP

Typeset by Graphicraft Limited, Hong Kong
Printed in Great Britain by Biddles Limited, Guildford and Kings Lynn

This book is dedicated to Emerald, Liam and Naomi
and to the memory of Rex Stainton Rogers

Contents

Notes on contributors

Ian Burkitt lectures in sociology and social psychology at the University of Bradford, UK. He is the author of *Social Selves* (1991) and his latest book is *Bodies of Thought: Social Relations, Activity and Embodiment* (1999).

Erica Burman is Professor of Psychology and Women's Studies in the Discourse Unit at the Manchester Metropolitan University. Her work is in the areas of feminist critiques of developmental psychology, critical reflections on psychological theory and practices, models of subjectivity and discourse. Her books include *Deconstructing Developmental Psychology* (1994), *Psychology Discourse Practice: From Regulation to Resistance* (co-authored, 1996), *Challenging Women: Psychology's Exclusions, Feminist Possibilities* (co-authored, 1996), *Feminists and Psychological Practice* (edited, 1990) and *Deconstructing Feminist Psychology* (edited, 1998).

Vivien Burr is Principal Lecturer in psychology in the Department of Behavioural Sciences, University of Huddersfield. Her previous publications include *An Introduction to Social Constructionism* (1995) and *Invitation to Personal Construct Psychology* (with Trevor Butt, 1992).

Trevor Butt is a senior lecturer in psychology in the School of Human and Health Sciences at the University of Huddersfield. He trained as a clinical psychologist and worked in the NHS before becoming a teacher. His published work is mainly concerned with personal construct theory. He has written about both its clinical applications and its elaboration as a social psychology. He is currently interested in the existential phenomenology of Merleau-Ponty, and its relevance to postmodern thought and constructivism.

John Cromby teaches psychology in the Department of Interdisciplinary Human Studies at the University of Bradford, UK. Before this he worked as a researcher in medical settings, including learning disabilities and drug addiction. His research has been concerned with issues of self, identity and subjectivity, and with educational applications of 'virtual reality' computer systems. He can be contacted via email at J.Cromby@bradford.ac.uk

Rom Harré graduated in mathematics and physics and then in philosophy and anthropology at the University of Auckland. He did postgraduate work in Oxford under J. L. Austin. His published work includes studies in the philosophy of both the natural and human sciences, such as *Varieties of Realism* (1986) and the trilogy *Social Being* (1979), *Personal Being* (1983) and *Physical Being* (1991). His current research interests have been concerned with the ways that language enters into all aspects of human life, including the sense of self (reported in *Pronouns and People*, 1990, with P. Muhlhausler) and the emotions. His most recent book in this area is *The Discursive Mind*, with G. Gillett (1994). He has also been involved in theoretical studies of the computational model of mind popularized as artificial intelligence. He is currently Professor of Psychology at Georgetown University, Washington, DC, and Emeritus Fellow, Linacre College, Oxford, UK.

Christine Kenwood is a graduate student in the Department of Psychology at the University of Victoria in British Columbia, Canada. She does research on verbal and non-verbal aspects of communication and is currently completing a thesis involving a critique of social constructionism.

Mike Michael teaches sociology at the Department of Sociology, Goldsmiths' College, University of London. His current research interests include the role of mundane technology in social ordering and disordering, and the public understanding of the new genetics. He has published numerous articles on the public understanding of science and critical social psychology. He is author of *Constructing Identities* (1996).

Marisela Montenegro is a graduate student at the Universidad Central de Venezuela and has developed participatory action research in the field of community social psychology in Caracas (Venezuela). She is currently a PhD student at the Universitat Autònoma de Barcelona and her present research topics include epistemology and applied psychology. She is co-author of the article 'Critical analysis of the concept of self management in community social psychology' (with A. León, N. Ramdjan and I. Villarte, in *Boletin de* *la Asociación Venezolana de Psicología Social*) and of 'The return of emotion in psychosocial community research' (with A. León, in *Journal of Community Psychology*).

David J. Nightingale teaches critical psychology in the Psychology Department at Bolton Institute. His research is concerned with the philosophical and theoretical underpinnings of social constructionism and critical psychology. He has published work on understanding and practising critical psychology, the teaching of social constructionism, the philosophy of social constructionism and the body. He is a member of the Radical Psychology Network (radical-psychology-network@mailbase.ac.uk) and Psychology Politics Resistance (he can be contacted at djn1@bolton.ac.uk or D.J.Nightingale@earthling.net).

Ian Parker is Professor of Psychology in the Discourse Unit at Bolton Institute, where he is course leader for the MSc in critical psychology. His books include *Deconstructing Psychopathology* (1995, with D. Harper, E. Georgaca, T. McLaughlin and M. Stowell-Smith), *Psychology and Society: Radical Theory and Practice* (1996, co-edited with R. Spears), *Psychoanalytic Culture: Psychoanalytic Discourse in Western Society* (1997), *Deconstructing Psychotherapy* (1999) and *Critical Textworks* (1999, with the Bolton Discourse Network). He is a member of Psychology Politics Resistance.

Joan Pujol is Senior Lecturer at the Universitat Autònoma de Barcelona. He has been lecturer at the University of Huddersfield and an Honorary Visiting Fellow at the University of Reading. His research combines material and discursive perspectives in the analysis of social issues ('As one in the web? Discourse, materiality and the Place of Ethics', with S. Brown and B. Curt, in I. Parker (ed.) *Social Constructionism, Discourse and Realism*, 1997). The areas covered involve technological and scientific discourse (*The Rhetoric of Technoscientific Discourse*, 1998, in Spanish), reproductive technologies ('A reading on human reproductive technologies', in C. Willig (ed.) *Deconstruction and Application*) and the construction of delinquency (*The Non-delinquents: How Citizens Understand Criminality*, with P. Garcia-Borés, M. Cagigós, J. C. Medina and J. Sánchez, 1995, in Spanish).

Rex Stainton Rogers completed his contribution to this book just before he died on 8 February 1999. His work was as a critical psychologist and a critical theorist more generally. He will be particularly remembered as the instigator of 'Beryl Curt' – the acorporeal collective author of *Textuality and Tectonics* (1994) and other publications – as well as for the careers of many critical psychologists that he nurtured. He will also be fondly remembered for his ability to turn 'half' into an art form, as an outstanding breakfast chef, and for the mischievous pleasure he took in making trouble.

Wendy Stainton Rogers is also a founding member of Beryl Curt (*Textuality and Tectonics: Troubling Social and Psychological Science*, 1994, is Beryl's magnum opus). She is a senior lecturer in the School of Health and Social Welfare at The Open University, and teaches and researches in three main fields: childcare, health psychology (both from a critical perspective) and critical theory more generally. She is particularly interested in applying criticality in ways that influence action, ranging, for example, from its impact upon social policy and professional practice in areas such as child protection, to challenging established methods of funding and evaluating research within contexts such as the Research Assessment Exercise.

Penny Standen joined the University of Nottingham after completing a PhD in ethology, first to lecture in the Department of Psychology and then, in the Department of Psychiatry, to set up a course to teach psychology to medical students. During this time most of her research focused on psychological factors associated with health, illness and the delivery of health care. An appointment as Reader in Health Psychology and Learning Disabilities at Nottingham has allowed an indulgence in two of her interests: the place of disability in society, and computers and IT. She is currently carrying out research on the use of computers by people with learning disabilities.

Carla Willig is Lecturer in Psychology at City University, London. Her research is concerned with the relationship between discourse and practice, particularly in relation to risk-taking. She has published journal articles and book chapters on the discursive construction of trust and sexual safety, and she has contributed to the debate about relativism and realism in social constructionist psychology. She is the editor of *Applied Discourse Analysis: Social and Psychological Interventions* (1999).

Foreword

Recent years have seen a transformation in the social sciences and in the language that researchers use to make sense of action and experience. This transformation has also opened up a space in academic institutions for reflexive questioning about what that language does in the world. Critical research on discourse, text and the social construction of things that were once taken for granted has inspired work across the disciplines, including cultural studies, psychology, sociology and human geography. It is now time to take stock of what we have accomplished and where we are going with this work, and so these three books review social constructionist perspectives in order to explore new ground creatively.

We accomplish three things: produce a clear theoretical overview of social constructionist frameworks; move our understanding of textuality beyond language; and embed analysis of discourse in an account of practice. There is a different emphasis in each book: Nightingale and Cromby's *Social Constructionist Psychology* surveys existing work and gathers together critical reflections on the conditions and limits of research on language; Parker and the Bolton Discourse Network's *Critical Textwork* elaborates and extends the compass of research to many kinds of textual domain; and Willig's *Applied Discourse Analysis* consistently and provocatively asks through a range of examples how such research can be made useful.

There are fruitful overlaps, with examples of discourse analysis, discussions of types of text and theoretical reflections on the social construction of meaning in each. Together the books address different facets of a common task – they take forward critical social constructionist research on discursive practice.

Ian Parker
Professor of Psychology
Bolton Institute

Preface

We (John and David) met at a conference in 1994. We discovered that although we were both broadly sympathetic to social constructionism we none the less felt that, at least in its current formulations, it was also flawed. We found that we shared concerns over constructionism's failure to account adequately for important aspects of the human condition – in particular, notions of the self, embodiment, materiality and power. Together, we came to realize that two features of social constructionism (its intense focus on language and its tendency to adopt an all-encompassing relativism) made it unable to theorize the human condition adequately. We welcomed constructionism's acknowledgement that individuals are fundamentally enmeshed within social, cultural and historical processes, but did not believe that it was helpful simply to reduce individuals *to* these processes.

We spent some time discussing and writing about these issues, we gave lectures, presented conference papers and symposia about them and argued about them with our colleagues, students, loved ones, friends and acquaintances (to the distress and yawning politeness of the latter three). We constructed the responses we received as falling into two broad categories. The first type was loosely supportive: we were applauded (not literally, at least not very often) for attempting to engage with issues of the 'real' that are difficult, if not impossible, to reconcile with the relativism of many constructionist frameworks. We found these responses useful and encouraging. But the second type of response was less appreciative. We were accused of 'mounting a backlash against constructionism' (rather than an attempted reconstruction). We were damned for having no data (a strangely empiricist critique from those committed to a constructionist world view). And we were accused of political naivety for apparently not realizing that our perspective is, or will herald a return to, essentialism.

While we were not surprised that people did not agree with us, we were taken aback by how thoroughly, and how often, they seemed to misunderstand what we said. It is our belief that the majority of these unproductive exchanges can be explained in terms of a failure to get beyond the 'it's real, no it's not' talk that seems to surface all too often during these debates; a failure to explain adequately the terms we (realists and relativists alike) use; a failure to explore the consequences of the claims we make; and a failure to acknowledge why it is we would wish to make them.

This book is an attempt to explore these debates in more detail. In it, we and the contributors try: to demonstrate the theoretical limitations of current accounts; to explore alternative accounts of ourselves, our bodies and the world in which we live; and to examine how these issues could be incorporated into both the theory and practice of social constructionism. To this extent we are proposing a way forward, a partial reconstruction of social constructionism. However, we also recognize that our position is thoroughly grounded in the circumstances of its own construction: it is a response. While social constructionism has made great progress in destabilizing and challenging the often oppressive and hegemonic practices of mainstream psychology, we believe it has now reached an impasse. Its strength as a critique is simultaneously its undoing as a framework for its own future development. With this in mind we do not think that this book, or the various perspectives expressed within it, represents *the* answer to these problems. It is a collection of signposts rather than a clearly marked destination, a possible way to move social constructionism forward instead of around in circles, or even backwards. We hope you find it useful.

David J. Nightingale, Bolton Institute
John Cromby, University of Bradford

1 What's wrong with social constructionism?

JOHN CROMBY AND
DAVID J. NIGHTINGALE

Introduction

There is a sense in which the aims of this book may already be compromised by its very existence, a sense in which even as you read this you are open to an argument that potentially undermines much that we have to say. Let us explain.

The theme of this book is that it is time for social constructionist psychology to loosen its almost exclusive focus on language and discourse, and begin to include other vital issues. This chapter identifies three issues that social constructionism (for the most part, and with some honourable exceptions) currently fails to adequately consider: embodiment, materiality and power. But how do we demonstrate this? Do we bundle together into boxes examples of embodiment (toenails, dead sharks in formaldehyde), materiality (blades of grass, sticks and stones) and power (hmm: perhaps a miniature Panopticon, made from matchsticks by homeless people and sold to get money for food)? Do we give these boxes to our publishers with a request to distribute them, since in their *immediacy* (see Patten 1981) they make our point more forcibly than any argument we could possibly contrive? We do not. Instead, we write a book – and in so doing, move on to the very territory we are identifying as problematic and insufficient.

In short, we are well aware that language does things. We accept that what follows is a story, and that alternative stories could be told. One such story would tell how social constructionism is a powerful and growing influence in psychology today. It would describe how theorizing and debate is both innovative and vigorous, as constructionists advance social explanations for an increasing range of phenomena: attitudes, memory, personality, emotions, the 'self'. This story would tell how the status of these phenomena as qualities or properties of individuals has been challenged. It would describe how the methods typically used by constructionists (discourse and conversation analysis, Q-sorts, ethnography) are increasingly acceptable to mainstream psychologists, and are now commonplace on undergraduate courses. It would show how constructionist ideas are being applied in practice in areas such as health psychology, counselling and therapy, developmental and educational psychology. In passing, it would mention that some of constructionism's most determined advocates now enjoy high esteem in academic circles. Let us emphasize now that this account of social constructionist psychology is one that we enjoy and frequently retell – it is, in our view, a rattling good yarn. But the purpose of this book is to tell a slightly different story. It has many of the same characters and settings as the one outlined above, but the plots diverge at crucial points. Moreover, you'll be glad to hear that our story has at least the potential for a much happier ending.

Our story begins with the observation that despite the charms of the tale of progress and consolidation outlined above, there are some things *wrong* with social constructionist psychology. Many of these problems are an inevitable result of the ways in which social constructionism has developed over the past 15 years or so. In particular, we believe that the 'discursive turn' – constructionism's strong emphasis on the role of language in the constitution of both world and person – has produced a corresponding lack of attention to other significant elements of human life. The kinds of things we will be talking about here include:

- the influences of embodied factors (from missing limbs to cold sores) and personal–social histories (from idyllic childhoods to abusive incidents) upon social situations and individual activity;
- the ways in which the possibilities and constraints inherent in the material world always already shape and inform the social constructions we live through and with;
- the power of institutions, governments and multinational corporations, and the inequalities that arise from those structural features of society usually described under terms such as 'capitalism' or 'patriarchy'.

Other problems, we suspect, arise either from strenuous efforts to bring into the linguistic arena these missing elements, or from misguided attempts to downplay their significance. The excessive wordiness, conceptual confusion, abstraction and indeterminacy of some social constructionist writing (Searle 1995) may be due at least in part to such striving.

In this chapter we will discuss embodiment, materiality and power in more detail, arguing both that these elements are not reducible to discourse and that those approaches which treat them as though they were purely discursive are erroneous. This necessarily implies that *our* constructionism will attempt to include what we will call, for the sake of convenience, the 'real'. Of course, this does not mean that we expect the booming, buzzing confusion of the ecosystem, or still less the embodied or physiological aspects of subjectivity, to show themselves here, unrepresented and unmediated. It simply means that we will not make any universalizing assumptions about their ontological status, or lack thereof. However, since questions of ontology are both shaped by moral or political imperatives and informed by academic debate and scientific research (consider, for example, the ontological status of 'schizophrenia'), we simultaneously reserve the right to question the ontological status of chosen aspects of our world in the future. Moreover, at times, we will explicitly call upon the 'real' to support our arguments – in contrast to many other constructionists, for whom the only reality that appears unproblematically is that of discourse. This means that we must also summarize another story called 'the realism–relativism debate'. But first, to make clear that we 'really' are social constructionists, we must briefly say what we think is *right* with social constructionism.

What's right with social constructionism?

Gergen (1985) described social constructionist psychology in terms of its qualities, interests and principles, providing something of a 'manifesto' for constructionists. Yet Burr (1995) points out that what unites the various people who describe themselves as social constructionists is no more than a 'family resemblance', and Potter (e.g. 1996) emphasizes that there is no one type of psychology which could be described as social constructionist, and that constructionism is itself a construction. Danziger (1997) describes two strands of social constructionist psychology: a 'dark' version, which attends to issues of power and subjectivity and is rooted in the work of Foucault; and a 'light' version, which attends to the minutiae of discourse and social processes and descends from speech act theory, ethnomethodology and deconstruction. Like other psychologies, then, social constructionism contains disparate and sometimes conflicting ideas (including those expressed here). But this disagreement and debate should not be allowed to obscure the broad consensus that has emerged between the many writers who all place one or more of the following principles at the core of their psychology. Below, we sketch what we see as the principal areas of broad agreement, together with outlines of the disagreements that surround them.

The primacy of social processes

Social constructionists argue that the world we experience and the people we find ourselves to be are first and foremost the product of social processes. Neither God nor individual consciousness but society itself is the prime mover, the root of experience. It is the social reproduction and transformation of structures of meaning, conventions, morals and discursive practices that principally constitutes both our relationships and ourselves. This implies that language, both as the dominant carrier of categories and meanings and as the medium which provides much of the raw material for our activity, is central. Rather than asserting this as an item of dogma, we prefer to provide evidence for the primacy of the social, and employ German critical psychology for this. Tolman (1994: 86–92) summarizes how an evolutionary perspective leads us necessarily (at this point in the evolution of our species) to privilege the social realm over other determinants of human life.

Although it seems that all constructionists must subscribe to some version of this argument, there is disagreement about the extent to which it can be applied. Some (e.g. Edwards and Potter 1992; Edwards *et al.* 1995) seem to believe that when we talk about 'reality' we can only be referring to the world we discursively construct, that 'there is nothing beyond the text'. Others (e.g. Harré 1990) accept that there is a real world beyond the text, but argue that what we can know of that real world is a sub-world or *Umwelt* restricted by the physiological, sensory apparatus of our species. Within those restrictions our world is always socially constructed – again, primarily through language.

Historical and cultural specificity

History provides extensive evidence that cultures change over time, while social anthropology demonstrates that they vary greatly from place to place (and note that, to the extent that evidence from these disciplines is accepted uncritically, this is already a realist argument). This variation does not only mean that the things we (think that we) know could be different. It also means that the ways we could find them out and the things that we would count as 'proof' may also be different. Being 'real' about constructionism leads us to emphasize that it isn't just our ways of talking about the world that vary: the subjectivities of the actual, living people that are constituted in and from those ways of speaking will vary, along with the cultures that produce and sustain them. For example, feminists and critical theorists have drawn attention to how dominant notions of 'women' and 'the person' in contemporary Western society fit all too neatly with the demands of patriarchy and capitalism. Such notions are much more than just ways of representing people; they become, in their elaboration, determinants of social practices in which we make and find ourselves as the subjects of patriarchy and capitalism, or alternatively as their opponents. In both cases, patriarchy and capitalism become influences to which we must attend.

Realism aside, what is contentious here is the extent of this variation. Some constructionists emphasize the significant differences that can be found even between neighbouring countries, or the important cultural shifts that can occur within one lifetime, and argue that any and all aspects of existence may be subject to enormous variation. For example, Geertz (1979: 229) writes: 'The Western conception of the person as a bounded, unique, more or less integrated motivational and cognitive universe, a dynamic centre of awareness, emotion, judgement and action, organised into a distinctive whole and set contrastively against other wholes and against a social and natural background is, however incorrigible it may seem to us, a rather peculiar idea within the context of the world's cultures.' Other constructionists simultaneously emphasize the consistencies and continuities that endure between and across cultures (such as widespread and enduring oppression based around gender or sexuality) and argue that these commonalities must also be explained. Geertz (1973: 126) also writes: 'At least some conception of what a human individual is, as opposed to a rock, an animal, a rainstorm or a god, is, so far as I can see, universal.'

Knowledge and activity are intertwined

As Burr (1995: 5) puts it, 'knowledge and social action go together'. We pose the questions we do and frame the answers we obtain in ways which are fundamentally, profoundly and intimately related to the activities we carry out. We actively seek to explore aspects of our world, in particular ways for particular purposes, and in so doing create knowledge which we then take as the 'truth' about the world. But other activities carried out for other purposes might have produced alternative 'truths'. So knowledge is inextricably linked to, and emerges as a product of, activity and purpose. However, an extreme version of this argument would say that there can be no facts which are true in every culture and for all time. While some constructionists are happy to accept this possibility, others find it more useful to believe that some things are still more 'true' or 'right' than others. The disagreement, then, is about the extent to which all knowledge is always local and particular, versus the extent to which it may also be grounded in aspects of the world that precede or transcend local human beliefs and activity.

A critical stance

The understanding that knowledge is relative and also emerges from practice gives constructionism a powerful critical impetus, placing it in opposition to the positivist, empiricist tradition of science, which assumes that 'facts' can be gathered by disinterested and neutral observation. However, as some observers have pointed out, this critical impetus has given rise to two distinct strands of social constructionist critique (Danziger 1997; Parker 1997a). One strand promotes a relativism that does not give rise to any explicit political activity (see Gill 1995), but is nevertheless opposed to the positivist tradition which still informs most of mainstream psychology. The other strand holds that while social constructions are relative, they are not arbitrary, but emerge through social processes that are already shaped by influences such as power relationships and material resources. The two strands share an emphasis upon the socially constructed and therefore malleable nature of our world, but differ in the extent to which they use this understanding as grounds for political (as opposed to philosophical or methodological) critique.

The realism–relativism debate

Social constructionists all agree that social processes, particularly language, are central to everyday life and experience. They all endorse notions of historical and cultural change, and accept that knowledge and activity are intimately related. They are all critical of the beliefs, methods and techniques of mainstream psychology, and advocate in their place alternative models of the person, research and practice. Yet within this consensus there are also significant disagreements, to do with locating the limits of social constructionism and quantifying the contribution (or establishing the existence) of extra-discursive influences. In recent years these questions and their various answers have coalesced to produce what is described as 'the realism–relativism debate'. Since this debate provided much of the impetus for this book and is a recurrent (if often implicit) theme within it, we will now briefly sketch its contours and some of its implications (for a more complete account see Parker 1997b).

Realism is the doctrine that an external world exists independently of our representations of it (Searle 1995). Representations include perceptions, thought, language, beliefs and desires, as well as artefacts such as pictures and maps, and so include all the ways in which we do or could know and experience the world and ourselves. Relativism repudiates this doctrine, arguing that since any such external world is inaccessible to us in both principle and practice, it need not be postulated or considered. It might appear at first glance that social constructionism must be inherently and exclusively relativist. We have already described and endorsed its historical and cultural relativism, and its understanding of the way that knowledge is both part and product of social action. Gergen (1985) also mentions the theory dependence of observation, the impossibility of 'proving' the theory of logical induction by any means other than induction itself and the existence of paradigm shifts in the 'hard' sciences, all of which seem to demand a relativist stance. However, the existence of extra-discursive influences, and the need to ground critique and to understand continuity as well as variability, have led some to propose a realist ontology for social constructionism – whether in Harré's notion of the *Umwelt* or in the critical realism of Parker (1992) and Willig (1997; Chapter 3 in this volume).

The most forthright celebration of relativism in social constructionist thought is provided by Edwards *et al.* (1995). Their eloquent paper calls relativism the 'quintessential academic position', and says that as such it is the only proper ground for inquiry in the human or social sciences. To demonstrate the value of relativism, the authors identify two 'bottom-line' arguments commonly used against it in the social sciences: the existence of 'things' such as furniture, as demonstrated by hitting a table ('It's real!'); and the 'fact' of death, suffering, illness and disease. Then they set out to show how, far from being real things in themselves, both death and furniture are socially constructed.

Along the way, they identify two complementary dilemmas. The first occurs at those moments when exasperated realists clout the furniture in order to demonstrate its physical existence to pedantic relativists. Edwards *et al.* argue that 'not only words signify. The table-thumping does its work as meaningful action, not mere behaviour . . . Rocks, trees, furniture are not *already* rebuttals of relativism, but become so precisely at the moment, and for the moment, of their invocation . . . We term this the realist's dilemma.' Second, there is the relativist's dilemma, which occurs because relativism 'must treat everyone's views as equally valid . . . it offers no grounds for caring one way or another on anything moral, political or factual.' Thus, Edwards *et al.* argue that both realists and relativists are compromised, albeit in slightly different ways: 'While realists shoot themselves in the foot as soon as they represent, relativists do so as soon as they argue. To argue for something is to care, to be positioned, which is immediately non-relativist.' Edwards *et al.* conclude that these two dilemmas produce an impasse, the way out of which is to adopt relativism as 'a non-position, as critique or scepticism, not as a positive statement opposed to realism. Relativism is offered as a meta-level (or one more step back) epistemology that can include and analyse realism and relativism alike, viewed as *rhetorical practices.*' On this analysis, relativism thus appears to gain a (weak) victory over realism, because it is proposed as a *resolution to* rather than a *component of* this debate (Davies 1998 summarizes this argument).

It is our view that insofar as this paper succeeds, it does so in three ways. First, Edwards *et al.* deploy a wide range of more or less subtle academic strategies and grammatical, rhetorical and textual devices to blur the experiential distinction between 'things' and 'words', a strategy which (at least implicitly) derives academic legitimacy from Derrida's assertion that there is nothing beyond the text. This is significant, since Derrida himself has acknowledged the possibility of a reality *before* the text in Levinasian ethics (Critchley 1992), and, according to Searle, has said that 'all he meant by the spectacular declaration that there is nothing outside of texts is the banality that everything exists in some context or other' (Searle 1995: 160; see also Derrida 1988: 136). Nevertheless, by muddying the distinction between word and world, Edwards *et al.* place the onus of proof firmly in the realist camp, and then claim an impasse when realists are forced to deploy rhetorical devices in their attempts to provide it. However, the apparent impasse only arises because although it is reality that provides the conditions that make the discussion possible, the discussion itself – as discussions must – takes place in the relativist arena of representations, of discourse.

Such a move is identified and criticized by Searle (1995), who points out that the demand for a proof of realism 'already somehow presupposes what is challenged'. Searle observes that one can easily establish whether a given English sentence is grammatical, but one cannot establish whether the English language itself is grammatical because English itself sets the standards for grammaticality in English. He suggests that attempts to prove realism by argument have a similar character: external reality frames them and makes them possible, but (as Edwards *et al.* successfully demonstrate) does not appear within them in unmediated or non-occasioned ways. Searle argues that it is misguided to take this as a proof of relativism, since 'realism is thus not a thesis nor an hypothesis but the condition of having certain sorts of theses or hypotheses.' It is the failure to acknowledge this point that produces the impasse in which Edwards *et al.* find themselves.

Second, Edwards *et al.* provide a convincing demonstration of the strengths of relativism, showing how it insists that all apparent truths can be challenged: indeed, their argument is at its strongest when they show how relativism 'offers an ever available lever of resistance. It is potentially liberating, dangerous, unsettling, with an appeal that is enduringly radical: nothing ever *has to be* taken as merely, obviously, objectively, unconstructedly true.' But this universal utility, which they claim as one of relativism's strengths, is simultaneously its greatest weakness. This is because the deconstructive methods that Edwards *et al.* advocate, and that depend for their universal applicability upon a totalizing and universal relativism, are double-edged swords which dissolve all solutions as remorselessly as they dissolve the problems from which they arise (Burman 1990). The history of critical thought shows that both realism and relativism are typically deployed strategically. Writers ground their critiques in aspects of the world they wish to make or remain real and, from this grounding, relativize aspects of it that they want to question or deny (see Held 1980; Fay 1987). Which aspects of the world are to be relativized and which 'real-ized' is a choice typically shaped by moral, political or pragmatical precepts, not epistemology or ontology.

So the difficulty is not with relativism *per se*, since, as Edwards *et al.* point out, relativism is essential to critical thought and academic work; rather, the difficulty is with their attempt to use relativism to provide theoretical closure. Edwards *et al.* want to relativize everything, all at once, to wish away the tiresome, brute facts of existence – as though the material world and our own embodied natures did not already bestow structure, limits and potentials on the social constructions that our analyses identify. Such omnipotent fantasies might be viable if the thoroughly malleable realm of discourse was autonomous and self-constituting, but this is simply not the case. Discourse is always already situated in a material world; it is always already the product of embodied beings. This means that we simply cannot construct the world any old way we choose, and if we persistently attempt to do so we are ultimately more likely to come to the attention of psychiatric services than to gain academic approval. Moreover, realizing that our world is socially constructed need not force us to adopt a promiscuous and unbridled relativism. Social constructions are all around us, and include such diverse features as racism, marriages and marriage guidance, government policies, governments themselves, child abuse, crime, disease, psychology, including social constructionist psychology, buildings, people and cities (to name but a few). *None of these things are any the less real for being socially constructed*, although the dominance of the processes of construction, as compared to other influences, may vary from one to another.

Third, the arguments put forward by Edwards *et al.* benefit from their resonance with the postmodern *Zeitgeist*, in which relativism is sometimes elevated almost to a point of principle. Relativism informs postmodern art and literature through questions about the intrinsic value of 'great' works and in the rise of new and challenging forms (Foster 1985; Taylor 1987); it appears in recent challenges to the authority and value of science (Holton 1993; Gross and Levitt 1994); and it gains political credibility in the fragmentation of mass movements and the corresponding emphasis on heterogeneity, pluralism and the ineluctable diversity of experience (Arac 1986; Callinicos 1989; Eagleton 1995). In this context, questions about the value of relativism are often seen as the thin end of a wedge that might reintroduce problems (for example, those of objectivism, essentialism and naive realism) that postmodernism seems to have transcended. Thus, there is in postmodern culture a largely uncritical acceptance of relativism, which helps to block or undermine any attempts to reincorporate the 'real', the extradiscursive. In this sense, relativism is not just a theoretical perspective or philosophical claim. Relativism is simultaneously a culturally offered rhetorical resource that can be drawn upon to disparage 'realist' arguments (as unsophisticated, as failures to understand the subtleties or nuances of relativists' claims and so on), and so avoid the need to take seriously the entirely reasonable questions that are being raised. With this in mind, the final chapter of this book offers a 'deconstruction' of relativism, and begins to develop a set of principled arguments to assess critically and challenge relativism's dominance.

Instead of attempting to universalize relativism, we believe that we should now embark upon the far more difficult and dangerous task of attempting to forge a coherent and grounded social constructionism that explains the world, in all its extra-discursive intransigence and mess, since only in this way might we contribute to its progressive transformation. To illustrate the need for such an approach, we will now discuss some issues that a wholly discursive (and hence relativist) social constructionism is unable to address adequately.

Embodiment

The human body is a site of birth, growth, ageing and death, of pleasure, pain and many things (like mild hunger or being tickled) that fall between. It is an object of desires, whether aesthetic, erotic or narcissistic. It is a bearer of features, from *retroussé* noses and pigeon chests to skins of different hue and primary and secondary sexual characteristics. It is a biological machine that provides the material preconditions for subjectivity, thought, emotion and language. With other bodies it makes possible physical interaction of all kinds, from passionate kissing to senseless killing. Bodies are celebrated in dance, honed in exercise and disciplined in Foucault, they are mended and modified by surgery and adorned by practices such as tattooing and piercing. Bodies differ, not just in their characteristics but in their capabilities: not all can touch fingers to their toes or dance all night, some struggle even to walk unaided, while others (blind, deaf and mute) can see, hear or speak no discourse. Bodies are the intimate place where nature and culture meet, they are the external boundary and principal mass of the mind–body–brain system that we call a human being. They are lumpy, smelly, messy, unreliable and ultimately destined to self-destruct.

Such bodies are difficult to find in social constructionism, which tends to dismiss the body while simultaneously appearing to address it by providing detailed analysis of the discourses of bodily matters. Studies of discourse typically proceed as though their raw material was not already the product of embodied beings, in seeming ignorance of the fact that talking is not the only form of interaction. In continually either ignoring the body or treating it as mere metaphor or text, social constructionism obscures and downplays the significance of its functional, physiological, hormonal, anatomical and phenomenological aspects. Not only does constructionism have no notion of the body to call its own, it views other approaches to the body with deep mistrust, branding them as biologistic, cognitivist or essentialist. It then has little choice but implicitly to reduce the speaking bodies we meet and find ourselves to be to mere discursive traces, transcribed echoes of their actual fleshy substance.

We do not deny that our understanding of embodiment benefits greatly from an analysis of the ways in which discourses and cultural practices are written on and through the body. Nor do we suppose that the body can be simply and unproblematically incorporated into an overarching constructionist framework. The spectres of Cartesian dualism, biological reductionism and essentialism continue to haunt the body, just as surely as its obstinate meatiness weighs down the airy flights of its discursive construction. We accept that bringing the body into social constructionism will cause problems, but emphasize that leaving it out has already done so. In ignoring the extensive evidence that the body's biological and physiological substrate differentially acts back upon or interacts with socially obtained discourses, constructionism has implicitly adopted a 'uniform plasticity' of the human body (Nightingale 1999). All aspects of all bodies must be so similar, so malleable before discourse, that they may as well not be there: if the body can be anything, it might as well be nothing.

There is a further aspect of embodiment about which social constructionism is largely silent, that is that subjectivity itself is embodied. The subjectivity that is 'me' inhabits one particular lump of flesh and no other such lump, and so appears in the context of one, and only one, personal–social life history. Let it be clear that in drawing attention to this issue we are not advocating a lapse into individualism, since it is through personal–social histories that such factors as class, gender and race enter subjectivity and discourse as experiential (rather than mere categorical or indexical) influences. Rather than continue along the neo-behaviourist path of pretending that subjectivity does not exist, we prefer to acknowledge and attempt to understand how subjectivity is constituted through embodied interactions, material possibilities and personal–social histories.

[handwritten marginal note: This is where Mead left out part of James.]

Materiality

Materiality refers to the elemental, physical nature of the world in which we are embedded, its 'thing-ness' and solidity. In addition to the human bodies already more specifically discussed above, it includes the physical (as opposed to conceptual or discursive) aspects of tables, rocks, tape recorders and transcripts, books like this one, rivers, mountains, oceans, planets and the dizzying curvature of the space–time continuum. Materiality is the wetness of water, the coldness of ice, the viscosity of oil and the grittiness of sand. It is the weight of lead and the lightness of feathers, the fragrance of tree flowers in the spring and of burning leaves in the autumn. Materiality embraces the distribution of resources, the location of bodies, the organization of space and the irreversible fact of time.

While all these things may appear in discourse, as they do here, they are not reducible to it. Even the existence of distinctions that appear in some languages but not others, such as the many words for snow in the languages of Greenland, does not demonstrate that discourse can be divorced from materiality. Something that speakers of English would call snow (and Greenlanders might call *qanik*, *pukak* or *apirlatt*, according to its age, texture and which dialect they spoke) would fall from the sky in certain atmospheric conditions, whether we had words for it or not. Far from demonstrating the ephemeral status of the material world, as is sometimes claimed, this example demonstrates both the diversity of human culture and the rootedness of social, discursive constructions in the material world and the activities of everyday life.

Materiality matters because it both creates possibilities for, and puts constraints upon, the social constructions by and through which we live our lives. Most fundamentally, the ecosystem that supports life is a necessary precondition for any and all social constructions, discursive or otherwise. This ecosystem is both dynamic and variable, yet the dominant trend in social constructionism is to treat materiality as simply uniform and hence to ignore its contribution to the processes of social construction. Murphy (1995) is critical of this stance, arguing that it is only maintained by the use of 'rhetorical avoidance strategies' and a neglect of comparative research that would allow materiality to emerge as a factor. He suggests that denying materiality makes social constructionism appear unconvincing, and leads to a spurious over-statement of the social that results in errors of reification.

Power

Power is a term swathed in confusion, with multiple and sometimes mutually exclusive definitions. Even confining ourselves to the social sciences, power is variously seen as a personal attribute or characteristic, as the implementation of strategies or the use of resources, as a commodity that can be 'seized', as a structural feature of societal relations and as a property that flows from and through the use of discourses acknowledged (at least by those who wield them) to be 'true'. But however power is defined, there is a failure in some strands of social constructionist work to theorize it adequately and take account of its influence. This failure is closely related to the two issues previously described. While constructionism does not adequately address embodiment and materiality and continues to consign subjectivity and personal–social history to its margins, it cannot include power. Embodiment and power are intimately related, as Foucault shows and the experiences of those whose bodies are considered to deviate from acceptable norms graphically illustrate. Power is a material issue too, from interpersonal violence through access to resources and on to the existence of armies and weapons of mass destruction. Power is essential to an understanding of subjectivity, since the personal–social histories from which it emerges are always moulded and shaped by power relationships. Evidence for this in everyday life is provided by research on gender, race and disability; and, *in extremis*, by studies of the effects upon individuals of sexual and physical abuse.

Of course, we are not suggesting that social constructionists have ignored power. As we described above, there are two strands of social constructionism, which diverge in part around this very issue. The relationship of power and discourse is central to the work of Foucault, and permeates the work of those constructionists influenced by his ideas (e.g. Hollway 1989; Parker 1992; Mama 1995; Burman *et al.* 1996). Power is also acknowledged in Gergen's notion of 'warranting voice' (Gergen 1989). Yet it is our contention that power is always and already a significant factor in the processes of social construction, whether it is acknowledged or not, since it is forever present in the interactions and relations which constructionism studies. For example, the analyses of racist discourse described by Potter and Wetherell (1987) are interesting precisely because of the history of oppression and exploitation that they recall and reproduce. Power appears in and operates through discourse, and to this extent discourse analytic methods may usefully map its contours and processes. However, unless discourse is then situated in the material, embodied context that actually gives it meaning (Parker 1992), such analyses will remain paradoxically incapable of fully addressing their own significance (as Wetherell and Potter 1992 in fact seem to acknowledge). Conversely, the simultaneous denial of both materiality and embodiment makes it easier for constructionists to ignore power relationships, contributing to the tendency to conceal power identified by Billig *et al.* (1988).

Conclusion

The intense focus on language and discourse has served social constructionism well so far, and determined efforts to deny the significance of influences 'beyond the text' were perhaps strategic necessities in the earliest phase of constructionism's development. However, such strategies have outlived their usefulness and are now causing more problems for constructionism than they solve: the discursive turn is threatening to become a discursive retreat. Continuing to ignore or downplay embodiment and materiality may eventually create the conditions for the tide of knowledge and practice simply to sweep social constructionism away. The many psychologists who have recourse to notions of embodiment and materiality, both in their practice and in their everyday lives, are unlikely either to resign *en masse* or wholly to transform their approach simply because constructionism refuses to believe in them. It seems far more likely that social constructionism will simply make itself irrelevant and trivial, and so waste the valuable gains it has made.

Structure of the book

Following this introduction, this book is organized into three main parts followed by a concluding chapter. The first part, 'A critical analysis of theory', explores some alternative theoretical foundations for social constructionism, and discusses ways in which the issues described here can be informed by debates and critiques in other disciplines. This paves the way for Part II, 'Materiality and embodiment', which moves beyond the purely linguistic by engaging with specific aspects of materiality and of our embodied natures. Part III, 'A critical analysis of practice', then assesses the significance of these debates within a number of practical domains. However, the reader should note that to some extent the distinctions we draw between these three parts are often blurred by the specific content of individual chapters. All the chapters reference theory (in one way or another), all are concerned with real (material and embodied) issues and all are concerned with the practical implications of the claims they make.

Part and chapter summaries

Part I

In Chapter 2, Ian Parker demonstrates the need for theory as a tool, both to deconstruct (or take apart) the common-sense understandings we have of ourselves and our world, and to construct frameworks that might facilitate the development of a progressive, critical psychology. To this end he explores the contribution that *humanism* can make, both to our understandings of ourselves and others, and to our work as critical psychologists. He also explores the tensions that arise between humanism (as a critical theoretical resource), humanistic psychology and its functions in mainstream psychology, and critical psychological theory and practice.

Next, Carla Willig agrees that social constructionism allows us to show that knowledge is historically and culturally situated. However, she is concerned that it offers nothing by way of an alternative, no principled basis for the replacement of current forms of knowledge by more liberating concepts. She demonstrates that while contemporary constructionist accounts allow us to *describe* certain 'regimes of truth' (particular forms of knowledge) they do not then permit an analysis of their 'origin and maintenance'. To solve this problem, she argues that critical psychology must move towards a 'wider historical materialist analysis of society', which understands subjectivity and action as grounded in the real conditions of their origin. She concludes that *critical realism* provides a suitable theoretical framework for such 'non-relativist social constructionist work'.

In Chapter 4, Mike Michael discusses the parallels between theoretical debates within psychology and those within other areas of the human sciences. He suggests that social constructionist psychology can progress only if it moves towards forms of analysis that can incorporate both the 'real' *and* the 'constructed'. To achieve this, he proposes a heterogeneous analysis that necessarily draws upon resources from disciplines outside of psychology. The 'paradisciplinarity' he suggests would allow an analysis of the biological *and* material *and* discursive aspects of our experience; not as mutually exclusive frames of reference, but as supplementary accounts that serve to 'help or support each other'. He illustrates his claims through a discussion of the various disciplinary and theoretical resources we might use to conduct a paradisciplinary analysis of the 'couch potato'.

Part II

Part II explores the notions of materiality and embodiment, not as the transient functions or reductive consequences of language, but as fundamental components of human existence. In admitting the material and the embodied, we move beyond an analysis of 'language as merely words' and begin to consider the ways in which language is underpinned, structured and supported by aspects of our worlds that both inform and transcend the purely discursive.

In Chapter 5, Ian Burkitt draws our attention to the ways in which power, language and practice are embedded within (material and embodied) social relations that transcend the purely linguistic. He discusses these issues with reference to two 'versions' of social constructionism; a 'light' version, where 'life is constructed in discourse', and a 'dark' version, where discourses are embedded in pre-existing relations of power. He suggests that both accounts are partial, in that both deny the fundamentally relational aspects of our existence. He concludes that social constructionism must move beyond a purely linguistic analysis, towards an analysis of the transformational nature of 'social relations and joint practices'.

Joan Pujol and Marisela Montenegro (Chapter 6) explore the tensions between discursive psychology's epistemological stance (relativism regarding knowledge and the world) and realist's ontological claims regarding a pre-existing external reality. Through a discussion of critical realism, they develop a parallel approach 'inspired by the work of Donna Haraway and actor network theory'. They attempt to transcend the 'segregation between discourse and materiality' by viewing knowledge as neither an objective *nor* a subjective understanding of the world, but as a form of political action brought into being 'by the interaction of the position of the researcher and of what is researched'.

In Chapter 7, Rom Harré explores the ways in which social constructionism and the notions of materiality and embodiment fundamentally presuppose one another. He demonstrates that the character of the symbolic world (the way in which we talk about the world) is dependent upon our shared conceptions regarding our embodied and material nature, and that, as such, our talk is always grounded in the material and embodied conditions of its production. He concludes that embodiment, far from being epiphenomenal to discourse, is a necessary condition for the very possibility of discourse.

Next, Vivien Burr argues that social constructionism's focus upon language has led it to neglect the person as an experiencing subject, in particular the experiences of selfhood and embodiment. Drawing upon a phenomenological analysis (Merleau-Ponty), she suggests that important aspects of our lives are situated 'outside' of language, in an extra-discursive realm of experience 'constructed in and expressed through embodiment'. Through a discussion of embodiment, art and dance she explores the ways in which the body 'can have its say' – the ways in which its experiences may be represented as something other than words.

In Chapter 9, Trevor Butt also draws upon phenomenology to discuss the ways in which emotions may be reframed as embodied phenomena rather than either hardwired cognitive responses (mainstream psychology) or linguistically based, locally contingent, moral and social behaviours (social constructionism). He sees phenomenology as a way of reconciling the objectivism of realism and the idealism or relativism of social constructionism; not to privilege one over the other but to reconcile them by placing the 'focus *between* the person and the world rather than within either'.

In Chapter 10, John Cromby and Penny Standen endorse social constructionist critiques of 'the self', but argue that some notion of the embodied person must still be retained by constructionists. They demonstrate that social constructionism's denial of the self leads to a loss of ecological validity, a blindness to the material factors and personal–social histories that constrain identities, and difficulties in adequately theorizing subjectivity. They argue that social constructionism's denial of the self merely serves to deepen and entrench the very dualisms it seeks to overcome, and begin to suggest ways in which a suitably constructionist model of the self might be formulated.

Part III

Here, the focus is on the ways in which these debates are played out in practice. How are these debates already grounded in real world issues? What impact do they have upon the practical and political concerns of their various participants? What use can theoretical accounts be put to?

In Chapter 11, Erica Burman provides a feminist commentary upon both this book and the project it represents. She demonstrates that while these debates can be pursued as academic or theoretical issues, their deployment or utilization is often grounded in pragmatic political concerns that transcend the disciplinary boundaries of both psychology *and* social constructionism. Through an analysis of feminist theory and practice she shows that feminist contributions are often marginalized and under-represented. She concludes that 'feminist work offers an example of a critical current in psychology struggling to resist disciplinary dynamics of incorporation which merits the attention, if not emulation, of social constructionists.'

Christine Kenwood (Chapter 12) discusses the impact of social constructionism upon psychotherapeutic practice. She demonstrates that social constructionism has mounted a successful challenge to mainstream accounts of 'mental illness' as individual pathology, through its emphasis upon the *social* development of mental distress. However, she expresses two related concerns. First, constructionist accounts are often ambiguous regarding what is meant by the term 'social'. Her concern is that certain versions of constructionism appear to privilege the micro-social arena of interpersonal activity, to the neglect of macro-social or structural problems within society. Second, such micro-social accounts are often couched in relativist terms that are neither desirable nor sustainable within the psychotherapeutic environment.

In Chapter 13, Wendy and Rex Stainton Rogers examine some of the dilemmas that arise when social constructionist ideas are applied in professional practice. They explore, with reference to child abuse and child protection, the ways in which constructionist ideas and perspectives are always enmeshed within practical and political concerns. They argue that although many child protection practitioners are often sceptical of constructionist ideas, in that to 'challenge everything' seems to make practical action problematic, a move towards constructionist ideas is now necessary for two reasons: first, to explore the increasing difficulties regarding the definition of abuse; second, properly to locate these issues within a moral framework that positivist research often denies.

Concluding chapter

The aim of this introductory chapter was to provide a foundation for the rest of the book by specifying what we see as the deficits in contemporary constructionist accounts. In it, we identified aspects of our experience that exclusively linguistic analyses can neither describe nor explain; namely, embodiment, materiality and power. We also suggested that an adherence to an all-encompassing relativism both demands and supports a neglect of these issues. Accordingly, in the final chapter we return to relativism and attempt to expand upon our introductory critique. We describe some fundamental theoretical and practical problems associated with relativism, discuss some of the ways in which realist alternatives are often misconstrued and finally suggest some of the ways in which social constructionism might now begin to incorporate the 'real'.

References

Arac, J. (1986) *Postmodernism and Politics*. Manchester: Manchester University Press.

Billig, M., Condor, S., Edwards, D., Gane, M., Middleton, D. and Radley, A. (1988) *Ideological Dilemmas: A Social Psychology of Everyday Thinking*. London: Sage.

Burman, E. (1990) Differing with deconstruction: a feminist critique, in I. Parker and J. Shotter (eds) *Deconstructing Social Psychology*. London: Routledge.

Burman, E., Aitken, G., Alldred, P. *et al.* (1996) *Psychology Discourse Practice: From Regulation to Resistance*. London: Taylor and Francis.

Burr, V. (1995) *An Introduction to Social Constructionism*. London: Routledge.

Callinicos, A. (1989) *Against Postmodernism: A Marxist Critique*. Cambridge: Polity Press.

Critchley, S. (1992) *The Ethics of Deconstruction: Derrida and Levinas*. Oxford: Blackwell.

Danziger, K. (1997) The Varieties of Social Construction, *Theory and Psychology*, 7(3): 399–416.

Davies, B. (1998) Psychology's subject: a commentary on the relativism/realism debate, in I. Parker (ed.) *Social Constructionism, Discourse and Realism*. London: Sage.

Derrida, J. (1988) *Limited, Inc*. Evanston, IL: Northwestern University Press.

Eagleton, T. (1995) *The Illusions of Postmodernism*. Oxford: Blackwell.

Edwards, D., Ashmore, M. and Potter, J. (1995) Death and furniture: the rhetoric, politics and theology of bottom-line arguments against relativism, *History of the Human Sciences*, 8(2): 25–49.

Edwards, D. and Potter, J. (1992) *Discursive Psychology*. London: Sage.

Fay, B. (1987) *Critical Social Science*. Cambridge: Polity Press.

Foster, H. (1985) *Postmodern Culture*. London: Pluto Press.

Geertz, C. (1973) *The Interpretation of Cultures*. New York: Basic Books.

Geertz, C. (1979) From the native's point of view: on the nature of anthropological understanding, in P. Rabinow and W. Sullivan (eds) *Interpretative Social Science*. Berkeley: University of California Press.

Gergen, K. J. (1985) The social constructionist movement in modern psychology, *American Psychologist*, 40(3): 266–75.

Gergen, K. J. (1989) Warranting voice and the elaboration of the self, in J. Shotter and K. J. Gergen (eds) *Texts of Identity*. London: Sage.

Gill, R. (1995) Relativism, reflexivity and politics: interrogating discourse analysis from a feminist perspective, in S. Wilkinson and C. Kitzinger (eds) *Feminism and Discourse: Psychological Perspectives*. London: Sage.

Gross, P. and Levitt, N. (1994) *Higher Superstition: The Academic Left and Its Quarrels with Science*. Baltimore: Johns Hopkins University Press.

Harré, R. (1990) Exploring the human Umwelt, in R. Bhaskar (ed.) *Harré and His Critics: Essays in Honour of Rom Harré, with His Commentary on Them*. Oxford: Blackwell.

Held, D. (1980) *Introduction to Critical Theory: Horkheimer to Habermas*. Berkeley: University of California Press.

Holton, G. (1993) *Science and Anti-science*. Cambridge, MA: Harvard University Press.

Mrs. Green's
natural market

HAPPY HOLIDAYS FROM MRS. GREEN'S
EASTCHESTER, NY   10583

```
          WAFFLE.BUCKWHEAT W        2.29 F
          WAFFLE.BUCKWHEAT W        2.29 F
          DELI.                     4.49 F
0.46 lb @ 1.39 /lb
T     TANGERINES                     .64 F
   **** TAX       .00  BAL          9.71
C MO  20% EMPLOYEE DISC             1.94-F
   **** TAX       .00  BAL          7.77
        CASH                       20.02
        CHANGE                     12.25
        COUPONS TENDERED   1.94
TAL NUMBER OF ITEMS SOLD =   4
/19/02  3:03 PM 0002 02 0119 2130
```

IT HAS BEEN A PLEASURE SERVING YOU!
     YOUR CASHIER WAS MANILIA
Your Local One Stop Organic Market
THANK YOU ** PLEASE COME AGAIN **
NE (914)472-0111 FAX(914)472-0624

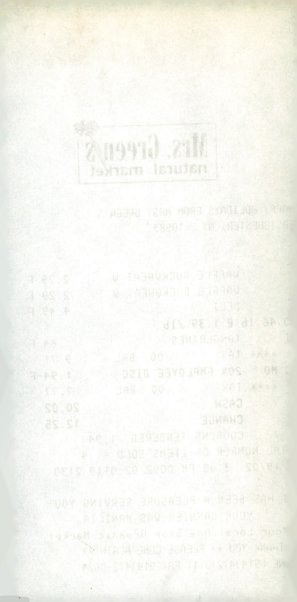

Hollway, W. (1989) *Subjectivity and Method in Psychology: Gender, Meaning and Science*. London: Sage.

Mama, A. (1995) *Beyond the Masks: Race, Gender and Subjectivity*. London: Routledge.

Murphy, R. (1995) Sociology as if nature did not matter: an ecological critique, *British Journal of Sociology*, 46(4): 688–707.

Nightingale, D. J. (1999) Bodies: reading the body, in I. Parker and the Bolton Discourse Network (eds) *Critical Textwork*. Buckingham: Open University Press.

Parker, I. (1992) *Discourse Dynamics: Critical Analysis for Social and Individual Psychology*. London: Routledge.

Parker, I. (1997a) Discursive psychology, in D. Fox and I. Prilletensky (eds) *Critical Psychology: An Introduction*. London: Sage.

Parker, I. (1997b) *Social Constructionism, Discourse and Realism*. London: Sage.

Patten, B. (1981) A Blade of Grass, in *Love Poems*. London: Hutchinson.

Potter, J. and Wetherell, M. (1987) *Discourse and Social Psychology: Beyond Attitudes and Behaviour*. London: Sage.

Potter, J. (1996) Discourse analysis and constructionist approaches: theoretical background, in J. T. E. Richardson (ed.) *Handbook of Qualitative Research Methods*. Leicester: B. P. S. Publications.

Searle, J. (1995) *The Construction of Social Reality*. London: Penguin.

Taylor, B. (1987) *Modernism, Postmodernism, Realism: A Critical Perspective for Art*. Winchester: Winchester School of Art Press.

Tolman, C. W. (1994) *Psychology, Society and Subjectivity: An Introduction to German Critical Psychology*. London: Routledge.

Wetherell, M. and Potter, J. (1992) *Mapping the Languages of Racism*. London: Harvester Wheatsheaf.

Willig, C. (1997) Social constructionism and revolutionary socialism: a contradiction in terms? in I. Parker (ed.) *Social Constructionism, Discourse and Realism*. London: Sage Publications.

PART I

A critical analysis of theory

2 Critical reflexive humanism and critical constructionist psychology

IAN PARKER

Introduction

This chapter is about the role of humanism, interpretation and reflexivity in critical psychology. *Humanism* has many connotations (depending on what it is being contrasted with), but always emphasizes the status, import- ance, powers and achievements of people – rather than emphasizing, say, the socio-cultural resources they draw upon. In psychology, humanism is associated with holistic approaches to the person, which emphasize the subject's agency, rationality and self-awareness. Of course, we would like to be subjects of this kind, as close as possible to things in the world and to the things we do, self-present and transparent to our own natures. The problem is that as soon as we start to use language, our experience becomes mediated and complicated. The discourses and practices that make it pos- sible for us to be human beings in a culture make any understanding we have of ourselves ambiguous and confused. Things and events do not speak directly to us. Human life is necessarily complex and contradictory, so we need to *interpret* what is going on. Common sense is not adequate to this task, since it is precisely commonly used language that betrays and misleads us when we try to use it to understand ourselves; instead, we must use theory.

One of the key contributions of constructionism in critical psychology is that it draws attention to the way discourse works ideologically. This is why some of us draw upon Michel Foucault's (1976, 1981) description of the emergence of certain 'regimes of truth', which seem to give us clear and simple answers about our nature, but actually bind us all the more firmly into relations of power. If we adopt this kind of critical constructionist approach, humanism is problematic – and humanistic psychology even more so. Humanism appeals to a 'self' under the surface that can be transparent to itself and communicate directly with others (Knight 1961; Ayer 1968). Foucault's work suggests that this 'self' serves an ideological purpose, bolstering the illusion of free and equal communication, which helps to mask the operation of power. Nevertheless, in this chapter I will argue that we still need to hold to some variety of humanism, one that is grounded in an understanding of social practice if we want to do progressive work in and against the discipline. This will necessitate taking the role of interpretation seriously, both in our understanding of ourselves and in our analysis of the social construction of our psychology. It also requires us to be *reflexive* when we use theory: to make our theories and analyses able to accommodate our *own* selves and activities (see also Cromby and Standen, this volume, Chapter 10).

Along with culturally grounded humanism and theoretically informed interpretation, then, we need a form of critical reflexivity. Foucault is often treated as an archetypal anti-humanist (e.g. Racevskis 1983) and is used quite correctly to argue against the 'rational unitary subject' of mainstream psychology (Henriques *et al.* 1984). However, I will argue that his work is helpful here, for it provides a way of reflecting on discourse that is embodied, sensitive to forms of power and able to connect theory and practice. Towards the end of the chapter I will outline three themes which flow from these arguments and which should be part of a critical reflexive humanist approach in constructionist psychology.

Problems in psychology and in humanist alternatives

Psychology is about problems. That is to say, the motive behind most research in psychology is a struggle to understand something that does not seem quite right, to make sense of an issue that is problematic. Sometimes that struggle to understand involves problematizing, making strange something that appears too self-evident, too coherent. Then we have to break down the phenomenon into its component parts to see what they do and where they come from.

Breaking up is hard to do

This is where critical research comes in. The dynamic of debates over alternative critical approaches in psychology has been to direct our attention inwards at psychology itself, and the struggle to understand how the discipline works and where it comes from is a vital part of critical reflexive work (Prilleltensky and Fox 1997). Yet there is a paradox here, for critical researchers have often been concerned with a holistic understanding of phenomena and a respect for the integrity of experience. Mainstream psychology has been dehumanizing in its theory and practice, and so humanism has become attractive as an alternative. We find humanism advanced as a 'third force' in North America psychology in the 1960s (Wann 1964; Bugental and Thomas 1967), and humanist sentiments are important in the 'new paradigm' arguments later on. We find some version of humanism, for example, in the demand that we should 'for scientific purposes treat people as if they were human beings' (Harré and Secord 1972: 18), and in the attention to subjectivity in qualitative research (e.g. Reason and Rowan 1981; Banister *et al.* 1994).

The dominance of empiricist and positivist agendas in psychology, and of North American versions in particular, was challenged at the end of the 1960s and beginning of the 1970s. The 'crisis' in modern social psychology heralded a dissatisfaction with 'silent' psychologies across the discipline and a sensitivity to the importance of language in human activity (Parker 1989). Human beings are not silent, but conduct most of their psychological activity through speaking. The 'turn to language' as a 'new paradigm' opened a space for critical research and, in particular, for an interest in discourse as the structuring material of human understanding and practice (Parker 1997).

Ethnomethodology, symbolic interactionism and ordinary-language philosophy were among the micro-sociological resources mixed together in the new paradigm (Harré 1979). Researchers who have had some contact with sociology are often dismayed to find that ideas that seem so innovative to psychologists – and now much qualitative research, discursive psychology and social constructionism is added to the list – are actually quite old, recycled items. A lack of attention to coercion and conflict still marks some recent appropriations from sociology, including ideas from the sociology of scientific knowledge and conversation analysis (Potter and Wetherell 1987; Edwards and Potter 1992; Antaki and Widdicombe 1998). We need to hold on to these issues, to appreciate that when language is structured into discourses it is structured such that spaces are permitted for certain things to be said by certain people, and such that certain subject positions are allowed and others proscribed. Phenomenology has been an important resource in these arguments, for it urges us to focus on the meanings that people make and on varieties of experience of living as psychological beings (Richardson and Fowers 1997). This focus, and the respect for individual meaning making, characterizes both the worst and the best of humanism.

Breaking with humanism

It seems to be in contradiction to humanist values to demand that we should break things up, that we should pull apart our discipline and its methodological apparatus in the name of good critical research. We can address this paradox in two ways, beginning with the understanding that it is not good enough to turn to a simple humanism as a reaction to the mechanistic picture of people that is peddled by traditional psychology. Such simple humanism does not tend to question the way in which subjectivity is constructed because it is so concerned with respecting people's experience. If we want to challenge the dehumanization of 'subjects' by the discipline we cannot take experience, and the meaning people attribute to things' at face value.

The first reason why it would be a mistake to do so is that all too often we find psychological models and processes reproduced in miniature in people's everyday lives. Many critical researchers who take a social constructionist position argue that this is not because those models and processes are real and psychology has 'discovered' them, but because psychological knowledge is now part of the structure of common sense (Harré 1983; Shotter 1993). When people talk about accessing their memory as if it were a storage machine, or about debugging relationships as if they were systems, for example, they are doing precisely that, *talking* about their experience and behaviour in a particular way. Cognitive psychology and computer modelling may then seem appropriate to understand those mental processes, but we need to explore where that talk has come from in the first place instead of assuming that we have revealed something about thinking. Similarly, when people talk about family rivalries in their childhood to explain their experience, or refer to unconscious reasons for things they do, we need to ask where those ways of talking come from and what function they serve.

There is a point here that we will pick up again later, which is that the accounts that people give of their own and others' mental states are structured. The advantage of social constructionism in psychology is precisely that it homes in on that point, rather than accepting psychological phenomena as they appear directly and immediately to us. We need some theoretical understanding of how they are structured, what role they play in culture and what role psychology plays in forming those accounts. It is most important, too, that we hold on to the point that our research should focus on the accounts themselves, rather than discovering hidden mental machinery beneath the surface.

The second reason why we cannot take experience and meaning at face value is that we thereby miss or gloss over the very work of contradiction in psychology. For all the competition between the two, popular humanism shares with psychology the idea that coherence or consistency is the bedrock of human reality and of good theory about it. In humanist defences of human beings against so-called scientific explanations of behaviour, this is played out in the figures of 'integrity', 'growth' or 'self-actualisation' (e.g. Rogers 1961; Maslow 1973). In mechanistic psychological investigations, which often violate human understanding, we see it played out in the obsession with consistency in theories or assessment schedules. The principle of 'parsimony' in psychological theorizing, in which the simplest, most economical explanation for phenomena is favoured, is just one expression of the attempt to filter out the messiness of mental life and the complex accounts we develop to make sense of it. Contradiction, inconsistency, ambiguity and ambivalence are the stuff of human psychology, and once we can take them on board we can better understand why the discipline of psychology is itself so incoherent and fragmented.

The problem with humanism is exacerbated when it becomes turned into a humanist psychology (e.g. Rowan 1994; Greening 1998). Humanist values are crucial to any hope for progressive social change, and they underpin Marxist critiques of dehumanization in capitalist society, for example (Novack 1983). However, in the hands of psychologists, they become a warrant for the reduction of social processes to the level of the individual (e.g. Nevill 1977). It is for this reason that feminists, who have helped to maintain humanist values in a dehumanizing world, have been scathing about what humanistic psychology does to devalue connections between women's experience and political struggle (e.g. Lerman 1992; Waterhouse 1993). We need to contrast humanistic psychology, which performs the same kind of ideological victim-blaming as the rest of the discipline, with the standpoint of a more complex critical humanism.

Construction and interpretation

Humanistic psychologists often pretend that psychological reality is clear and simple, and that we can feel it directly. Traditional psychologists make the same mistake when they think that observation and measurement are the keys to good science, and their approach culminates in empiricism, which simply collects and collates what can be observed. However, there is a problem, which is that there is always an 'interpretative gap' between representations of the world, which include all our observations and constructions of behaviour and feelings, and the things themselves (see also Pujol and Montenegro, this volume, Chapter 6). Three forms of the gap have been described in the sociology of scientific knowledge by Woolgar (1988), and what he calls the 'methodological horrors' are irresolvable in empiricist research. These horrors are 'inconcludability' (in which every representation can always be augmented by further different displays of the phenomenon as a kind of data), 'indexicality' (in which every description is so tightly tied to specific contexts that the description must change as soon as it leaves the particularity of a phenomenon) and 'reflexivity' (in which the position of the researcher affects the phenomenon). Reflexivity operates by virtue of the indexicality of things and is manifest in the way our statistical descriptions may be useful but are also always inconcludable. These look like problems for traditional psychology, but we should see them as vital processes and resources for addressing real-world problems, and for problematizing the real world.

Methodological horrors

Inconcludability draws our attention to the way a complete description of a phenomenon is impossible. There is always more that could be said, always a further layer of theoretical and meta-theoretical reflection that could be added. A social constructionist approach focuses on the way certain descriptions become 'real' for people, and on opportunities for change. A review, a critical review, then a synthesis of different positions and then a critique are dialectical building blocks of knowledge in any scientific community (including psychology). Despite this being a necessary characteristic of academic work, it is usually dealt with by writing it off as trivial. This problem also emphasizes the importance of interpretation in research. Humanistic psychology closes the gap by trying to reach the 'authentic' real 'things in themselves', at which point interpretation can come to a halt.

The term 'indexicality' helpfully reminds us that an explanation is glued to the circumstances in which it is used. Words, phrases and complete accounts are never independent of context, and we can make sense of them only in relation to a specific occasion or set of occasions. This is why social constructionism always locates its descriptions in specific contexts, rather than pretending to find universal realities lurking under the surface. This indexicality of meaning and explanation is a consequence of the interpretative gap, so it highlights the ubiquity of interpretation. One conventional way of dealing with this is to treat it as a simple technical problem, one that someone else will deal with. Humanistic psychology also tries to close the gap by finding underlying 'essential qualities' of experience that exist independent of context.

The third methodological horror, reflexivity, reminds us that our observations are affected by us as observers, by our relationship to what is observed. This goes beyond the way our preconceptions draw attention to certain things and lead us to disregard others, to the way our place in the same field of experience as the research object recreates what it is possible for us to say about it. An acknowledgement of reflexivity, then, sets in train a spiral of reflections upon the changes that an awareness of us as observer brings about. Psychology once again usually finds it simpler to ignore reflexivity, or to sideline its importance as a philosophical problem, as if it were simply not our department. Here, humanism has been useful in prompting us to take reflexivity seriously, but it also opens up some problems for us. For at the very moment it provokes us to turn around and reflect on our place in the world and our work as psychologists, it threatens to lead us into a spiral of self-questioning that prevents us from taking a position. There is just such a danger in relativist forms of social constructionism, which focus on language and play with it, instead of doing something practical and critical with it.

Implications for research

Critical research transforms the methodological horrors into methodological virtues by taking indexicality, inconcludability and reflexivity seriously as part of social and mental life and of the process of creating and critiquing knowledge. This has been very important for the development of qualitative research in psychology (Banister *et al.* 1994).

Some of the endemic problems that beset traditional research in psychology can only be addressed by breaking from empiricism and, instead, working with the interpretive gap. Ecological validity, for example, is treated as a problem because empiricist psychologists are trapped in a chain of reasoning which says that the only way we can make the experiment more like the real world is to isolate and control it further (Brunswik 1947). This line of argument is often supplemented by one which says that the greater the number of instances of subjects or behaviour that are collected, the better you will be able to find a fit between the findings here and the reality out there. Another example is that of 'demand characteristics', which are treated as a problem when they are conceptualized as aspects of the research situation that prompt the 'subject' to guess what the hypothesis is and respond according to that guess (Orne 1962). Here, empiricists are faced with the impossible task of setting up a situation in which subjects must simply behave as if they too were empiricists, as if they had no theories about what they were doing and what was being done to them. A third problem is sometimes introduced to manage this, which is to turn the power of the empiricist spotlight onto the subject and look for 'volunteer characteristics', which determine why people who turn up to take part in experiments not only are younger, brighter, friendlier and less conservative but also display a strong need for approval (Rosenthal 1965). Another level of interpretation is thus added to account for the peculiarity of psychological research results, but it is one which is designed to ensure that the deliberate self-conscious activity of interpretation itself is still screened out. Here, it is the subject that is seen as the problem, not what *we* are doing.

To work with the interpretive gap is to open up the questions of ecological validity, demand characteristics and volunteer characteristics again
in a different way, but now to keep them open rather than getting nervous
about their danger to science. Ecological validity is the core to questions
of validity in general in psychology, and can be addressed by exploring and
specifying in detail the particular characteristics of the phenomenon in question. Surely what are called 'demand characteristics' are the necessary pre-
requisites for research to take place, and it is useful to reflect on the ways
in which the 'interviewee' or 'research participant' is invited to puzzle and
theorize about the research question. To talk of volunteer characteristics is
a rather clumsy and mechanistic way of drawing attention to the particular
qualities of the case in question, whether that case is a person, a group, an
institution or an ideological form. Critical researchers often prefer intensive
case studies for the very reason that they permit them to respect the specificity
of the problem, of participant involvement and of the material collected.
Some writers in the philosophy of science would argue that an intensive
case study is actually the key to good research in the natural sciences, and
that psychology should learn about what really happens there if it wishes to
be scientific itself (Harré and Secord 1972). These ways of approaching the
problems do not plug the interpretive gap, but they do explore what creative work is done to manage its enduring reality in social and mental life
and its reflections in action and experience.

However, we also need to reflect on reflexivity, for although humanist
approaches encourage us to take reflexivity seriously, we need to ground it
in an understanding of power and social practice.

Reflexivity, politics and power in psychological research

One of the symptoms of relativist discourse in psychology is that there is
often a simple appeal to 'reflexivity' to solve problems of politics and power
in the discipline (e.g. Potter 1998). Some writers in the tradition of discourse analysis also appeal to reflexivity, even though they are otherwise
extremely suspicious of anything that looks therapeutic, to the extent that
talk of subjectivity of any sort is accused by them of slipping into humanistic psychology. Reflexivity is often felt to be a kind of space that we can
escape into, as if we could then look upon the discipline from a distance, or
reflexivity is sometimes even thought to be a solvent in which the abusive
aspects of psychology can be dissolved. The activity of thinking back and
thinking around an issue, and situating oneself, which is a valuable and
necessary part of deconstructive and discursive therapeutic work, is thought
to illuminate all problems and, in that very process, solve them.

I am caricaturing a bit here of course, but what I want to draw attention
to is the mistake sometimes made by radicals in the discipline when they

imagine that simply to turn around and reflect on what we are doing, as researchers or practitioners, is enough. I should also quickly point out that I am not impugning critical reflection on our practices, and I want to draw a contrast between reflexivity as such and a critical reflection. While reflexivity is something that proceeds from within the interior of the self, and participates in all of the agonizing confessional work that Foucault (1976, 1981) so brilliantly describes, critical reflection traces the subjective investments we make in our everyday practice, and traces them to the networks of institutional power that contain us. While reflexivity can be a passive contemplative enterprise that all too often succeeds in paralysing individuals as they take responsibility for the pain and troubles of a painful and troubling set of circumstances, critical reflection is an active rebellious practice that drives individuals into action as they identify the exercise of power that pins them into place and the fault lines for the production of spaces of resistance.

Foucault, practice and counter-practice

Some of the most critical work in psychology threatens to fall into passive reflection on the discipline, and this even goes on in the name of an analysis of power and resistance. A case in point is the way in which Foucault's work is sometimes reinterpreted, so that instead of being a threat to power it becomes an avoidance of political action (e.g. Minson 1980; Soyland and Kendall 1997).

Foucault is particularly important to us because his description of surveillance and confession in Western culture, which accounts for the development of the 'psy-complex' (Ingleby 1985; Rose 1985), comes from the very heart of the discipline. It is often forgotten that Foucault was a psychologist by training, and that his analysis of individual identity was grounded in clinical experience in psychiatric wards and prisons (Parker 1995). Foucault's work marks a turning point, both in the way that the objects of psychology may be conceptualized and in the methods we may use to understand those objects. His founding concerns were how we understand and experience abnormality and distress. The ways we account for different modes of psychological function must now also include a reflection upon the network of classifications that divide what is normal from what is not (Parker *et al.* 1995). Psychology is a powerful actor in this network, a network Foucault saw as made up of what he termed 'dividing practices'. His approach emphasizes the ways in which the theory and practice of psychology meet in correctional, therapeutic and welfare settings to specify how personal experience is to be defined and treated.

The ways we conceptualize the work of psychology, and the significance of what Foucault (1977) was to call 'counter-practice' in and against the discipline, also remind us that he was an exemplary 'engaged intellectual'. Many of us now using his work in psychology have come to see that it just not possible to do so in good faith unless we also develop a counter-practice. The organization Psychology Politics Resistance is the product of many different strands of political opinion (Reicher and Parker 1993), but important among those strands is the spirit of Michel Foucault. It is appropriate that this is how his work as academic and activist appears again today in the world of psychology.

I would want to hold on to some variety of reflexive activity as prerequisite for, and necessary accompaniment to, politics outside and inside psychology. The critical reflection I have described carries with it the best and most progressive elements of reflexivity. Like any other approach, we use Foucault as part of a transitional strategy to bring psychologists up against the barriers to change in the discipline. Foucauldian discursive approaches assist that activity of reflection on the barriers constructed in the institutional discourse of psychology.

Constructing critical reflexive humanism in psychology

We have arrived at the point where we can draw together some of the problems that psychology poses and reconstruct them as issues that critical research can address. Perhaps one of the main outcomes of this process of critical reflection on the way psychology inhibits the work of interpretation is that it allows us to formulate more clearly what more we want out of good research. When the discipline defines what 'science' is in a restricted way which pretends to model itself on the natural sciences, it also defines what desires we permit ourselves to express, and, as a consequence, we can easily forget what led many of us into psychology in the first place.

Let us conclude, then, with a review of key points for a critical constructionist psychology. Some versions of discursive psychology that have been imported from psychology's close neighbours, in particular from sociology and micro-sociology, have often failed to take these issues seriously, and sometimes we have just been left with something that masquerades as a progressive alternative but is actually dismissive of the problems psychology poses and itself maintains. I will describe three components to more useful research.

Agency and social action

We need to take subjectivity seriously, but we need to take that a step further to look at how the subjectivity of the researcher affects and interconnects with that of the researched, and, in particular, what forms of agency are facilitated or blocked in the process (Parker 1998). An attention to subjectivity should not be a licence for individual navel-gazing, and this means that it should be considered as a relational issue, not one that simply resides in the individual. There have been attempts to emphasize agency in alternative psychology over the past decade, but often the appeal to the individual has been too simple and voluntaristic.

While symbolic interactionism has made a useful contribution to psychological notions of self-identity, and drawn attention to the ways in which meanings are shared symbolic resources (Mead 1934), we need to be cautious about the conceptions of agency that have been imported with it. It is all too easy simply to assert that human beings are endowed with agency, or even to say that this is produced out of interaction with significant others. A further step should surely be a thorough account of the ways in which different forms of consensus are maintained in symbolic interaction, and the way agency operates as much through resistance as through the uncomplicated exercise of a mysterious human gift. The attention to subjectivity, then, leads us to ask for fairly sophisticated accounts of agency.

Interpretation and theory

If we are to take as our starting point the always already interpreted nature of social and psychological reality, we need to take the next step and look for theoretical frameworks that can assist in comprehending accounts. Interpretation is guided by implicit theories of the self and the world, even when one tries to avoid theorizing. For example, one of the mistakes of ethnomethodology (drawn in from micro-sociology during the paradigm crisis debates) was to pretend that one could dispense with grand theory because it always reified activity and treated 'accomplishments as things' (Garfinkel 1967). This refusal of theory leads us into mere descriptions of behaviour, which all too often amount to little more than mindless empiricism (Harré 1981).

Psychologists who turn to critical research sometimes eschew theory altogether, as a reaction to the dehumanizing models of human beings that they have had to put up with. The assertion of a simple humanism and defence of uncomplicated subjectivity against psychological fake science sometimes then goes alongside a refusal to develop any account which does not completely accord with the immediate felt life experience of research participants. Ethnomethodology is one of the end points, one of the culs-de-sac, of this line of reasoning. An understanding of the power psychological models enjoy cannot be developed if you refuse to go beyond everyday accounts, and if you treat all theory as totalizing and reifying. So, as a way of managing the interpretive gap we need to develop useful theory.

Reflexivity, knowledge and power

The accounts we gather in critical research, the language we study and the language we study it in are all forms of knowledge which distribute rights to know and rights to speak to different people in different social positions. The role of science, for example, as a master discourse, a form of knowledge that is privileged over common sense, is very much at issue in psychology as a discipline that likes to think of itself as a science. There have been attempts to conceptualize the relationship between different forms of knowledge, and the ways in which the distribution of representations of the world operates ideologically to open up or close down certain forms of action. The shift from individual cognition to the study of shared 'social representations' in an influential current of French research has been particularly important, to the extent that writers in the 'new paradigm' claimed that they too were always studying social representations. There is also a concern with the ways reified and consensual forms of knowledge function in society and give to social actors frameworks to understand themselves (Moscovici 1976).

Nevertheless, it must be said that much of this work tends to reify science as if it were a special knowledge, rather than looking at the institutions in which it is embedded, the ways in which it operates in the service of power through discursive practices, and we need to take care not to idealize consensual universes as the 'other' to science. All forms of knowledge need to be thrown into question, treated as problematic, and we need to attend to the way knowledge is intertwined with power. This would be a third component of good emancipatory research.

Social constructionism has been invaluable to the development of critical psychology, and it invites us to reflect on the way each and every psychological experience we have is constituted in forms of discourse and practice rather than given and to be taken for granted. It leads us to interpret the complexity of human life and ask how it has come to be the way it is, rather than adopting assumptions that are relayed through common sense and that then feel as if they must be true. It also means that if we are to be humanist in our work we have to be so in a more theoretically sophisticated way than is advocated by humanistic psychology. We need a complex humanism, a good deal of interpretation underpinned by theories that take power seriously and a critical reflexivity that is embodied and grounded in forms of practice.

References

Antaki, C. and Widdicombe, S. (eds) (1998) *Identities in Talk*. London: Sage.
Ayer, A. J. (ed.) (1968) *The Humanist Outlook*. London: Pemberton.

Banister, P., Burman, E., Parker, I., Taylor, M. and Tindall, C. (1994) *Qualitative Methods in Psychology*. Buckingham: Open University Press.

Brunswik, E. (1947) *Systematic and Unrepresentative Design of Psychological Experiments with Results in Physical and Social Perception*. Berkeley: University of California Press.

Bugental, J. and Thomas, J. (1967) *Challenges of Humanistic Psychology*. New York: McGraw-Hill.

Burman, E., Aitken, G., Alldred, P. *et al.* (1996) *Psychology Discourse Practice: From Regulation to Resistance*. London: Taylor and Francis.

Derrida, J. (1978) *Writing and Difference*. London: Routledge and Kegan Paul.

Edwards, D. and Potter, J. (1992) *Discursive Psychology*. London: Sage.

Foucault, M. (1976) *Discipline and Punish: The Birth of the Prison*. Harmondsworth: Penguin.

Foucault, M. (1977) *Language, Counter-memory, Practice: Selected Essays and Interviews*. Oxford: Blackwell.

Foucault, M. (1981) *The History of Sexuality, Volume I: An Introduction*. Harmondsworth: Penguin.

Garfinkel, H. (1967) *Studies in Ethnomethodology*. New York: Prentice Hall.

Greening, T. (1998) Five postulates of humanistic psychology, *Journal of Humanistic Psychology*, 38(1): 9.

Harré, R. (1979) *Social Being: A Theory for Social Psychology*. Oxford: Basil Blackwell.

Harré, R. (1981) The positivist–empiricist approach and its alternative, in P. Reason and J. Rowan (eds) *Human Inquiry: A Sourcebook of New Paradigm Research*. Chichester: Wiley.

Harré, R. (1983) *Personal Being: A Theory for Individual Psychology*. Oxford: Basil Blackwell.

Harré, R. and Secord, P. F. (1972) *The Explanation of Social Behaviour*. Oxford: Basil Blackwell.

Henriques, J., Hollway, W., Urwin, C., Venn, C. and Walkerdine, V. (1984) *Changing the Subject: Psychology, Social Regulation and Subjectivity*. London: Methuen.

Ingleby, D. (1985) Professionals and socializers: the 'psy complex', *Research in Law, Deviance and Social Control*, 7: 79–109.

Knight, M. (ed.) (1961) *Humanist Anthology*. London: Pemberton.

Lerman, H. (1992) The limits of phenomenology: a feminist critique of the humanistic personality theories, in L. S. Brown and M. Ballou (eds) *Personality and Psychopathology: Feminist Reappraisals*. New York: Guilford Press.

Maslow, A. (1973) *The Farther Reaches of Human Nature*. Harmondsworth: Penguin.

Mead, G. H. (1934) *Mind, Self and Society: From the Standpoint of a Social Behaviorist*. Chicago: Chicago University Press.

Minson, J. (1980) Strategies for socialists? Foucault's conception of power, *Economy and Society*, 9(1): 1–43.

Moscovici, S. (1976) *La Psychanalyse: Son Image et Son Public*, 2nd edn. Paris: Presses Universitaire de France.

Nevill, D. D. (ed.) (1977) *Humanistic Psychology: New Frontiers*. New York: Gardner Press.

Novack, G. (1983) *Humanism and Socialism*. New York: Pathfinder Press.

Orne, M. T. (1962) On the social psychology of the psychology experiment: with particular reference to demand characteristics and their implications, *American Psychologist*, 17: 776–83.

Parker, I. (1989) *The Crisis in Modern Social Psychology, and How to End It*. London: Routledge.

Parker, I. (1995) Michel Foucault, psychologist, *The Psychologist*, 8(11): 214–16.

Parker, I. (1997) Discursive psychology, in D. Fox and I. Prilleltensky (eds) *Critical Psychology: An Introduction*. London: Sage.

Parker, I. (1998) Qualitative data and the subjectivity of 'objective' facts, in D. Dorling and L. Simpson (eds) *Statistics in Society*. London: Arnold.

Parker, I., Georgaca, E., Harper, D., McLaughlin, T. and Stowell-Smith, M. (1995) *Deconstructing Psychopathology*. London: Sage.

Potter, J. (1998) Fragments in the realization of relativism, in I. Parker (ed.) *Social Constructionism, Discourse and Realism*. London: Sage.

Potter, J. and Wetherell, M. (1987) *Discourse and Social Psychology: Beyond Attitudes and Behaviour*. London: Sage.

Prilleltensky, I. and Fox, D. (1997) Introducing critical psychology: values, assumptions, and the status quo, in D. Fox and I. Prilleltensky (eds) *Critical Psychology: An Introduction*. London: Sage.

Racevskis, K. (1983) *Michel Foucault and the Subversion of Intellect*. Ithaca, NY: Cornell University Press.

Reason, P. and Rowan, J. (eds) (1981) *Human Inquiry: A Sourcebook for New Paradigm Research*. Chichester: Wiley.

Reicher, S. and Parker, I. (1993) Psychology politics resistance – the birth of a new organization, *Journal of Community and Applied Social Psychology*, 3: 77–80.

Richardson, F. C. and Fowers, B. J. (1997) Critical theory, postmodernism, and hermeneutics: insights for critical psychology, in D. Fox and I. Prilleltensky (eds) *Critical Psychology: An Introduction*. London: Sage.

Rogers, C. (1961) *On Becoming a Person: A Therapist's View of Psychotherapy*. London: Constable.

Rose, N. (1985) *The Psychological Complex: Psychology, Politics and Society in England 1869–1939*. London: Routledge and Kegan Paul.

Rosenthal, R. (1965) The volunteer subject, *Human Relations*, 18: 389–406.

Rowan, J. (1994) *A Guide to Humanistic Psychology*, 2nd edn. London: Association for Humanistic Psychology in Britain.

Shotter, J. (1993) *Cultural Politics of Everyday Life*. Buckingham: Open University Press.

Soyland, A. J. and Kendall, G. (1997) Abusing Foucault: methodology, critique and subversion, *British Psychological Society History and Philosophy of Psychology Section Newsletter*, 25: 9–17.

Wann, T. W. (ed.) (1964) *Behaviorism and Phenomenology: Contrasting Bases for Modern Psychology*. Chicago: Chicago University Press.

Waterhouse, R. (1993) 'Wild women don't have the blues': a feminist critique of 'person-centred' counselling and therapy, *Feminism and Psychology*, 3(1): 55–71.

Woolgar, S. (1988) *Science: the Very Idea*. Chichester: Ellis Horwood.

3 Beyond appearances: a critical realist approach to social constructionist work

CARLA WILLIG

Chapter aims

Anglo-American academic and applied psychology is deeply reductionist. Dominant psychological theories construct categories such as personality types, cognitive styles or psychopathologies, which are conceptualized as independent variables and thus as potential causes of physical and psychological effects, such as behaviour patterns or symptoms. Social constructionism draws attention to the role of language in the construction of explanatory categories and exposes the way in which research practice creates rather than reveals evidence in support of such categories. As a result, constructionist accounts allow us to challenge positivist reductionist science. This is particularly helpful in relation to psychology, where positivist constructs such as 'intelligence', 'personality' and 'mental illness' are used to divide, discipline and oppress people (e.g. Parker *et al.* 1995). Within this context, social constructionist thought can be empowering because it provides a way of challenging dominant categories and their associated practices.

Constructionist ideas, however, are generally used in order to deconstruct positivist categories without putting alternative, and arguably liberating, concepts in their place. In other words, social constructionism functions predominantly on the level of epistemological critique of the taken-for-granted, but not as social critique of the (socio-economic/material) structures that support positivist categories. As a result, contemporary social constructionism has created a conceptual, and consequently also a political, vacuum.

I would argue that what is needed is an account which not only suggests that things could be different but is capable of explaining why things are as they are and in what ways they could be better. We need to continue to deconstruct contemporary social constructions but we also need to account for their emergence and to trace their psychosocial effects. We need to continue to analyse the complex dynamics involved in the operation of dominant categories and practices, but we also need to begin to recognize the human potential for the transcendence of constraining constructions and to attempt to identify the social conditions which facilitate such a move.

In this chapter I aim to:

- demonstrate that there is no necessary connection between social constructionism and a relativism which denies the possibility of human emancipation;
- identify ways in which social constructionist research can be part of a critical realist project;
- provide some guidance as to the type of psychological research such a perspective requires.

In order to achieve these aims, I draw on the work of psychologists and natural scientists who work with Marxist concepts and methods. A historical-materialist analysis of society, together with a dialectical approach to science, offers a way of politicizing social constructionist work.

Introduction

Foucault's work has become a major reference point for social constructionist writers in psychology (e.g. Parker 1992; Burr 1995). Foucauldian discourse analysis represents one of two dominant approaches to the analysis of texts in social constructionist psychology. Potter and Wetherell (1995) differentiate between a focus on discourse practice and a focus on discursive resources. The former derives from work in conversation analysis and is primarily concerned with what people do with their talk and writing (i.e. its action orientation), such as blaming, excusing, disclaiming. The latter approach draws on the work of Foucault, and it is used in order to explore the ways in which discourses construct subjects and objects. Foucauldian discourse analysis allows us to draw attention to the ways in which different versions of reality are constructed through language. It reminds us that things could always be different, that there are alternative ways of describing an event and that, therefore, every discourse can be deconstructed. As a result, identities and subjectivities are never fixed but are always open to renegotiation and/or resistance.

Deconstructionist psychology can be experienced as empowering because it provides a way of undermining dominant (oppressive) categories and their associated practices. However, Foucault himself recognized the limitations of this type of deconstructionist work. First, Nellhaus (1997) draws attention to the fact that Foucault only claimed to have described systems of discursive ground rules ('epistemes') and that they still needed to be accounted for (Foucault 1980: 113). Second, Fox (1997) points out that Foucault did not have time to address fully his later concern with the way in which discursive subjects become persons: that is, 'the history of how an individual acts upon himself, [in] the technology of the self' (Foucault 1988: 19). In other words, Foucauldian discourse analysis allows us to trace changes in social constructions and to speculate about their implications for subjective experience; however, it does not allow us to account for their emergence and maintenance, and does not help us to understand the dynamics of the self. These absences have allowed social constructionist work in psychology, as elsewhere, to become associated with a relativist position. Here it is argued that since any version of events can be deconstructed, there can be no version which gives us a superior understanding of 'reality'. 'Truth' is not inherent in an account; rather, it is culturally and historically negotiated. I would argue that a social constructionist perspective need not necessarily entail relativism. Social constructionist work needs to become part of a wider historical materialist analysis of society, which is capable of moving beyond a description of 'regimes of truth' and which begins to account for their origin and maintenance. Such an analysis should also allow us to explore human subjectivity and its dynamic processes of self-formation.

Accounting for constructions: beyond appearances

A non-relativist variety of social constructionist research needs to do two things. It needs to provide detailed and comprehensive descriptions of the discourses available to groups and individuals, and of the various ways in which these discourses are deployed and with what consequences. This part of the research is concerned with giving a voice to participants, with documenting accounts of subjective experience. The next step, however, involves an analysis of the conditions (historical, social and economic) that gave rise to and/or made possible these documented subjective accounts and the discourses which constitute them. Subjectivity does not directly reflect the conditions of its origin; however, there is a relationship between the two which can be explored. Particular meanings are made possible by some conditions and not others. For example, Parker (1992: 37–41) identifies material constraints upon discursive change, including direct physical coercion and the material organization of space. He argues that forms of talk require appropriate spaces in which to be practised and elaborated, and that these are not always available. It is important, however, to avoid a reductionist reading according to which the relationship between material conditions and subjectivity is directly determined. Rather, we need to acknowledge the role of 'practice' as a mediator. 'Practice' here refers to individuals' (or collectivities') interpretations of and interactions with the conditions within which they find themselves. Every situation offers more than one possible way of relating to it. Individuals (or collectivities), through their actions, can realize different possible futures inherent in one and the same situation. They can make it something different. It follows that subjectivities, and the discourses which constitute them, are not determined but are accommodated by the material conditions within which they arise. A non-relativist social constructionist psychology needs to be able to explain the processes that mediate such accommodation. Such a psychology needs to be able to explain why a particular individual (or group) makes a particular sense of his or her social environment and how this particular sense-making feeds back into and thus shapes the social environment.

Potentialities

A key concept in the development of a non-relativist social constructionist psychology must be that of 'potentialities'. Potentialities are possible futures that can be accommodated by the present. The concept of 'potentialities' is grounded within a dialectical approach to science (e.g. Levins and Lewontin 1985). Such an approach requires that we abandon the dominant reductionist analytic method in favour of a systems analysis. Levins and Lewontin (1985) argue that reductionist Western science is unable to study intrinsically complex systems because: (a) it isolates parts as completely as possible before studying them; (b) it ignores properties of complex wholes as 'noise' and excludes them from theory and explanation; and (c) it allocates relative weights to separate causes, thus making it difficult to study the nature of interconnectedness. By contrast, a dialectical approach to science maintains that objects or systems are not composed of fixed natural units. 'Parts' have no independent existence as parts and can, therefore, not be studied as such.

Instead, 'the correct division of the whole into parts varies, depending upon the particular aspect of the whole which is in question' (Levins and

Lewontin 1985: 272). For example, a single species may be part of two communities, without thereby joining those communities into one. Parts can be parts only when there is a whole for them to be part of. It follows that the properties of parts have no prior alienated existence but are acquired by being part of a particular whole. Thus, what appears to be the 'same' unit may display very different characteristics in different contexts. Similarly, a whole can become part of a bigger whole, and what was once a part of something bigger can function as a smaller whole. In the same way, subject and object as well as cause and effect can take each other's place within a system. For example, an action such as getting drunk can be a response to an event such as losing one's job, but can in turn become the cause of future developments, such as not getting another job.

Practice

A dialectical view of the world allows us to recognize that social life constitutes the material basis of human experience, and at the same time to acknowledge that social conditions do not directly determine human experience. Rather, they offer a range of possible ways of being which when taken up by social actors transform social life and the possibilities it offers in the future. In other words, the social environment cannot be reduced to an objective, external set of stimuli; instead it is the social conditions of life *as appropriated by the individual* that constitute his or her environment. It is in this sense, according to Holzkamp (1997: 59), that the social environment (*Umwelt*) can be said to be objective, yet at the same time unique and personal to the individual.

The concept of 'practice' is concerned with the mechanisms by which potentialities are realized. Newman and Holzman (1997) draw on the work of Vygotsky in order to develop their notion of performed activity. According to Vygotsky, speech does not express, but completes thought. This means that speaking takes thought beyond what it is, it takes us beyond ourselves and it allows us to grow. In Vygotsky's words, we become who we are by being who we are not (Newman and Holzman 1997: 110). This happens because speaking as a social activity involves relational activities which require that others relate to us as though we understood. In other words, we learn the rules of social performances (e.g. of speech, of games, of conversation) by playing the game. Thus, 'practice' is not about putting something we know into practice but about creating something new. That something, in turn, depends upon the possibilities afforded by the social environment and our ability to tap into them. Newman and Holzman (1997: 129) acknowledge that social performances become 'commodified, routinised and rigidified into behaviour'. As a result, we often act out fixed roles and fail to take up possibilities for development.

Change and transformation

An emphasis upon potentialities and practice provides us with the means of theorizing change and transformation. If social structures offer possibilities for action, rather than determine behaviour, our task is not only to explain why someone did what he or she did but also to identify what else he or she could have done. We can explore the range of potentialities offered by any one situation and we can trace their implications for individual (and collective) experience. As a result, we become concerned with creating a particular future as well as with accounting for the present. This is because potentialities can only ultimately be identified through their realization. This means that analysis must be combined with intervention if it is to be successful. Binns (1973: 5) argues that 'objective truths are not uncovered so much as created. It is in the act of us making them that they become revealed. To attempt to reveal them first and only later to act is to remove practice from where it belongs – within the theory of knowledge.' However, it is important to remember that structures are constraining as well as enabling, and that the range of possibilities for action, though always larger than their realizations, is always also limited. That is to say, we cannot create just any reality.

Discourse, subjectivity and practice: an example

Let us take a closer look at Holzkamp's discussion of racism in order to illustrate the application of non-relativist social constructionist psychology. German Critical Psychology aspires to be a science of the subject (*Subjektwissenschaft*). It conceptualizes the individual as a rational and responsible agent rather than as a mere recipient of and respondent to stimuli and social influences. Critical Psychology attempts to theorize people's determination through their conditions of life and their simultaneous personal responsibility for these conditions. It does this through the concept of 'premises for action'. Premises for action are derived from structures of meaning (or discourses) that are available in the culture. Individuals generally attempt to realize their interests from within such structures of meaning, even though it is possible to challenge, subvert and transcend them. Thus, individuals always act rationally, that is to say with good reason, although their actions are not necessarily actually in their own interests. Let us apply these ideas to the phenomenon of individual racism.

Holzkamp (1997) argues that in order to understand and challenge individual racism we need to start from the point of view of those who express racist ideas and/or who adopt racist practices. This is in keeping with critical psychology's status as a science of the subject. Thus, racists become the subject of the research, not its objects (as is the case with theories which

propose that early childhood experiences, authoritarian personality structures or irrational emotions lie at the root of individual racism). Here, we
listen to and take note of the ways in which individuals use dominant
discourses, including institutionalized racist discourses, in order to define
and realize their interests. This is followed by an exploration of the premises for action derived from the discourses used and their implications for
their users' ability to act in the future. For example, the attempt to extend
one's own possibilities for action at the expense of others (e.g. through
dominating others) can strengthen the restrictions faced by the subject in
the first place (through isolation and the loss of partners in the struggle to
extend shared possibilities for action). In this way, premises for action
are problematized and the tensions between the individual's short- and
long-term interests identified. Throughout this process, the 'subjects' of the
research remain partners in conversation. The objects of research are the
discourses rather than their users. The research process, however, must not
stop once racist discourses have been identified and explored. The next step
involves the search for higher order, or wider, discourses of which racist
discourse forms a part. For example, majority–minority discourse includes
racist discourse, but it constructs a much wider range of 'person categories',
including 'homosexuals', 'the mentally ill', 'the elderly', 'the unemployed',
'the poor', 'criminals', 'the disabled', 'the homeless' and many more. These
categories are, of course, not mutually exclusive, and an exploration of
minority–majority discourse demonstrates that it is capable of positioning
even its users as members of minority groups and thus of legitimating their
own marginalization. It follows that the use of racist discourse is not in
the long-term interests of its users since it strengthens and perpetuates
majority–minority discourse, which is capable of marginalizing everyone.
Holzkamp points out that the labelling and condemnation of 'racists' is
itself dependent upon majority–minority discourse, a form of 'marginalization in the name of the fight against marginalization' (Holzkamp 1997:
296), and that it is therefore unlikely to eradicate individual racism. Instead,
he recommends the collective transcendence of racist discourse through the
realization that it does not actually serve the interests of its users but that
it disempowers, disciplines and divides all its users. In this sense, Critical
Psychology advocates a form of reflexive action research which allows individuals to reflect upon the grounding of their actions in structures of meaning and to identify alternative ways-of-being afforded by those structures.

Discourse: its role and status

Discourses contain a range of subject positions which in turn facilitate and/
or constrain certain experiences and practices. Discourses mediate between
objective conditions of life and the individual's subjective experience of
these conditions. For example, within a Catholic discourse, the individual is

positioned as the passive recipient of the trials and tribulations of mortal life, and is expected to carry his or her cross with humility and resignation. From within this discourse, adverse circumstances constitute a challenge and an opportunity for the faithful to display qualities of meekness and endurance. By contrast, discourses of modernity which construct human beings as progressively gaining control over nature define adverse circumstances as a problem to be solved and as an opportunity to deploy the human qualities of rational thought and forward planning. Thus, what are in one sense the same objective material conditions (e.g. food shortages) constitute different social environments (*Umwelten*) for individuals who ground their responses to them in different structures of meaning: that is, in different discourses.

According to Holzkamp (1997), institutionalized discourses constitute societal structures of meaning which contain opportunities and constraints in relation to action. These can be uncritically adopted by individuals but they can also be reflected upon, challenged, subverted and ultimately transcended. Individuals' actions are grounded within and through these structures of meaning. In this way, they become premises for action. Subjectivity is, therefore, equated with the ability to act (Holzkamp 1997: 400). Thus, individual actions are not caused by societal conditions but they are grounded in them and mediated by them. Conditions of life, as experienced by the individual through discourses, provide reasons for the individual's actions. It follows that from a non-relativist social constructionist point of view, meanings are afforded by discourses, accommodated by social structures and changed by human actors.

Critical realism

I have argued that in order to become part of a non-relativist project, social constructionist research needs to begin to account for the social constructions it deconstructs. This involves the identification of 'action spaces' provided by the material and historical relations between individual and society, and the diverse ways in which these are discursively constructed. It also includes an analysis of 'social-historical forms of economic, political, juridical and ideological structures in terms of the relative possibilities for action that the various class-and-position-specific life worlds contain' (Maiers and Tolman 1996: 112). Such an analysis is important because it demonstrates that social constructions are grounded within, yet not directly reflective of social structures, and because it identifies the opportunities for as well as the limitations on human action.

A non-relativist approach to social contructionist research needs to adopt a critical realist position with regard to the question of 'knowledge'. Critical realism subscribes to epistemological relativism only insofar as it acknowledges 'the impossibility of knowing objects except under particular descriptions' (Bhaskar 1978: 249). This echoes the dialectical insight dis-cussed earlier, that parts have no independent existence as parts and that there is no one correct way of dividing a whole up into parts because this depends upon which particular aspect of the whole is being studied. How-ever, critical realism maintains ontological realism by proposing that events (observable and experienceable phenomena) are generated by underlying, relatively enduring structures, such as biochemical, economic or social struc-tures. These cannot be directly accessed but they can be detected through their effects. These intransitive structures do not directly determine out-comes; rather, they possess tendencies, or potentialities, which may or may not be realized. Therefore, the objective of critical realist science is not to predict outcomes but to explain events as the specific realizations of struc-tural possibilities.

From within this perspective, then, social constructions and discourses cannot be independent from material structures; rather, they are historic-ally and culturally variable ways of making different kinds of sense of the phenomena and events generated by intransitive structures.

Motivation: making sense and fulfilling needs

It is important to acknowledge that the perspective developed above depends upon the assumption that human beings actively manipulate their environment in order to fulfil their needs.

While neither 'environment' nor 'needs' is an objectively defined non-discursive entity, the motivation to act in what one perceives to be one's interests is assumed to be universal. For example, Osterkamp (1997: 11) refers to the '*a priori* of Critical Psychology', which states that 'one cannot consciously violate one's own interests', while Maiers and Tolman (1996: 112) adopt the premise that 'no one is knowingly his or her own enemy'. Maiers and Tolman (1996: 111) define the 'material *a priori* of human self-consciousness, of interpersonal understanding and thus also of subject-scientific knowledge' as follows: 'An individual's action becomes, in principle, intelligible for others on the basis that no one acts consciously contrary to his or her vital interests as he or she understands them.' Such an under-standing of human motivation is grounded within a Marxist conception of 'human nature'. Although Marx emphasized the plasticity of human nature, its ability to accommodate a large variety of practices and experi-ences, to the point of claiming that 'All history is nothing but the continu-ous transformation of human nature' (Marx 1975), he also maintained that the realization of human freedom is not an abnegation of our needs but their properly human fulfilment. Thus, productive activity, imposed upon us by natural necessity as the fundamental condition of human survival and development, offers the possibility of human fulfilment and gratification. Meszaros (1970) distinguishes between 'inherently human needs' and alienated, or 'abstracted', needs. The latter, such as the need for money or power, are historical needs which tell us more about the society within which they emerged than about human beings. They are in conflict with the social nature of human beings and they are limitless: that is, they can never be satisfied. By contrast, 'inherently human needs' are the needs of a social producer and transformer of the conditions necessary for survival, including socio-economic institutions. They include the need to have some control over these conditions.

Another, perhaps more controversial, assumption is that human beings act rationally in the sense that their actions are purposive rather than expressive. Even though human action can appear irrational or senseless to an outside observer, according to this perspective, individuals always have reasons for acting the way they do. Moreover, these reasons are always contemporary in that they are grounded within structures of meaning which mediate between the environment and the individual's experience of it. In other words, human action is rational from within the structures of meaning individuals use in order to realize their interests as they perceive them. In this sense, emotions are rational, too, because they are associated with structures of meaning, or discourses. Emotional experiences are practices which are bound up with discourses, rather than independent biological or psychological entities (e.g. Averill 1985; Holzkamp 1997: 334–7). As such, they can be nurtured and learned, they can fulfil functions and serve purposes, and they can potentially be transcended. Emotional practices, like discourses, can be impediments to the realization of the individual's long-term interests while being functional in the short term: that is, within a restrictive mode (see Maiers and Tolman 1996: 111–12). For example, the expression of jealousy is designed to secure a partner's attachment but is likely to succeed only in preventing his or her departure in the short term.

Research practice

Non-relativist social constructionist research constitutes a challenge to its practitioners. It requires a strong interdisciplinary orientation, the ability to work with others who may not agree with us and the willingness to take responsibility for the social and political consequences of our work. The seven dimensions discussed below constitute the basic ingredients of such research. They are presented as a sequence of stages of research; however, they can be constructively integrated in practice.

Documentation of subjective experience

First of all, we need to document individuals' subjective life experience. This is to say, we need to start from the standpoint of those whose actions we aim to understand. This part of the research requires that we listen carefully to how people describe their experiences, how they account for their actions and how they make sense of others' behaviour. A lot of qualitative research stops at this point. Having given participants 'a voice', having documented their subjective experience of a particular situation, the researcher is content simply to systematize the data in some way (e.g. through grounded theory or phenomenological methods). Alternatively, discourse analysis may be carried out, in which case the research is completed once prevalent discursive constructions and their action orientations have been identified. This type of qualitative research is associated with a relativist position which suggests that different ways of seeing the world can be, and ought to be, documented but cannot be explained. Non-relativist social constructionist research, however, needs to move beyond documentation and towards explanation.

Discourse analysis of these

The next step within our research programme involves collective discourse analysis of the accounts collected earlier. Here, participants in the research engage in critical reflection on the texts they have produced. They identify discourses they have drawn on in their accounts, they explore the positionings which these discourses contain and trace their implications for practice and experience. This includes the identification of opportunities for action that are offered by the discursive constructions of objects and subjects produced by the accounts. In addition, limitations and constraints on action and experience are also identified. Crawford *et al.* (1992) provide a useful discussion of collective discourse analysis as a research method.

Identification of alternatives

Having explored the discourses that structure their accounts, participants attempt to formulate alternatives to these. This is to say, they try to think of other ways in which they might have 'read' their experiences. In order to facilitate this task, participants may wish to draw on other sources, such as historical writings, cross-cultural writings or other forms of literature. Alternatively, this phase of the research may involve discussions with groups of people whose experiences differ from those of the participants. Again, positionings, opportunities for action and implications for practice and experience of these alternative discursive constructions are identified.

Exploration of the relationship between discourses and institutions

Parker (1992) draws attention to the fact that discourses are implicated with the structure of institutions. Discursive practices reproduce the material basis of an institution and thus reinforce the power of the institution. For example, the racist discursive practice of checking passports at airports reproduces the material basis of the institution (in this case, the nation state) and thus reinforces its power. The next phase of our research programme, therefore, requires an exploration of the institutional grounding of the discourses identified earlier. Here, we need to establish which institutions are reinforced by the discourses we use and which institutions may be challenged or undermined by them (see Parker 1992: 17–18).

Exploration of the historical emergence of discourses

Discourses have histories as well as relationships with each other. In order really to appreciate the ways in which discursive constructions position us and with what consequences, we need to be aware of the historical contexts in which they emerged and which, in turn, they helped to constitute. For example, the recent emergence of a discourse of commerce within the traditional public service sector in the UK, whereby rail users, students and patients have become 'customers' instead of clients, who expect 'value for money' instead of care, was part of a wider project of privatization initiated by the Conservative government in the 1980s. The final step in our collective discourse analysis, therefore, involves the tracing of our discourses' histories, the identification of their conditions of emergence and their changes over time.

Analysis of the material basis of discourse

Closely related to an exploration of the historical emergence of discourses is an analysis of the material basis of discourse. Here, we need to establish a link between what can be said and thought, and the structures that can accommodate such discourse. In other words, we need to ask what the world must be like for those ideas and activities to be possible (see Bhaskar 1979). For example, Nellhaus (1997) discusses the materials and practices through which discourse is produced, and he argues that changes in material communication practices cause epistemic shifts. He suggests that the emergence of print culture encouraged introspection, individualism and social atomism, with the reader viewing the world from isolation. He argues that 'our analytical imagination is strongly shaped by our most basic and frequent experiences of receiving and producing knowledge – that is, by the practice of communication' (Nellhaus 1997: 10). An analysis of the material basis of discourse requires a careful exploration of the ways in which forms of material and social organization shape forms of discourse.

Formulation of recommendations for practice to bring about change

Finally, and arguably most importantly, our research must be applied. This is to say, our collective discourse analysis must generate recommendations for practice. It must have something to say about how psychological, social and/or political practice can be improved. For example, if our object of analysis is racist discourse, then we would expect our analysis to tell us something about how racist discourse and practice may be eradicated.

There are (at least) two ways in which collective discourse analysis informed by the above guidelines can impact upon social life. First, its involvement of participants as co-researchers means that the research is not 'about' but rather 'for' its participants. This is to say, the purpose of the research is to explore the relationship between participants' subjective experience of life and their conditions of life, with the aim of extending participants' opportunities for action (e.g. Holzkamp 1997: 36–7). Through the exposure of the limited functionality of participants' discursive strategies and through the identification of alternative, less restrictive, practices, participants are able to identify and access 'action spaces' that increase their control over the circumstances which govern the quality of their lives (Maiers and Tolman 1996: 113–14). In this sense, collective discourse analysis is a form of action research that aims to empower its participants (see also Willig 1998). Second, the insights generated by collective discourse analysis in relation to discursive positionings and their implications for opportunities for action can be used outside of the group that produced them. For example, if it is the case that the use of a discourse of addiction on the part of smokers constitutes an obstacle to giving up smoking (Gillies and Willig 1997), it follows that such constructions should not be used within a health promotion context. Similarly, if discursive constructions of 'trust' position their users as the potential victims of their partners (Willig 1995, 1997), it could be argued that such constructions should not form part of safer sex education materials. This is because opportunities for action and the structures of meaning within which they are grounded, having been identified by a research group, are potentially generalizable to others in comparable life situations (Holzkamp 1983b). While it is important to acknowledge that there are a number of serious risks associated with the 'application' of psychological research (see Willig 1999), a non-relativist social constructionist research programme of the kind outlined in this chapter must be committed to interventionist work.

Conclusion

In this chapter, I have explored the possibility of non-relativist social constructionist work. I have attempted to demonstrate that social constructionist research need not necessarily be associated with a relativism which denies the possibility of human emancipation. Instead, I have argued that social constructionist research can be part of a wider historical materialist analysis of society that allows us to move beyond appearances and their deconstruction, and enables us to account for constructions and to transcend their limitations.

I have concluded by providing a brief outline of the basic ingredients of a critical realist research programme for the study of subjectivity. I have proposed that such a programme must take the form of action research and that it must be committed to intervention.

Acknowledgement

I would like to thank Pete Green for many constructive discussions of the questions addressed in this chapter.

References

Averill, J. R. (1985) The social construction of emotion with special reference to Love, in K. J. Gergen and K. E. Davis (eds) *The Social Construction of the Person*. New York: Springer Verlag.

Bhaskar, R. (1978) *A Realist Theory of Science*, 2nd edn. Brighton: Harvester Press.

Bhaskar, R. (1979) *The Possibilities of Naturalism*. Brighton: Harvester Press.

Binns, P. (1973) The Marxist theory of truth, *Radical Philosophy*, 4: 3–9.

Burr, V. (1995) *An Introduction to Social Constructionism*. London: Routledge.

Crawford, J., Kippax, S., Onyx, J., Gault, U. and Benton, P. (1992) *Emotion and Gender: Constructing Meaning from Memory*. London: Sage.

Foucault, M. (1980) *Power/Knowledge: Selected Interviews and Other Writings 1972–1977*. New York: Pantheon.

Foucault, M. (1988) Technologies of the self, in L. H. Martin, H. Gutman and P. H. Hutton (eds) *Technologies of the Self: A Seminar with Michel Foucault*. London: Tavistock.

Fox, N. J. (1997) Is there life after Foucault? Texts, frames and *differends*, in A. Petersen and R. Bunton (eds) *Foucault Health and Medicine*. London: Routledge.

Gergen, K. J. (1995) Social construction and the transformation of identity politics. Paper presented at the New School for Social Research, New York.

Gillies, V. and Willig, C. (1997) 'You get the nicotine and that in your blood' – constructions of addiction and control in women's accounts of cigarette smoking, *Journal of Community and Applied Social Psychology*, 7: 285–301.

Holzkamp, K. (1983a) 'Aktualisierung' oder Aktualitat des Marxismus? Oder: Die Vorgeschichte des Marxismus is noch nicht zuende, in *Aktualisierung Marx: Argument-Sonderband AS 100*. Berlin: Argument Verlag.

Holzkamp, K. (1983b) *Grundlegung der Psychologie*. Frankfurt: Campus Verlag.

Holzkamp, K. (1997) *Schriften 1. Normierung, Ausgrenzung, Widerstand*. Berlin: Argument Verlag.

Levins, R. and Lewontin, R. (1985) *The Dialectical Biologist*. Cambridge, MA: Harvard University Press.

Maiers, W. and Tolman, C. W. (1996) Critical psychologe as subject-science, in I. Parker and R. Spears (eds) *Psychology and Society. Radical Theory and Practice*. London: Pluto Press.

Marx, K. (1975) The poverty of philosophy, in K. Marx and F. Engels, *Collected Works, 6.* London: Lawrence and Wishart.

Meszaros, I. (1970) *Marx's Theory of Alienation.* London: Merlin Press.

Nellhaus, T. (1997) Communication structures as modes of production. Conference paper to the Inaugural Conference of the Centre for Critical Realism, 'Critical Realism and the Human Sciences', University of Warwick, 30 August.

Newman, F. and Holzman, L. (1997) *The End of Knowing. A New Developmental Way of Learning.* London: Routledge.

Osterkamp, U. (1997) Vorwort, in K. Holzkamp, *Schriften 1. Normierung, Ausgrenzung, Widerstand.* Berlin: Argument Verlag.

Parker, I. (1992) *Discourse Dynamics. Critical Analysis for Social and Individual Psychology.* London: Routledge.

Parker, I., Georgaca, E., Harper, D., McLaughlin, T. and Stowell-Smith, M. (1995) *Deconstructing Psychopathology.* London: Sage.

Potter, J. and Wetherell, M. (1995) Discourse analysis, in J. A. Smith, R. Harré and L. Van Langenhoven (eds) *Rethinking Methods in Psychology.* London: Sage.

Willig, C. (1995) 'I wouldn't have married the guy if I'd have to do that' – heterosexual adults' accounts of condom use and their implications for sexual practice, *Journal of Community and Applied Social Psychology,* 5: 75–87.

Willig, C. (1997) The limitations of trust in intimate relationships: constructions of trust and sexual risk taking, *British Journal of Social Psychology,* 36: 211–21.

Willig, C. (1998) Constructions of sexual activity and their implications for sexual practice: lessons for sex education, *Journal of Health Psychology,* 3(3): 383–92.

Willig, C. (ed.) (1999) *Applied Discourse Analysis: Social and Psychological Interventions.* Buckingham: Open University Press.

4 | A paradigm shift?
Connections with other critiques of social constructionism

MIKE MICHAEL

Caricature I

Realists on one side, social constructionists on the other, the battle lines are drawn. Despite the utmost adherence to the conventions of politeness that pervade academic writing (Myers 1989), let us see how this war of attrition might proceed.

Realists want to admit a reality-in-itself – things, processes, powers – that serves as a ground for critique. Without holding in place some baseline, some condition, some truth, any discourse that claims to be critical, aspires to offer hope, or traces the marks of resistance, unravels. For without this groundedness in the stuff of the real, a critical discourse is itself a 'mere' social construction – a concoction of linguistic repertoires, narratives, tropes, discourses and so on that constitutes the real in an effort to render honourable effects (see, for example, Bhaskar 1989; Parker 1992).

Social constructionists respond by repeating that the real is constructed. However sophisticatedly this real is portrayed – say, the intransitive realm

– it is still constituted through language, it still draws upon the discursive resources that circulate in 'our' culture. The 'real' is thus never a ground, always a topic for argumentation (Shotter 1992), and the argument for the real is always open to a discourse analysis that interrogates the textual techniques by which discourse analysis and social constructionism are derogated, and the need for a real displayed (Potter 1992; Edwards *et al.* 1995).

The realist says: 'You, the social constructionist, are shaped by the real – your very approach reflects the condition of your class faction (e.g. Douglas 1986) or the more or less parochial political battles that you fight within academia (e.g. Horigan 1988).'

The social constructionist replies: 'You, the realist, are using the "You, the social constructionist, are shaped by the real – your very approach reflects the condition of your class faction or the more or less parochial political battles that you fight within academia" discourse.'

Ad infinitum.

Caricature II

Social constructionists are pure of mind, clear of thought. Always they ask: '*How* did you do that? How did you organize such and such bits of language to accomplish such and such?' Realists are pure of heart, immersed in ethics. Always they ask: '*What* are you doing? What enables, or even causes, you to say and do that? What are the consequences of such saying and doings?'

In *Purity and Danger*, Mary Douglas (1966: 35) defines dirt as 'matter out of place': it is stuff that is found in places it does not belong. But this 'belongingness' is a cultural criterion – if something escapes the classificatory systems that characterize a culture, is anomalous, then it is impure, a source of danger, an abomination (see also Bloor 1978). Social constructionists find the realists dirty: they bring the 'what' into the domain of the 'how'. To adapt Douglas, this is 'discourse out of place'. She writes, 'Shoes are not dirty in themselves, but it is dirty to place them on the dining-table' (p. 35). The real is not dirty in itself (we all make assumptions about the real), but it becomes dirty when it enters into a discourse analytic perspective without being the topic of analysis itself. Realists find the social constructionists an abomination: like the pig or camel in the abominations of Leviticus, they are 'cloven-hoofed but are not ruminant' (Douglas 1966: 55): that is, they claim to practice a politics (say, to unpick the discursive structures of racism or sexism), but do so without grounds, without a real from which to critique.

Complexities

The foregoing caricatures serve as bald statements of the key antagonisms between social constructionism and realism. However, throughout the social sciences we find examples where realism and constructionism seem happily to cohabit in the same text. In other words, strains of realism and constructionism are bound together to produce apparently seamless narratives. Sometimes this cohabitation is an honourable fudge. Sometimes, the very process of cohabitation becomes a topic in its own right. Let me expand upon and illustrate each of these configurations (though, as will become apparent, they are by no means discrete).

Honourable fudges

By honourable fudges I want to suggest that in some versions of discourse analysis (and social constructionism more generally) there is a tacit reliance upon some version of the real. The reasons these dependencies are 'honourable' are at least two-fold: (a) they serve to inform the reader of the sorts of background knowledge necessary to understand what is going on in the rest of the text, a realist account of the historical context to which the analysed discourse contributes (e.g. a history of racism in New Zealand by Wetherell and Potter 1992); (b) a realist account of sufferings, oppressions, injustices serves as a way of grounding the radical import of the discourse analysis, it shows how particular forms of discourse contribute to those sufferings, oppressions, injustices.

Within social psychology and elsewhere, discourse analysis has been deployed in the uncovering of the linguistic resources and techniques involved in the production of 'bad' social processes: racism (Wetherell and Potter 1992), sexism (Wetherell *et al.* 1987), heterosexism (Kitzinger 1987), conservative views of crowd behaviour (Potter and Reicher 1987), over-individualistic accounts of self (Widdicombe 1993). These, we can say, entail what Turner (1996), in reference to the practice of social constructionism in medical sociology, calls 'weak constructionism' (see also Sismondo 1993, regarding the versions of social constructionism in social studies of science). For Turner (1996: 29), 'while the relativism of the sociology of knowledge and deconstructionism is a useful critical starting point for social inquiry it is not necessarily its conclusion.' And this is what we find in the listed discursive analyses. Each of these 'deconstructs' 'bad' discourses (quite rightly in my view), but in the process such treatments assume 'good' discourses that are not the object of such deconstruction. Such discourses might construe particular social arrangements or forms of selfhood that are 'left-liberal' or radical, and as the tacit 'others' of bad discourses they cannot be analytically scrutinized, for that would raise doubts about the 'badness' of the target discourses. Let me clarify with similar examples from another area, environmental sociology.

Yearley (1991) argues that 'environmental problems' should be regarded as socially constructed: they are the upshot of particular discursive activity by certain groups. In contrast, when he comes to discuss the environmental problems of the 'developing' world, these are not so problematized. One could say that the former deconstruction serves to problematize the construction of 'environmental problems' by certain elites to the exclusion of other groups; the latter realist account serves as a buffer against any deconstruction of 'environmental problems' in the 'developing' world. Beck (1992) argues that environmental problems are the social constructions of scientists, especially insofar as many of the dangers we currently face are beyond our senses. At the same time he assumes that such risks are real. The constructionist dimension stresses the lay public's dependency upon scientific elites in 'identifying' and combating such dangers, while the realist allows that public a certain autonomy. In Wynne's (e.g. 1991, 1992, 1996) analysis of the impact of the Chernobyl fall-out upon Cumbrian sheep-farmers, we find another version of this asymmetrical application of realism (or relativism). The scientists of the Ministry of Agriculture, Fisheries and Food are seen to generalize their science (e.g. techniques for the measurement of radiation on land) to an unfamiliar domain: the Cumbrian fells. As a result, the social constructedness of their techniques become exposed; the farmers, with their more authentic or grounded experience of the local terrain, know already that such techniques will not work (that is, their knowledge is real). Subsequently, Wynne (1996) has argued that he never meant to suggest that their knowledge was any less constructed than that of scientists; his main point is that the 'body language' of institutions such as MAFF (Wynne 1991), insofar as it signals the dismissal or marginalization of the understandings of publics such as the farmers, alienates such constituencies. What are required are more 'transparent' institutions that acknowledge the uncertainties and contingencies of their science. Yet this eminently 'good' suggestion (to my mind) also assumes a real. On the one hand, this is concerned with the capacity of public to accommodate such contingencies and uncertainties. On the other, it is concerned with a view that some version of dialogism between expert and lay is the appropriate form of exchange (all else being distortion).

Now, I think these 'honourable fudges' are 'fudges' only as long as one aspires to some sort of epistemological purity, or, rather, a reflexivity that encompasses the relation between, the cohabitation of, the real and constructed. Instead of fudge, let us call it epistemological eclecticism: this seems perfectly reasonable in the context of tactical narrative manoeuvres in which the discourses of dangerous or powerful others need to be deconstructed from the perspective of a particular standpoint (see Harding 1986). Problems arise, as we have seen, when these very analytic tools are turned upon the practitioners of such eclecticism. I will now consider some of those writings that have directly attempted to excise this unreflexive 'eclecticism', or 'fudging'.

Cohabitation as a topic, or forms of prioritization

There are various ways in which the cohabitation of the real and the constructed can be explicitly formulated. In this section I want briefly to consider those treatments that prioritize either the real or the constructed.

The real can be seen as a logical prerequisite for the very practices of social construction. Thus, Harré (1992) and Knorr-Cetina (1988) both cite the local – the conversation or the micro-situation – as a necessary assumption for social constructionist accounts. These 'sites' comprise an inescapable realm where the socially constructing activities of humans are conducted. Without these, according to such authors, it is difficult to see how social constructionism could be 'coherently' conceptualized. For Collins (Collins and Yearley 1992a, b), arguing against Latour's and Callon's (e.g. Callon 1986; Latour 1991) importation of non-humans as actors that contribute to the process of technoscientific production (including scientific knowledge), we are only equipped to know social processes. Such a 'social realist' position entails an empirical argument. It is to these social processes – modes of argumentation, forms of discourse, dynamics of negotiation – that we, as competent social beings ourselves, have a 'direct' empirical access. Reflexivists such as Mulkay (1985) and Ashmore (1989) also demonstrate the dependence of constructionist accounts upon the real (and vice versa). For example, within the sociology of scientific knowledge, in showing that the establishment of replication in science is a social accomplishment, constructionists themselves depend upon an unscrutinized version of social replication, this time of cases or instances of the social construction of scientific replication. Here, in contrast to the preceding forms of cohabitation, cohabitation of the real and the constructed is effectively treated as textual co-dependency, through which convincing social constructionist accounts are socially constructed. Social constructionism takes priority.

Critical realists, we might say, are happy to entertain the cohabitation of the real and the constructed, but prioritize the real because it offers a 'base' from which to be moral or political. Without rehearsing, yet again, the debate between critical realists and social constructionists, we can, albeit superficially, interrogate this political/moral dimension of critical realism's warrant by considering Soper's (1995) critique of Benton's (1993) critical realist take on environmental politics. For Benton there is something like an intransitive realm inhabited by 'those "deep structures" of physicality and its causality whose processes are constantly at work in the world' (Soper 1995: 157). That is to say, nature's causal powers are the bases of all ecological activity, spanning human and non-human, animate and inanimate. The laws of such a nature serve as constraints upon what is humanly and technologically possible. To struggle against them either makes us look foolish or invites calamity (or both). These reals of the intransitive realm are thus meant to serve as a 'base' which places a moral/political obligation upon us to do, or not do, certain things. Now, Soper readily acknowledges that such an assumption is vital to ecological politics: environmentalists need to assume limits set by such a nature, in order to argue against the instrumental use, or argue for the conservation, of nature. However, she also notes a number of problems with Benton's realist scheme. First, these limits are highly elastic – the experts themselves cannot reach a consensus over what they might be. This is a typical constructionist argument. What is the use of presupposing a realist 'base' if even experts who supposedly have a more direct access to it cannot agree among themselves on the nature of this nature? However, as we have seen in the section on 'honourable fudges', those constructionists committed to doing a certain sort of politics will happily deploy a real in some form or other. A more important insight furnished by Soper is that this version of 'real nature', the 'contents' of such an intransitive realm, cannot necessarily warrant a protective (or precautionary) environmental politics. This is because these causal powers, embodied in, for example, the laws of physics, are so abstract, or rather pertain to such a deep level of nature, that 'nature . . . is indifferent to our choices, will persist in the midst of environmental destruction, and will outlast the death of all planetary life' (Soper 1995: 159–60). As such, this level of the 'natural' has little to do with the 'natural' that environmentalists are asking us to protect, or conserve. The point is that such a real has to be carefully pitched if it is to serve its normative purpose. But, of course, as soon as we begin to talk in terms of careful pitching we return to social constructionism.

In this all too schematic section, I have sketched a number of ways in which the real and the constructed can be forced to cohabit. However, as we have seen, in these textual households one or other turns out to be the dominant partner. While the old dualism is directly addressed, it is simultaneously reasserted in the form of a hierarchy. What happens when we try to dispense with such hierarchies?

Caricature III

In his meditation on the meanings and materialities of ecological catastrophe, Michel Serres (1995) begins with a striking, poignant image from Goya, in which two men are engaged in a battle with sticks while sinking into a mire. Serres's point is that they are practising a social contract while ignoring, or negating, the contract that they have with nature (which, of course, they cannot do). Let us imagine that one antagonist is 'The Realist', the other 'The Social Constructionist'. How might we characterize them? Are they fighting humans? Or are they sinking humans?

They are both.

Entering a new paradigm

Hilary Rose (1993) has argued that the antagonism between constructionism and realism is a manifestation of the patriarchal predilection for 'either/or' forms of discourse. Perhaps if the humans in Goya's representation were women they would embrace and wallow, rather than fight and be swallowed. For Rose, the alternative to 'either/or' is 'both/and'. The paradox is, of course, that this move begins to repeat the patriarchal predilection: *either* practice an 'either/or' discursive form *or* engage in a 'both/and' alternative. But then again, if one suggests that *both* 'either/or' *and* 'both/and' are accommodated in our accounts, we again exclude, this time at a meta-level, the 'either/or'.

Ad infinitum.

This is a pattern that reflexive sociologists of scientific knowledge, such as Ashmore and Mulkay, have delighted in laying bare. Yet is it of consequence (Collins and Yearley 1992a, b)? Instead, let us begin by assuming heterogeneity: both the real and the constructed, the material and the semiotic, the human and the non-human play their part in the production of an event, an account, a process.

A paradigm (Kuhn 1970) can be thought of as a model of scientific understanding that is a form of dogma. When such paradigms are overthrown, it is not new 'facts' (anomalies) that do the overthrowing, for what is to count as a 'fact' would be in dispute (e.g. Feyerabend 1975). Rather, change occurs because of, for example, the persuasive prowess of key scientists advocating the new paradigm. The realist and social constructionist perspectives might be thought of as opposing paradigms, more or less irreconcilable (incommensurable). Each would find the heterogeneity suggested above unpalatable. Or, rather, either could recuperate a heterogeneous account, translating it into its own terms. Perhaps what is required is a leap of faith, or, rather, an openness to persuasion, that has as much to do with the materialities and meanings of career in academia and the like, as the brilliance of the rhetoric of the advocate of heterogeneity. That is to say, and as a first exemplification of such heterogeneity, the persuasiveness of a paradigm centred upon heterogeneity is to be sought in heterogeneity: the circulation of documents (championing by publishers, conferences in exotic locales, the existence and relative aesthetics of relevant websites etc.); the career trajectories of readers, especially the next generation of academics who must make their mark; the modesty and/or mystique of the language through which such heterogeneity is expressed; and so on and so forth.

Cohabitation as heterogeneity

A form of writing, a form of analysis that is ready to encompass the real and the constructed: that is the 'new paradigm'. It is by no means a coherent endeavour: there are serious divides and divisions, there are divergent accounts of what sort of politics is being offered in these heterogeneous accounts and there are troublesome differences in the analytic resources that are brought to bear (concrete and situated, or abstract and universal?). Having noted these (healthy) difficulties, what holds this range of efforts together is what we might call a 'studied indifference to epistemology'. The purification of knowledge is not an aim. The real and the constructed (and their accompanying epistemologies) are not transgressed – they are jumbled. Let us briefly consider two important examples of the 'new paradigm'.

With Haraway (1995, 1997), we assume heterogeneity: we are the products of associations that are always irreducibly material and semiotic. In addition to intertextuality, we can talk of intermateriality; in addition to subject (human)–object (things) relations, we can talk of object (human)–subject (things) relations. We are the playthings of composite discourses; we are structured by a world of shifting signifiers. But we are also materially composite – caught in a network of natures and technologies. We are cyborgs, with all the promise and terror that such a condition holds (see Haraway 1991; Prins 1995). But we are also biologically composite: our guts are full of useful bacteria, our cells could not function without mitochondria, which once were, possibly, symbionts, or parasites even. And, further, we are individuals operating a grubby politics, carrying our biographical baggage. That includes the analyst whose knowledge is always situated, always partial, always conditioned by local heterogeneity. So when Haraway writes, she mixes things up. Her texts juxtapose narratives, characters and metaphors; her accounts draw upon the scientific, the semiotic, the historical, the sociological, the biographical in a sort of mosaic that aspires to neither resolution nor hierarchy.

Where is the real and constructed here?

With Michel Callon, Bruno Latour and John Law, we assume heterogeneity. A different strategy this time. What is to count as agent, as sign, as material, as object is the outcome of the network – that heterogeneous configuration of agents, signs, material and objects through which pass other agents, signs, materials and objects, making the configuration more or less durable (see Michael 1996a, b, for a summary of their actor–network theory; see also Pujol and Montenegro, this volume, Chapter 6). While Haraway's account implies a juxtaposition of various discursive and representational forms derived from different genres (including different disciplines spanning the social and natural sciences), actor–network theory has developed a neutral terminology (of actants, associations, translation, hybrids etc.) by which to capture the heterogeneity of elements that contribute to the production of certain knowledges, technologies, humans and nonhumans. Actor–network accounts are likewise local, contingent, situated. For Law (1994) this means, with Haraway, practising a careful modesty. For Latour (1988) this means practising a careful sequestration of such contingency and situatedness. One's aim is to persuade – to do politics – and, as Michael (1997) has noted, ironically, one needs to be modest about modesty lest it becomes the latest rhetorically potent textual form.

To practise this heterogeneity, we can no longer rest peacefully within our disciplines. Harawayan and actor–networkish texts must span the disciplines – at the very least, social and natural sciences become interwoven in these accounts. But there can be no easy integration of different disciplines as the above perspectives tacitly suggest. In contrast to such terms as cross-disciplinary, transdisciplinary and interdisciplinary (see Roberts and Good 1993), perhaps we might prefer 'paradisciplinary', for this conveys the sense that there is no possibility of fusion, but a 'beside-ness' among disparate disciplines. In such accounts these disciplines textually 'help' or 'support' each other, in the sense that what we are presented with is the interweaving of different registers that evoke complexity (and not some spurious comprehensiveness). But always this should be a pragmatic, contingent and reflexive arrangement, in the sense that the individual disciplines and their configuration, or juxtaposition, signal their situatedness (and not some spurious coherence) in professional, political, cultural (etc.) networks (after all, paradisciplinarity is itself marked by the very heterogeneity it practises).

Caricature IV

Let me attempt, albeit superficially and tentatively, to put this paradisciplinarity into practice.

What is the couch potato?

In stereotype, we see something like a junk food guzzling indolent dissipating before the television, which, remotely controlled, emits a continuous incoherent stream of images.

The couch potato is the object of the realist medical gaze. In its unhealthy habits – its lack of exercise and abominable diet – lies, at the very least, the ever-increasing risk of cardiovascular disease. It is the object of a realist medical sociological gaze that asks who the couch potatoes are. They are the poor, the unemployed, the disenfranchised. But it is also a point of contention, for whatever risks are accrued in such bad habits, there are always uncertainties. The correlations and risk factors that are presented by the health promotion professionals confront a lay epidemiology which has available to it counter-instances: Uncle Charlie, say, who smoked and drank and ate fat without regard and lived to 108; young Charlie, who exercised and ate healthily and did not own a television and died at the age of 30. So we have a medicine keen to ensure the health of the population. However, in the process, according to Foucauldians, this project can be seen to be engaged in the policing of the body of the human and the body of the population to produce individuals and groups better adjusted to the needs of the economy, the state. Yet it also meets with resistance – the practices of the couch potato can be represented as pleasures that subvert such disciplinary endeavours.

To discourse analysts, the couch potato is perhaps a narrative character, something we might deploy simultaneously in excusing ourselves and blaming ourselves: we should not be couch potatoes but such a state of being is in the nature of contemporary society. So, we analysts do some interviews, and trawl the Internet and the expert and popular media and derive a variety of discourses, or linguistic repertoires, or metaphors, or tropes, or narratives. For example, the above discussion of the medical gaze and lay epidemiology could be recounted in the terms of discourse analysis. Popularly, in the broadsheets, we might find that the couch potato is both a thing of derision and a condition into which one routinely slips in the light of modern pressures: fractions of the middle classes are ashamed of, and resigned to, this (temporary) mode of comportment. But the couch potato might also be an emblem of certain subcultures, most obviously youth cultures of 'slacking'. Certainly, on the Web, we find that on the homepages of some American football fan clubs there is a self-identification with the couch potato. We also find that the couch potato is a commercial prospect – the identity of a particular consumer and the icon for a particular market niche. Couch Potato Investments Inc. thus promises an ease of investment that appeals to the very sedentariness, or, rather, the desire for an easy life (in the dual sense of physical and financial), embodied in the figure of the couch potato. As a final example, the couch potato is a commercial prospect for personal computer companies that offer new technological media beyond, or additional to, the television through which to practise being a couch potato.

There are other realist sociological understandings of the couch potato. For example, if a key fixture of the couch potato is the remote control, it contributes to the terrain on which gender relations are played out. As Morley (1992) has noted, the control of the remote control is a point of contention within families, men typically monopolizing possession. Moreover, the style of use of the remote control can also lead to fractious relations: men's propensity to channel hop with the aid of the remote control is often a cause of complaint from women who would prefer prolonged, undisturbed viewings of particular programmes. With the mention of channel hopping, we can also address how the ease of access to multiple, fractured, fragmented images structures (post)modern consciousness. So, the remote control serves as one technological tool (out of very many – see, for example, Gergen 1991) through which we are exposed to a disorderly parade of signs. Our selves might become 'saturated', as Gergen has phrased it: 'a multiphrenic condition . . . in which one swims in ever-shifting concatenating and contentious currents of being' (Gergen 1991: 79–80). But this can also be viewed as a consumption of signs that refer only one to another, with no special connection to referents – reals – beyond (e.g. Baudrillard 1983). Our attention span diminishes, and what we become used to, what we desire, is the flow of signs – the surface, the spectacle of their rapid procession is what pleasures us. However, we can also suggest that the man of the family, through the very monopoly of the remote control's channel hopping facility, comes to reproduce the relations of power within the family. That is to say, in order to enjoy this luxuriant consumption of fragmented signs there needs to be in place a set of social, political, economic and cultural circumstances that enable such consumption. Thus, if there is something like a saturated self, this coexists with another social self that is endowed with the capacity to become saturated: the identity of the postmodern is couched within the practices and privileges of an indulgent consumer (e.g. Lury 1996). Ironically, as we have seen, such indulgence – represented in, for example, the figure of the couch potato ('the postmodern' is, perhaps, a more positive alternative) – can become discoursed into an emphatic form of warrant.

What is the couch potato? It is a cyborg, a hybrid, a monster. It spans the human and the technological non-human. In actor–network terms there is a delegation of body parts (the legs) to the remote control. The legs are unreliable: they get tired, they trip over cups and ruffled rugs, they need to be disciplined. In contrast, the remote control does not get tired (though sometimes the batteries need to be changed), and it does not miss its target (though sometimes it goes missing). The remote control also demands certain capacities in its user: fingers should not be too shaky or too large. As such, it acts as a moral agent, shaping the comportment of its human companion (see Latour 1992). But, of course, the remote control also embodies chains of humans and non-humans: those other technologies and people whose joint labour is congealed in the device. Just as the couch potato is a part of this 'retrospective' network, it is also a part of a 'prospective' network. In contrast to the optimistic, primarily female cyborg, whose complex engagement with(in) technoscientific networks opens up a space for transformation (Penley and Ross 1991), we have in the couch potato a retrograde, largely male cyborg who feeds into and mediates the worst excesses of these networks. According to Latour (1993), because of the 'Modern Constitution' – those very many discourses that in the modernist West have served to maintain a separation between the human and non-human – we have, unlike premodern societies, neglected to attend properly to the production of human–non-human combinations. So, does the couch potato comprise a hybrid which, in Latour's terms, is part of the unpoliced proliferation of hybrids that is threatening to overwhelm us?

As we have seen in certain accounts, this hybrid is indeed policed: for some it is a model of bad (human) living; for others it is the crux of a cherished identity. In both cases, it is a monster (see Law 1991) that is in constant need of practical localized policing, for the couch potato is also the site of numerous ironies that reflect the accidental coalition of technological designs and social circumstances. What are we to make of the remote control's affinity for the back of the sofa, when the couch potato is so cruelly disaggregated? The couch potato is at the effect of the fact that sofas are designed with removable seat cushions (that enable seat covers to be taken off for cleaning). One structuring assumption here is the nature of the hand: the remote control nestles neatly in the palm; the pliable gap between seat cushion and sofa back is perfect for fingers aiming to remove the former. The size of the remote control matches, more or less ideally, the space between sofa cushion and back. But even such incidental conformations are the subject of comment: as a contributor to the 'Top Tips' section of the adult comic *Viz* has suggested, why not attach a child's sock to one's belt to serve as a holster for the remote control?

The foregoing has been a tenuous example of the practice of paradisciplinarity. The layers of narratives, characters, metaphors and ironies collected above weave in and out of the real and the constructed. We find the real in, for example, the body: unhealthy medical bodies, retrograde political bodies, delegated body parts. We find the constructed in, for example, subcultural recuperations, lay epidemiologies, commercial audiences. More or less likely linkages have been drawn that explore the complexity of a seemingly simple figure: the couch potato. We have, unsystematically, traversed the borders of, and juxtaposed, a number of disciplines: medicine, sociology, cultural studies, technological design. But lest I give the impression that this new paradigm is a 'paradigm of no paradigms', the above text is no less the product of situated practice.

Caricature V

There is a hybrid-cyborg-monster comprised of a university employee, a sleeping cat, a mobile personal computer, a coffee table and a sofa over which are strewn academic and popular texts, print-outs from the Internet, pieces of paper on which are scrawled writing and doodles. There is a flurry of activity. Where is the A4 sheet with the notes for the conclusion? Beneath the motionless Wilma there is a scrap of paper . . .

References

Ashmore, M. (1989) *The Reflexive Thesis: Wrighting Sociology of Scientific Knowledge*. Chicago: Chicago University Press.
Baudrillard, J. (1983) *In the Shadow of Silent Majorities*. New York: Semiotext(e).

Beck, U. (1992) *The Risk Society*. London: Sage.

Benton, T. (1993) *Natural Relations*. London: Verso.

Bhaskar, R. (1989) *Reclaiming Reality*. London: Verso.

Bloor, D. (1978) Polyhedra and the abominations of Leviticus, *British Journal for the History of Science*, 11: 245–72.

Callon, M. (1986) Some elements in a sociology of translation: domestication of the scallops and fishermen of St Brieuc Bay, in J. Law (ed.) *Power, Action and Belief*. London: Routledge and Kegan Paul.

Collins H. M. and Yearley, S. (1992a) Epistemological chicken, in A. Pickering (ed.) *Science as Practice and Culture*. Chicago: University of Chicago Press.

Collins. H. M. and Yearley, S. (1992b) Journey into space, in A. Pickering (ed.) *Science as Practice and Culture*. Chicago: University of Chicago Press.

Douglas M. (1986) The social preconditions of radical skepticism, in J. Law (ed.) *Power, Action and Belief*. London: Routledge and Kegan Paul.

Douglas, M. (1966) *Purity and Danger*. Harmondsworth: Penguin.

Edwards, D., Ashmore, M. and Potter, J. (1995) Death and furniture: the rhetoric, politics and the theology of bottom line arguments against relativism, *History of the Human Sciences*, 8: 25–49.

Feyerabend, P. (1975) *Against Method*. London: Verso.

Gergen, K. J. (1991) *The Saturated Self*. New York: Basic Books.

Haraway, D. (1989) *Primate Visions*. London: Routledge and Kegan Paul.

Haraway, D. (1991) *Simians, Cyborgs and Nature*. London: Free Association Books.

Haraway, D. (1995) Cyborgs and symbionts: living together in the new world order, in C. H. Gray (ed.) *The Cyborg Handbook*. New York: Routledge.

Haraway, D. (1997) *Modest_Witness@Second_Millennium.FemaleMan.Meets_ OncoMouse: Feminism and Technoscience*. London: Routledge.

Harding, S. (1986) *The Science Question in Feminism*. Milton Keynes: Open University Press.

Harré, R. (1992) What is real in psychology? A plea for persons, *Theory and Psychology*, 2: 153–8.

Horigan, S. (1988) *Nature and Culture in Western Discourses*. London: Routledge and Kegan Paul.

Kitzinger, C. (1987) *The Social Construction of Lesbianism*. London: Sage.

Knorr-Cetina, K. (1988) The micro-social order: towards a reconception, in N. G. Fielding (ed.) *Actions and Structure: Research Methods and Social Theory*. London: Sage.

Kuhn, T. S. (1970) *The Structure of Scientific Revolution*. Chicago: Chicago University Press.

Latour, B. (1988) The politics of explanation – an alternative, in S. Woolgar (ed.) *Knowledge and Reflexivity: New Frontiers in the Sociology of Knowledge*. London: Sage.

Latour, B. (1991) Technology is society made durable, in J. Law (ed.) *A Sociology of Monsters*. London: Routledge.

Latour, B. (1992) Where are the missing masses? A sociology of a few mundane artifacts, in W. E. Bijker and J. Law (eds) *Shaping Technology/Building Society*. Cambridge, MA: MIT Press.

Latour, B. (1993) *We Have Never Been Modern*. Hemel Hempstead: Harvester Wheatsheaf.

Law, J. (1991) Introduction, in J. Law (ed.) *A Sociology of Monsters*. London: Routledge.

Law, J. (1994) *Organizing Modernity*. Oxford: Blackwell.

Lury, C. (1996) *Consumer Culture*. Cambridge: Polity Press.

Michael, M. (1996a) *Constructing Identities: The Social, the Nonhuman and Change*. London: Sage.

Michael, M. (1996b) Constructing a constructive critique of social constructionism: finding a narrative space for the nonhuman, *New Ideas in Psychology*, 14(3): 209–24.

Michael, M. (1997) Hybridising regularity: a characterology and chronography of the hudogledog. Paper presented to the Actor-Network Theory and After Conference, Keele University, 10–11 July.

Morley, D. (1992) *Television Audiences and Cultural Studies*. London: Routledge.

Mulkay, M. (1985) *The Word and the World*. London: George Allen and Unwin.

Myers, G. (1989) The pragmatics of politeness in scientific articles, *Applied Linguistics*, 10: 1–35.

Parker, I. (1992) *Discourse Dynamics*. London: Routledge.

Penley, C. and Ross, A. (1991) Cyborgs at large: interview with Donna Haraway, in C. Penley and A. Ross (eds) *Technoculture*. Minneapolis: University of Minnesota Press.

Potter, J. (1992) Constructing realism: seven moves (plus or minus a couple), *Theory and Psychology*, 2: 167–73.

Potter, J. and Reicher, S. (1987) Discourses of community and conflict: the organization of social categories in accounts of a 'riot', *British Journal of Social Psychology*, 26: 25–40.

Prins, B. (1995) The ethics of hybrid subjects: feminist constructivism according to Donna Haraway, *Science, Technology and Human Values*, 20: 352–67.

Roberts, R. H. and Good, J. M. M. (1993) Introduction, in R. H. Roberts and J. M. M. Good (eds) *The Recovery of Rhetoric*. Charlottesville: University Press of Virginia.

Rose, H. (1993) Rhetoric, feminism and scientific knowledge: or from either/or to both/and, in R. H. Roberts and J. M. M. Good (eds) *The Recovery of Rhetoric*. Charlottesville: University Press of Virginia.

Serres, M. (1995) *The Natural Contract*. Ann Arbor: University of Michigan Press.

Shotter, J. (1992) Social constructionism and realism: adequacy or accuracy?, *Theory and Psychology*, 2: 175–82.

Sismondo, S. (1993) Some social constructions, *Social Studies of Science*, 23: 515–53.

Soper, K. (1995) *What Is Nature?* Oxford: Blackwell.

Turner, B. S. (1996) *The Body and Society*, 2nd edn. London: Sage.

Wetherell, M. and Potter, J. (1992) *Mapping the Language of Racism*. Hemel Hempstead: Harvester Wheatsheaf.

Wetherell, M., Stiven, H. and Potter, J. (1987) Unequal egalitarianism: a preliminary study of discourses concerning gender and employment opportunities, *British Journal of Social Psychology*, 26: 59–71.

Widdicombe, S. (1993) Autobiography and change: rhetoric and authenticity in 'gothic' style, in E. Burman and I. Parker (eds) *Discourse Analytic Research*. London: Routledge.

Wynne, B. E. (1991) Knowledges in context, *Science, Technology and Human Values*, 16: 111–21.

Wynne, B. E. (1992) Misunderstood misunderstanding: social identities and public uptake of science, *Public Understanding of Science*, 1: 281–304.

Wynne, B. E. (1996) May the sheep safely graze? in S. Lash, B. Szerszynski and B. Wynne (eds) *Risk, Environment and Modernity*. London: Sage.

Yearley, S. (1991) *The Green Case*. London: HarperCollins.

PART II

Materiality and embodiment

5 Between the dark and the light: power and the material contexts of social relations

IAN BURKITT

In a recent review of social constructionist literature, Kurt Danziger (1997) has distinguished between what he calls 'light' and 'dark' social constructionism. In the light version, life is constructed in discourse and power is also embedded in that medium, so that removing barriers to the openness and multiplicity of discourse is a way of overcoming the inequalities within society. The dark version, on the other hand, sees discourse as embedded in relations of power that form systems of constraint which regulate social actions. Light social constructionism has been influenced by the 'linguistic turn' of the social sciences during recent decades, which is 'a turn away from linguistics, conceived as an independently formed discipline, towards examining the mutual coordination of language and *praxis*' (Giddens 1987: 80). Constructionists working in this vein emphasize the ongoing construction of meaning in everyday dialogues where discourse is used within joint activities or relationships (Harré 1993; Shotter 1993a, b; Gergen 1994). Although all the various light constructionists differ in their approach and orientation, they are united in a tendency to understand power, if they consider the issue at all, as a discursive product, the possession of a warranting voice (Gergen 1989). Dark constructionism differs in being influenced by the French philosophers of the 1970s and 1980s, in particular Michel Foucault, who claimed that power and knowledge always go hand-in-hand and that they are joined together in discourse (Foucault 1979: 100). Here, power is not reducible to the discursive, because it also takes the form of social relations or institutionalized practices in which discourses are lodged.

In this chapter, I do not want to argue for one form of constructionism over another, but to suggest that the issue of power relations needs to be taken account of in any form of social understanding. However, the Foucauldian conceptualization of power can often give the impression that humans are eternally trapped in constantly respun webs of power and domination, from which there is no historical escape. What I shall suggest, then, is that both dark and light versions of constructionism are inadequate on their own, and that we need to reconstruct a version which is more shaded and nuanced in its analysis of power. For me, power is important for three main reasons: first, a conceptualization of power relations helps to create links between the 'macro' levels of society (the economy, industry, political, bureaucratic or military institutions) and the 'everyday' world where interactions take place; second, an analysis of power can aid in understanding the connections between structure and agency, or, rather, the issue of the degree to which human actions are enabled and constrained by the 'social structures' we act within; third, I believe that analysing power relations overcomes the dualism that often appears in constructionism between the practical and the expressive realm (Harré 1993), or the non-discursive and the discursive. I will now elaborate these issues, centring the discussion on relations of power and expressive practices.

Constructionism and relations of power

In the work of Foucault (1979, 1982), power is not a 'thing' that individuals can gain, possess and then lose; instead, power has to be thought of as an interlocking series of relations which produce a configuration that appears to have a logic and strategy, but is designed by no single person or group. Power, then, needs to be understood 'as the multiplicity of force relations immanent in the sphere in which they operate and which constitute their own organization', and 'as the support which these force relations find in one another, thus forming a chain or system, or on the contrary, the disjunctions and contradictions which isolate them from one another' (Foucault 1979: 92–3). So power relations are not separate from the other forms of relations, such as economic, family or sexual relations, but are immanent in all of these; power is the product of these mutually supporting or opposing relations. The inequalities within them also give shape to the overall system of domination, which becomes established more widely.

This means, though, that in all these localized areas of power relations there is always resistance against domination. What defines a relation of power is 'that it is a mode of action which does not act directly and immediately on others. Instead it acts upon their actions: an action upon an action, on existing actions or on those which may arise in the present or future' (Foucault 1982: 220). In terms of the empirical analyses from which this conceptualization of power emerged, Foucault studied the asylums and prisons of the eighteenth and nineteenth centuries in Western Europe, and also the way in which the sexuality of children was regulated in schools and the family (Foucault 1965, 1977, 1979). It is in such institutional and everyday sites that we encounter the forms of constraint and the norms that guide our behaviour and conduct. Furthermore, it is here that spaces of knowledge open up in which discourses are created that act to regulate the conduct of individuals. The discourses on mental illness, criminality and sexuality that emerged in the past two centuries, and still dominate our lives today, are as much aimed at the regulation of conduct as at the liberation of individuals from sickness, crime or sexual repression.

However, one of the problems with Foucault's view of power is that, influenced by Nietzsche, he thought that one system of power and domination would simply be replaced by another through a process of eternal recurrence (Foucault 1986). Not only is this view unfounded in long-term historical analyses, it is also politically very conservative, offering little hope of making positive changes to social conditions. Foucault's analyses also portray individuals as regulated and subjectified by discursive practices, but tend to ignore the other side of the coin – that people are the joint authors of discourses within various contexts and situated interactions. In one of his later publications, Foucault (1982) suggested that humans are located not only in relations of power, but in relations of communication and relations that transform the real. Although he suggested that these relations were interconnected yet not identical to one another, he never explored communication or transformation in any great detail. These three types of relationship have implications for social constructionism, something I have outlined elsewhere (Burkitt 1998). More emphasis on relations of communication would lighten Foucault's dark vision of the limitations on human possibilities, and I will offer here the view of individuals as the authors of their own history, but ones who can author changes only under conditions that are given in their historical and material circumstances (to paraphrase Marx 1851). In this sense, I want to find a place between the dark and the light; to take account of power relations and the limits on human actions and yet to find ways of moving beyond them.

Certainly, the 'light' forms of social constructionism promote an active and agential view of the person. For Gergen (1994, 1997), discourse only functions in ongoing relationships, and it is here that language gains its meaning. The focus of analysis shifts from the underlying structures of language to the relational pattern in which language is employed. It is communities of related individuals who give meaning to the world and create the openings for new relational possibilities through dialogue and the refashioning of discourse. Furthermore, Gergen's account does something unusual for the lighter forms of social constructionism, by suggesting that discourse does not exhaust the possibilities for social or psychological analysis:

> Thus, while explicitly concerned with discourse, the attempt is to theorize more fully enriched patterns of relational performance (including the bodily activities of the participants, along with the various objects, ornaments and physical settings necessary to render these performances intelligible). In this sense, discourse is often central to the analysis, but spoken or written language does not exhaust the spectrum of concerns.
>
> (Gergen 1997: 740)

However, Gergen's view of relatedness includes every conceivable type of relation and their discursive and non-discursive forms of constant reconfiguration. He is wary, from this position, of 'grounding' relationships in any single concept, such as power. After all, to what does the concept of power refer? For Gergen (1994: 73) power is multiply constructed by different groups (Marxists, conservatives, feminists) and used for different purposes. However, if Foucault is right, power is more than just a concept mobilized by various interest groups – it is a fundamental effect of all relationships, and of the interlocking nature of many relational forms. In any relationship we care to think of – a political relation, between people at work, in the family, between lovers – power can manifest itself as an imbalance or inequality between those who are related. It is hard, in fact, to think of any relationship free of such imbalances and therefore of the opportunity to exercise power – of one or more related individuals beginning to structure the field of activity. Power does not simply move in one direction, with some individuals becoming more powerful than others. Each individual in a network of relations may have talents, abilities, capacities, opportunities or resources that give him or her leeway to take up a more powerful position or to resist the government of his or her actions. Further, in Gergen's own relational terms, power may be more than a discursive concept, itself having relational form, and, like all such forms, is not exhausted by linguistic explanation. The warden has more power than the prisoner because the warden has the keys to the cell; the Western world has such dominance across the globe because it possesses greater economic resources and military might, and a more extensive network of media, than smaller nations.

So power is more than just a concept: it is a relation between people and groups in which inequalities arise and actions are governed. There are non-discursive aspects to power as it figures within the various forms of relations and in the links between these relations, whether they support or oppose one another. However, most varieties of light constructionism isolate a form of expressive realm that can be uncoupled from power and social divisions. For Harré (1993), for example, humans live in a practical and an expressive order. The practical comprises the causal forces of nature and the more mundane aspects of work, while the expressive order is the one more dominant in most human societies: here, life is devoted to the expressive performances which aim to maintain the honour of the individual within the social group, winning him or her the respect craved from fellow social beings. The expressive order is a conventional rather than a causal one, meaning that it is governed by social conventions and moral rules through which individuals present themselves as the kind of people worthy of respect within that local moral order. For Harré, norms and conventions are central to the management of social action, but this is not seen as a form of government tied to relations of power; rather, moral norms play a positive role in turning individuals into responsible and autonomous agents, ones who can be held to account for their actions. Through this accountability, human actions become intentional and meaningful, for they are not 'caused' in any way by forces – either biological or social – of which the individual is unaware: instead, people use the same rules and reasoning procedures to construct their own actions as they use to account for them, meaning they are always intending what they do and say. All this is made possible through the discourses circulating in the expressive order, which leads Harré into his basic formulation that all social life is primarily composed of conversation.

Harré's position is framed by the work of micro-sociologists, such as Goffman and Garfinkel – who stressed the performative nature of social life and the tacit rules that are shared in society and script those performances – and by the philosopher Wittgenstein, with his concept of the 'language game'. Yet this allows Harré to 'bracket out' the more macro-social contexts of power relations, concentrating instead on the kinds of power exercised within the expressive order. This leads to the question 'How is the power of one person over another established and maintained discursively?', leaving aside the more sociological question of the hegemony of one social group over another (Harré 1993: 126). The problem for Harré, though, is that these two levels – the macro- and micro-social – are interconnected, in that the norms we use in everyday life are connected to power relations and the hegemony of social groups. For example, the norms of sexual conduct, which we use to guide our behaviour and to judge the actions of others, include a 'heterosexual hegemony', where sexualities and sex acts are demarcated into 'straight', 'bisexual' or 'gay' (to name but a few), and also classified on this basis as 'normal' or 'abnormal'. We regulate each other's actions according to these norms, but the way we either do this or rebel against it cannot be isolated from power relations at the macro level, where groups identifying themselves as heterosexual dominate those who are regarded as different.

On an everyday level, the operation of such regulatory norms may take a discursive form, such as disapproving words, gestures or looks, but it can also take a more physically violent form, like 'queer bashing'. Yet Harré (1993: 125) discounts physical forms of coercion as asocial, regarding only the discursive forms of power as fully social. Once more, this misses the vital connection between the macro- and micro-social in relations of power, for, as Elias (1978, 1982) demonstrated, the more expressive and performative styles of gaining and maintaining status came to prominence in Renaissance Europe, initially within the courts of the aristocracy. This could only occur as the means of violence were gradually monopolized in the form of professional armies, at first in service to the monarch and later to the state as a whole. This monopolization of the means of violence led to more and more pacified spaces being created in everyday life, beginning with the aristocratic court and spreading eventually to most aspects of social life. Yet the means of violence are not done away with but kept 'behind the scenes', reserved for use against a population if needs be (as they were in the general strike in Britain in the 1920s, or in the anti-Vietnam war protests in America in the 1960s).

This dislocating of relations of power from an 'everyday' level, so that they can somehow be kept analytically distinct from other forms of relations, is also evident in the work of John Shotter. He wants to distinguish

> the hurly-burly of everyday life (the multiplicity of partial orderings in everyday life), from the devices and institutions of the State, as well as from the economic mechanisms of production, distribution and exchange. These latter, as rule-governed patterns and structures of *official* social life, clearly exist and are empirically identifiable as such. But what I want to argue is that the unofficial, everyday hurly-burly of social life is not best thought of as consisting in particular, fixed and empirically identifiable structures and activities. It lacks, I want to claim, any fully developed nature at all; it is only partially structured and open, to a certain limited extent, to further development, to further shaping or reshaping by those involved in its conduct.
>
> (Shotter 1993a: 80–1)

There is a political and humanistic reason for Shotter's reluctance to characterize social life as structured and regulated by the state or the economy. He believes that most social thinkers have been concerned with the official, structured institutions of social life, presenting a view of social action as being highly organized and rendering 'rationally invisible' the chaos and disorder out of which social actors create regularity. By stressing order and regulation, most social theories construct a world in which joint action is highly constrained, when in fact it is more liberating to stress the disorderly, contested and still-to-be-made nature of everyday life in which all people play a part. What we take to be 'reality' and the 'structures' or 'things' that constrain our actions are the products of everyday conversation in which participants create orderly patterns out of the disorderly flux, or 'hurly-burly', in which they live. This social and political vision is intended to empower people, by stressing the fundamentally creative nature of everyday conversation and – by de-emphasizing official discourses and structures – opening up spaces for marginal or unofficial voices.

Although these political and humanistic aims are admirable, the potential effectiveness of Shotter's strategy and the understanding of social life inherent within it can be questioned. He is surely right to stress the partially structured nature of social life, but this does not mean that the regulations or constraints on action will disappear if we stop talking about them. While I agree that relations of communication are not completely synonymous with relations of power, so that dialogue can form a base of resistance and change, there are links between relations of communication and relations of power. For example, a heretical or unofficial discourse is often framed in terms of the official discourse or organization it is opposing, so it is difficult, if not impossible, to uncouple the linkage between them. Indeed, Volosinov (1986), from whom Shotter draws some of his ideas, stresses how unofficial discourses (or ideologies as he refers to them) always mingle with official discursive forms before they can be accepted and published more widely. These everyday discourses do create change, but they have to be formulated, in part, in terms of what already exists. People do make history, but under conditions not entirely of their own making – and these conditions are there whether we like it or not. If Volosinov is right, the already existing structures are the means through which something new is authored.

Moreover, relations of power and their crystallization in institutional form have not only a discursive life, but also a material existence that needs to be taken into account. Foucault illustrated how there are institutional sites and spaces where human behaviour is regulated by means that are non-discursive, such as surveillance. As Roy Bhaskar has said in an afterword to one of Shotter's books, 'one can accept that conceptuality is (uniquely) distinctive of human life, without supposing that it is exhaustive of it. "Being imprisoned" involves more than the negotiation of meanings; it means being physically excluded from certain spaces for a certain time' (Bhaskar 1993: 187). In this sense, some people within society are rendered relatively powerless, and overcoming this is not solely a question of making sure they are included in the multiplicity of voices in conversation. We need also to understand how the devices and institutions of the state and economy interpenetrate everyday life, which in turn feeds back into these structures, thus providing opportunities as well as constraints for everyday actors. Parker (1989: 151) has said that social psychology needs to be situated in a context where one can connect 'the expressive order with [the] physical, economic, and practical distribution of power in society'. This is closer to a Foucauldian view of power, where different forms of relations support or oppose one another, forming contexts for action that humans do not choose but in which they make their own history. It is also a move closer to a blending of the dark and light forms of constructionism.

This leads me to the second part of the discussion, for not only have some social constructionists uncoupled the expressive order from relations of power and their institutional sites, they have also severed the links between relations of communication and relations that transform the real. In other words, a world of conversation and discursive dialogue is posited against a material world that might, or might not, be 'out there'. This dichotomy is also related to the issue of power.

Expressive practices

The light versions of social constructionism often overlook the material contexts in which relations are located. Although Gergen acknowledges that patterns of action are located in such contexts, he also claims that social constructionism is 'ontologically mute' (Gergen 1994: 72): that is, it cannot pretend to provide descriptions of a world of things or beings because such descriptions are always linguistic constructions. Therefore, constructionism can neither affirm nor deny a world 'out there' beyond linguistic formulation. This is reflected in Shotter's warnings about the dangers of a 'things ontology', of believing that the way one talks about a thing somehow reflects its actual existence rather than the way it is talked of, and thus constituted, as real. However, even accepting these points, can we not also say that material contexts and things somehow play a role in activity and discourse without believing that we could ever have a definitive account of them? Should we not see material contexts and things as 'in here', within our practices and discourses rather than outside them? This would then begin to darken the horizons of social constructionism, for we would have to begin to consider that discourse does not produce everything we experience within our world, and that some aspects of our world may actually constrain the way we construct them linguistically.

Harré has tried to get to grips with this problem in his distinction between the practical and expressive orders, in which he demarcates a physical world of causal mechanisms (the practical) from a social world of conversation and conventions (the expressive). However, Harré also included work in the practical order, especially work to produce the means of subsistence, the things necessary to sustain human life. Humans need to eat in order to live, so our ancestors began cultivating crops to produce a regular supply of food; yet digging is related to cropping just as cause is related to effect in a causal mechanism, so the labour that goes into producing the means of subsistence can be regarded as part of the practical rather than the expressive order. Harré borrows the notion of the means of subsistence from Marx, but argues that whereas Marx made economic production the basis of his social theory, most human societies at most periods in history have devoted energy and concern more towards expressive activities than towards practical ones. The maintenance of honour and respect is a more pressing concern and a more interesting preoccupation than the realm of 'mere' necessity (Harré 1993: 30).

Although Harré is right to challenge the Marxist notion that all societies are grounded in an economic base which then crudely determines the cultural superstructure that arises from that base, his division between the practical and expressive maintains the same dichotomy, merely tipping it on its head in terms of importance. Furthermore, Marx claimed that labour was not just about the production of the means of subsistence, but also about the transformation of reality through labour. Thus, labour does not simply refer to the production of the means of subsistence, nor simply to industrial work, as Harré (1993: 30) takes it to mean: for Marx, labour referred to all human endeavours that transformed the ecological niche in which we live, and, as such, it was a basic means of human *expression*. Although human labour had become dehumanized, routinized and robbed of human expression, in Marx's view this was not something inherent in human labour itself, but was exactly the *result of industrialization and the power relations within capitalist society*. This was the basis of Marx's view that modern people are alienated, because work in the industrialized world has been robbed of its function as a means of expression and individuals have been reduced to the appendages of machines – like robots fixed into the mechanized rhythms of the assembly line (Marx 1848).

Thus, Marx actually challenged the notion of any fundamental division between a practical and expressive order. The work of a crafts person can be as expressive of social being as the dress and style of the dandy at court, or the interactants in an everyday conversation. Expressive practices need not be discursive in the conversational sense, they can also be practical in terms of the invention or creative use of an artefact to fashion an object or to transform some other aspect of the material world. As Ilyenkov (1977) points out, artefacts can be created objects, such as tools and utensils, or they can be symbols, such as signs, language or numerals. But all artefacts – whether objects, implements or signs – are meaningful in that they embody human practice and have significance for the social group. Ilyenkov's work also makes us realize that the sign may not be the privileged artefact which alone constructs the human world; artefacts more generally have been the instruments with which humans have fashioned a world in natural materials. This challenges the notion that discourse is in itself the primary means of social construction.

It also challenges the idea of a human realm somehow distinct from the natural, material or practical world. In both Harré's and Bhaskar's (1989) realist epistemology, there is a world outside of discourse composed of intransigent causal forces, distinguishable from the world of human expression and knowledge, which is transient and changes at a relatively fast pace. Yet if human constructive action is based not only in discourse that gives rise to knowledge, but in practical activity that changes the face of reality, then our societies, cultures and knowledges are not solely discursively based. That is, they arise from the transformation of materiality, which can no longer be regarded as an intransigent backdrop to discursive invention. We live in a world that is partly socially constructed, yet not through discourse alone: it is constructed from the practical–expressive activities of human beings within a socio-natural world.

Harré (1990, 1993) addresses issues of materiality by taking up von Uexkull's concept of the *Umwelt*, which is 'that part of the material world that is available as a living space to the members of the species by their specific modes of adaptation, such as distinctive perceptual and manipulative capacities. The same "total" world contains any number of possible Umwelten' (Harré 1990: 301). Within the human *Umwelt*, scientists create devices that constantly expand our perception of it; for example, microscopes allow us to view molecular particles. Thus, Harré's version of realism means that the knowledge we have of the world denotes 'real beings', entities or processes existing in the *Umwelt*, even though what we know of them may require revision as our explorations in the *Umwelt* continually expand it. We know that some of the things we encounter in the *Umwelt* are objective realities with an independent existence because they are only malleable and open to manipulation to a certain degree. Their stubborn refusal to bend to every theory or design humans may have for them attests to their relatively objective existence. On this basis Harré (1990: 352) continues his distinction between the practical and expressive, because 'Human life is lived with respect to two intransigent, imperfectly knowable "realities". As embodied beings we are located in physical space–time and have such powers as our material embodiment endows us with. But as psychological and social beings we are located in another world', the world of conversational reality.

The problem, though, is the question of how these two worlds interrelate. Harré has already given the example of how an artefact, the microscope, expanded the perception of the physical world and added to scientific discourse and knowledge. Yet the microscope itself was invented as part of scientific practice and expressive theoretical inquiry, so how can a distinction between two 'intransigent realities' possibly be maintained? Within the human *Umwelt* practical and discursive activity are fundamentally fused and it is impossible to separate them. The questions should be: how does conversation have material effects by sustaining human communities of practices that intervene in the world in order to change it; and how do those practices which expand the *Umwelt* have effects upon the discourse and knowledge of the community? As Ian Hacking (1983: 146) says, 'we shall count as real what we can use to intervene in the world to affect something else, or what the world can use to affect us.' Although Harré is aware that the human *Umwelt* is composed of both the physical environment and social meanings, we need to know how these combine in the totality of human experience; otherwise we end up in a social/material dichotomy which concepts like *Umwelt* could potentially overcome.

The problem for constructionism is that it is often based in a view of 'the unchanging character of nature', which 'fails to capture the dynamics of nature and the embeddedness of social projects and constructions in those dynamics' (Murphy 1994: 958). What this means is that we do not simply construct nature in our accounts of it, since the dynamics of nature themselves influence the accounts we construct. An example of this two-way relationship given by Murphy is the way in which scientific and technological interventions in the natural world have produced unintended outcomes in nature itself, which has 'reacted to such manipulation through high-technology accidents, the creation of pesticide-resistant and drug-resistant species, atmospheric change, etc.' (Murphy 1994: 971).

In order to avoid the dichotomy of the social and material, I propose that we should not view human experience as divided between two intransigent realities. Rather, we should conceptualize experience using the metaphor of five dimensions. I have adapted this metaphor from the work of Elias (1991), for whom the five dimensions were composed of the three dimensions of space (breadth, depth and height), the fourth dimension of time and the fifth dimension of the symbolic (which includes language and other signs). However, as I have already said of constructionism, I do not think that symbols alone can characterize what is unique about the patterns of human relations, action and knowledge: instead, it is the creation and development of artefacts that mark out what is distinctive about human life, and such artefacts include language, tools and other instruments or inventions. Language is not, then, the only mode for the transmission of knowledge. Once this is taken into account, I believe the dimensional metaphor is valuable because it allows us to think of different dimensions of human life that are distinct and cannot be reduced to one another, yet neither can they be separated. To imagine this, think of a three-dimensional image like a hologram: we are aware of the three dimensions, the experience of breadth, depth and height in the image, yet no one can say where any one of these dimensions begins or ends, nor can we identify a point where one dimension begins to segue into the others. So it is with space and time, for Einstein demonstrated how these two dimensions are inextricably linked, even though they are experienced as distinct.

This is also the case with the artefactual dimension and its blending with space and time. Take, for example, the symbolization of time, with which we are all familiar in terms of the various cultural artefacts we use to measure time: the seconds, minutes and hours of a clock, or the days, months and years on the calendar. Although these are purely artefactual markers, they are nevertheless connected to the dimensions of space and time in the *Umwelt*: the orbit of the earth, the cycle of day and night, the changing seasons which affect climate and environment. We are also aware of the general rate at which human bodies in our period of history age and eventually die, and in symbolic terms we can generally expect to last a little over the biblical three scores years and ten. The way we think about the duration of our lives, then, is composed of spatial, temporal and artefactual markers, and it becomes impossible to separate these out from one another. Could anyone say where the dimension of the artefactual measurement of time ended and some 'pure' dimension of time 'in itself' began? I think not, nor do I believe it would be fruitful to try, because life is irreducibly multidimensional.

This is a darker version of social constructionism because it suggests that human meaning is always situated in a material context and, although we can partly change the world through the use of artefacts, we can never completely transform the realms of space and time, in practice or in conversation. Some aspects of the world are always likely to limit discursive practices. However, transformation of the real is possible and, with the aid of artefacts, humans are able to change and gain knowledge of various aspects of the *Umwelt*. In this way there is much light in the darkness.

Conclusion

Arguing for a blending of dark and light forms of social constructionism allows for the possibility of conceptualizing humans as discourse users constructing a meaningful world within their social relations and joint practices. But much of this discursive and moral practice is devoted to constraint and regulation and the reproduction of existing relations of power, as well as being devoted to reconfiguring them by resisting forms of social hegemony and domination through the creation of heretical discourses and new social alliances. I have suggested here that we need to understand these two forms of action, reproduction and reconstruction, as being inherently linked. For example, in this book many authors are drawing from ideas outside of social constructionism in order to refashion constructionist ideas and practice. We are constrained to a certain degree in our writing by what is already there, yet we can synthesize ideas in ways that have the potential to create new possibilities.

Again with the material contexts of the *Umwelt*, humans are constrained in their constructive activities by the material living space we are adapted to, but only within constantly changing limits. Through relations and practices that transform the real, people can reshape the *Umwelt* and fashion artefacts that are not given in nature. Indeed, such artefacts are themselves at the core of relations that transform the real, becoming extensions of the human body as prosthetic devices which extend the perceptual boundaries of the *Umwelt* (as in the case of the microscope), or as technological instruments put to use in the transformation of materiality. Whether the *Umwelt* is unlimitedly expandable or transformable is a pragmatic question that will only be settled – or may never be settled – in practice. For now, all we can say is that despite the current limits on action, in both power relations and material contexts, there are innumerable relational possibilities that are open for the future.

References

Bhaskar, R. (1989) *Reclaiming Reality: A Critical Introduction to Contemporary Philosophy*. London: Verso.

Bhaskar, R. (1993) Afterword, in J. Shotter, *Conversational Realities: Constructing Life Through Language*. London: Sage.

Burkitt, I. (1998) Relations, communication and power: selves and material contexts in constructionism, in I. Velody and R. Williams (eds) *The Politics of Constructionism*. London: Sage.

Danziger, K. (1997) The varieties of social construction, *Theory and Psychology*, 7(3): 399–416.

Elias, N. (1978) *The Civilizing Process, Volume 1. The History of Manners*. Oxford: Blackwell.

Elias, N. (1982) *The Civilizing Process, Volume 2. State Formation and Civilization*. Oxford: Blackwell.

Elias, N. (1991) *The Symbol Theory*. London: Sage.

Foucault, M. (1965) *Madness and Civilization*. London: Tavistock.

Foucault, M. (1977) *Discipline and Punish: The Birth of the Prison*. London: Penguin.

Foucault, M. (1979) *The History of Sexuality, Volume 1*. London: Penguin.

Foucault, M. (1982) The subject and power, in H. L. Dreyfus and P. Rabinow (eds) *Michel Foucault: Beyond Structuralism and Hermeneutics*. Brighton: Harvester.

Foucault, M. (1986) Nietzsche/genealogy/history, in P. Rabinow (ed.) *The Foucault Reader*. London: Penguin.

Gergen, K. J. (1989) Warranting voice and the elaboration of the self, in J. Shotter and K. J. Gergen (eds) *Texts of Identity*. London: Sage.

Gergen, K. J. (1994) *Realities and Relationships: Soundings in Social Construction*. Cambridge, MA: Harvard University Press.

Gergen, K. J. (1997) The place of the psyche in a constructed world, *Theory and Psychology*, 7(6): 723–46.

Giddens, A. (1987) *Social Theory and Modern Sociology*. Cambridge: Polity Press.

Hacking, I. (1983) *Representing and Intervening: Introductory Topics in the Philosophy of Natural Science.* Cambridge: Cambridge University Press.

Harré, R. (1990) Exploring the human *Umwelt*, in R. Bhaskar (ed.) *Harré and His Critics: Essays in Honour of Rom Harré with His Commentary on Them.* Oxford: Blackwell.

Harré, R. (1993) *Social Being*, 2nd edn. Oxford: Blackwell.

Ilyenkov, E. (1977) *Dialectical Logic: Essays on Its History and Theory.* Moscow: Progress Publishers.

Marx, K. (1848) The Communist Manifesto, in D. McLellan (ed., 1977) *Karl Marx: Selected Writings.* Oxford: Oxford University Press.

Marx, K. (1851) The Eighteenth Brumaire of Louis Bonaparte, in D. McLellan (ed., 1977) *Karl Marx: Selected Writings.* Oxford: Oxford University Press.

Murphy, R. (1994) The sociological construction of science without nature, *Sociology*, 28(4): 957–74.

Parker, I. (1989) *The Crisis in Modern Social Psychology – and How to End It.* London: Routledge.

Shotter, J. (1993a) *Conversational Realities: Constructing Life through Language.* London: Sage.

Shotter, J. (1993b) *Cultural Politics of Everyday Life: Social Constructionism, Rhetoric and Knowing of the Third Kind.* Buckingham: Open University Press.

Volosinov, V. N. (1986) *Marxism and the Philosophy of Language.* Cambridge, MA: Harvard University Press.

6 'Discourse or materiality?'
Impure alternatives for recurrent debates

**JOAN PUJOL AND
MARISELA MONTENEGRO**

New developments in social theory are progressively being incorporated into the theories and methods of social psychology. Social constructionism (Gergen 1973, 1982, 1985) and discursive psychology (Potter and Wetherell 1987; Edwards and Potter 1992) are sensitive to these approaches, offering theoretical and methodological alternatives to mainstream psychology. A characteristic feature of these and related perspectives is the centrality of language, a distinctive feature compared to other traditions such as behaviourism or cognitivism.

The centrality of language dissolves some of the common dichotomies (such as internal/external, subjective/objective or relative/real) that have long been present in psychological literature and research. Instead of an individual or macro-social phenomenon, meaning production becomes a shared activity among social actors, where researcher and researched equally belong. Language has become a powerful metaphor for the understanding of social reality, and linguistic analogies inspire explanations for the origins, transformations and effects of the 'social'. From this perspective, language constitutes the final warrant for theoretical claims:

> Discursive psychology attempts to look at how events are constructed in the social and cultural arena along with the psychological implications for the study of people's evaluations and representations . . . Unlike attitude research and social representations theory, the focus is much more on everyday interaction, on talk and discourse, on the activities which people perform when they make sense of the social world and the resources (category systems, vocabularies, notions of persons, etc.) on which these activities depend . . . Discursive psychology shifts the emphasis away from the nature of the static individual to dynamic practices of interaction.
>
> (Potter 1996a: 150)

Discourse, all discourse and nothing but discourse

Alongside the gradual academic recognition that discursive perspectives are valid alternatives to cognitive approaches, dissatisfaction with the importance given to language has emerged. The limits of our world seem to be somehow different from the limits of our language. However, because language is our principal technology for the representation, construction and transmission of knowledge, descriptions of social reality and tests of the correspondence between these descriptions and the world (if such tests are relevant) must also be described linguistically. Accounts of the world display variability, construct reality and have discursive effects (Mulkay 1984; Potter 1996b). Therefore, the status of 'the reality behind language' (like attitudes or cognition) becomes either a topic for discursive research or a philosophical matter (Potter and Wetherell 1987: 181–2). The vigour and beauty of the argument come from its phenomenological logic. An alternative to describing the 'real world' is to describe 'the world as it appears'. But then, because the principal means of expressing reality in the academy is language, discourse becomes a *substitute* for 'the world-as-it-appears': the limits of our language become the limits of our world.

The naturalization of discourse as an object of research raises the problem of accounting for the origins of, alterations in and effects of those things called 'discourses'. The emergence and modification of discourses has to be located in participants' agency, in social structure or in the interaction between these two, as in Giddens's (1984) concept of *double structuration*. All these options require extra-discursive concepts, such as social structure or individual agency. Even if these concepts are themselves theorized as discursive, the interaction between discourses cannot be. To account for discourses, then, either a normative dimension (using concepts such as power, ideology or social structure) or an interpersonal dimension (like agency, intentionality, interaction or practice) needs to be introduced.

Trying to study the social world with language as its only metaphor puts discursive research in a paradoxical position: it has to understand the appearance and modification of discourses without referring to non-discursive entities.

Against the dissolution of reality into discourse, realist perspectives postulate a human independent reality affecting social life that informs and shapes social processes. Phenomenological perspectives may be correct in considering knowledge as a human product, but they do not consider the effect of objects on human cognitive possibilities (Bhaskar 1989: 25). Critical realism, a sophisticated version of realism, recognizes both the conceptual and the material components of social reality. While traditional forms of realism do not consider the constructed character of social reality, critical realism recognizes that social structures have conceptual aspects – although they are not reducible to them.

> Society then is the ensemble of positioned practices and networked interrelationships which individuals never create but in their practical activity always presuppose, and in so doing everywhere reproduce or transform. On this approach, while social structures are dependent upon the consciousness which the agents who reproduce or transform them have, they are not reducible to this consciousness. Social practices are concept-dependent; but, contrary to the hermeneutical tradition in social science, they are not exhausted by their conceptual aspect. They always have a material dimension.
>
> (Bhaskar 1989: 4)

In order to reconcile the constructed status of knowledge with the existence of an external reality, critical realism distinguishes between ontology and epistemology, arguing that 'how things are' may differ from 'how they appear according to the methods and techniques used'. While for naive relativism there is a clear link between language and reality, critical realism approaches this relationship with suspicion and distinguishes between its ontological and epistemological dimensions. Using this distinction, positivism is realist on both ontological and epistemological dimensions, and social constructionism is relativist on both. In contrast, critical realism recognizes that methods do not uncover reality (relativist epistemology), but rational analysis of phenomena can uncover it (realist ontology).

It is important to understand that this debate is not only academic, but also political. The identification of 'real' underlying factors for social problems either legitimates existing structures of power or grounds radical action against them, depending on the political utility of the factors identified. Moreover, the procedures used by both natural and social sciences to 'construct' facts have been exposed (Callon 1986; Latour 1991; Michael 1997; Knorr-Cetina 1997: 265). Relativism, by acknowledging that knowledge is constructed, challenges justifications for present structures of power and suggests that some utopias, given enough time and effort, can be accomplished. However, relativism is also criticized for leading to political inactivity, since 'if there is nothing outside the text, then there is no means to assert the existence of even the starkest material realities' (Wilkinson 1997: 184). Neither realism nor relativism offers answers applicable to all contexts, and more partial perspectives are needed: 'relativism is the perfect mirror twin of totalization in the ideologies of objectivity; both deny the stakes in location, embodiment, and partial perspective; both make it impossible to see well' (Haraway 1991: 191).

The dichotomies 'real/relative' or 'material/linguistic' are part of Western philosophical history (Potter and Wetherell 1987: 181). They comprise a structure of oppositions, such that utilizing one of the poles activates its related dimension. The search for underlying factors shaping social reality energizes elements such as 'realism', 'search for truth', 'natural', 'nature', 'identification of previous/causal variables', 'independence of human activity' and 'materiality'. The analysis of understandings of the social world energizes elements such as 'relativism', 'manifestation', 'construction of truth', 'artificial', 'social', 'posterior/consequence', 'dependence upon human action' and 'discourse'. Our argument is that constructing other demarcations for concepts such as real, manifestation, material or linguistic may enable us to break with these oppositions, making possible new forms of theory and research.

New metaphors for old dichotomies

Although discursive psychologists emphasize their differences from cognitivism, it may nevertheless be useful to highlight their similarities. Constructionist and discursive approaches can be considered as a radicalization of cognitive psychology, since they both view the social world as constructed. The difference between them is that the latter considers individual cognitive structures as 'unconstructed' (other than by physiology), while the former broadens the constructed character of social life to include the individual. It is informative that cognitive perspectives appear under the heading 'the construction of the social world' in some social psychology textbooks (e.g. Hewstone *et al.* 1996). Emphasizing these similarities, the label 'second cognitive revolution' for discursive perspectives may not be inappropriate:

> the word discourse is to be understood very broadly. Its usual implications of verbal presentation of thought and argument are broadened, to provide a handy word for all sorts of cognitive activities, that is, activities which make use of devices that point beyond themselves, and which are normatively constrained, that is, are subject to standards of

correctness and incorrectness. Language use is just one among the many discursive activities of which we are capable, if we broaden the use of the term in this way. My excuse for this innovation is that there is no one term which comprehends all the various kinds of things we might do that fall under the general prescription of being both intentional and normatively constrained. The second cognitive revolution is nothing other than the advent of discursive psychology!

(Harré 1995: 144)

The structure of arguments for the Cartesian *cogito* illuminates some of the dimensions underlying both cognitive and discursive psychology. In his *Meditations*, Descartes uses the logic of mathematics as a paradigm for reasoning to establish firm and permanent foundations from which knowledge can be built. The project negates the importance of the body for this enterprise, a point of departure that would constitute one of its conclusions:

To-day, then, since very opportunely for the plan I have in view I have delivered my mind from every care (and I am happily agitated by no passions) and since I have procured for myself an assured leisure in a peaceable retirement, I shall at last seriously and freely address myself to the general upheaval of all my former opinions.

(Descartes 1641: 45–6)

Other starting points would have led to different ends: if the project had begun from the perspective of a fragmented subject governed by the temporal truths of the passions of the body, its outcome would undoubtedly have been different. The 'indubitable foundation' that the *Meditations* tries to build comes from an act of *authority*, from the uncritical establishment of axioms such as distrust of the body as departure points.

The *Meditations* work hard to avoid the passions of the body, even though they address a question that desperately requires them: the question of one's existence. The apparent truth of the sentence 'I think therefore I am' is based on constructing an 'I' different from Descartes's body and using this 'I' simultaneously as an object and as a subject (Leyden 1963). The distinction between 'I' (subject) and 'Descartes' (object) is apparent when the *cogito* is reformulated as 'I think therefore Descartes exists'. It is the use of the pronoun 'I' that makes the assertion 'I think and I do not exist' appear self-contradictory, because it becomes a self-referential sentence (like 'This sentence is not true': Slezak 1983) and so leaves the content of 'I' undetermined (Herzberger 1970). Since the 'I' does not have any concrete content, its existence cannot be decided (Ayer 1953).

A second strategy consists of considering the body as unreliable and incapable of offering any valid knowledge. This rhetorical construction of the body makes statements like 'I can doubt that my body exists but not that I exist *ergo* I am not my body' appear acceptable. Similar prejudices could be directed towards 'the mind', as in 'I can doubt that a being exists whose essential nature is to think, but I cannot doubt that I exist, *ergo* I am not a being whose essential nature is to think' (Malcolm 1965). Neglecting the reality of the body as the starting point, and considering the human being as divided into two – body and mind – leads to the conclusion that mind is the final reality. The *Meditations* construct a unitary 'I' cemented by reason, whose principal activity is thinking. Body, on the other hand, is a material accessory that makes the 'I' possible, but is modifiable and change-able without affecting any relevant aspect of the 'I'. The lodger of the mind is the one who says 'I think therefore I am', the subject that has self-given reality and has deprived the body of its legitimacy to speak. Although cog-nitivism is closer than discursive perspectives to the *Meditations'* underlying assumptions, the following similarities can be traced:

- The Cartesian 'I', cognitive processes and (often) 'discourses' are ideal-ized entities belonging to everyone and no one. These entities are at the same time agents and subjects of actions (discourses effect, interact with and modify other discourses).
- Both use a phenomenological perspective ('the world from the perspect-ive of the actor') to justify the neglect of material elements of interaction outside people's consciousness.
- Both neglect the body as a valid source of knowledge.

The theoretical and practical implications of the Cartesian *cogito* are exemplified in the concept of reflexivity. The value of reflexivity comes from the particular perspective one achieves when analysing one's own activity. However, the notion of reflexivity does not take into considera-tion the position from which one can be reflexive. It does not consider the material conditions that make the reflexive act possible, implicitly assuming the existence of a space outside any material constraints. One can reflect from the future, from a different position or from a different perspective, but one cannot 'be reflexive'. In contrast, acknowledging that 'reflection is produced from certain material conditions' dissolves the paradox of the 'eternal reflexive loop'. Because 'cognition' or 'discourses' are idealized con-cepts, it is possible to take infinite positions in an ideal space, but this becomes impossible when embodiment is introduced. Discursive perspect-ives, although they emerged in response to cognitivism, nevertheless pre-suppose a researcher with no body and no place in the material world.

There is one major discourse, however, whose exclusion is shared by the dominant and successor traditions: both exclude the inherently embodied character of human endeavour . . . I insist that both the larger culture and this disciplinary interest, for the most part, have been con-cerned not with embodiment but rather with what I refer to as the object body: the body that is known, as a third person observer knows any object in the world. Little interest has been shown in embodied social practices, including, especially for the constructionist challenger, embodied discourse.

(Sampson 1996: 602)

One way forward involves constructing new metaphors to provide a different perspective on these issues. Inspired by the fiction of the cyborg (Haraway 1991), we suggest 'machines' as a base metaphor. Machines are human products combining discursive and material elements, i.e. both the design and the substance of the machine. Both material and discursive aspects are dependent on human activity and, therefore, relative. What the machine produces, on the other hand, does not depend on human activity (although it needs humans to exist): it depends on the interaction between discourse and materiality, between the design and the substance from which the machine is built. Just as material objects such as prisons, bicycles and tables have a discursive element, so discourses and verbal interactions are materially sustained. Words cannot 'exist' without some support (for example, the paper on which these words are printed). Considering reality (and also ourselves) as contingent productions blurs the distinction between 'real' and 'relative' because:

1 'Reality' is a consequence, not a cause. It is constituted through the interaction between discourses and materiality, but both elements are relative, as they are human dependent. Reality is a social production and, as such, artificial, as it is facilitated by human action.
2 'Reality' is independent of human action. It is the result of interactions between human products, but it is not the direct outcome of human actions. Everything is not possible because reality is not 'what we want' but a collateral consequence of our actions in the world. Reality is the *unintended consequence* of interactions among our constructions.

This perspective dislocates the traditional dichotomies, by defining both discourse and materiality as underlying forces that are not 'real' and by placing the limits of our world beyond the limits of language and materiality. Phenomena and reality are located in the same plane as a result of the assemblage between discourse and materiality, as elements independent of human action but impossible without humans. Nevertheless, we do not claim that this constitutes the correct form of understanding, but simply another version of the debate, a version that makes possible other forms of social theory and social research (like the work of Yardley 1996 or Stoppard 1998). Building other versions of the debate shows how discourse and materiality have been reified, and are separable analytically but not ontologically.

Implications for research

This solution may be significant at an ontological level, but it does not offer an epistemological answer or provide any methodological guidelines. There are perspectives, like actor–network theory (ANT) (Callon and Latour 1981; Latour 1987), that have already considered the difference between 'discursive' and 'material', 'nature' and 'technology' or even 'human' and 'non-human', as the product of processes of translation and purification (Michael 1997). Ethnographic research conducted under ANT considers objects such as computers as 'actants', as participants in the interaction. ANT research describes the processes of purification and networks of translation in the production of scientific knowledge, but does not resolve the problematic distance between researcher and what is being researched: 'In recounting an ANT story, where does the analyst situate him/herself?' (Michael 1997: 248). Further, the production of knowledge undertakes a process of purification that magnifies its linguistic dimensions. Although ANT research may treat objects as participants, dominant technologies of knowledge production based on writing and information demand a linguistic representation of what is observed, experienced and collected by the researcher. Current modes of academic production have inherited the Cartesian dichotomy between body and mind, and give priority to the latter.

The relationship between researcher, representation and reality has been an important topic in the hermeneutic tradition in terms of 'reader', 'text' and 'author'. A first approach would consider that language has an intersubjective character and the text constitutes the space where reader and author ('reality' and 'researcher') meet. Scheleirmacher considers that understanding emerges from the empathic action of taking the position of the author, reading the text such that the reader can understand and reconstruct the author's motives and implicit assumptions (see Gadamer 1960: 187). A good interpreter should be able to understand the author as well as, or even better than, the author understood himself. From this perspective, as the researcher partakes of the meanings already present in the text, he or she can understand them. This premise is used in discourse analysis to justify the interpretability of the texts analysed, relying on the linguistic competence of the analyst in order to understand the text under consideration (Potter and Wetherell 1987; Edwards 1996; Potter 1996b). Although the assumption that the researcher is linguistically competent in a particular society may work at a general level, it becomes problematic when we take into consideration the multiplicity of subcultures in a given society – one of which may include the researcher. Further, intercultural research would be difficult, if not impossible, since to understand the 'text' the researcher would need to suspend assumptions derived from his or her particular cultural position and replace them with the interpretive codes of the community under consideration.

Interpretation should consider the perspective from which the reader accesses the text, instead of denying it: 'Before we are detached, contemplative and theoretical; before relating to the world as radical externality . . . we are alongside and within an already significant world' (Stenner 1998: 61; see also Parker, this volume, Chapter 2). After all, as Heidegger points out, understanding is possible precisely because the researcher is located in a temporal and spatial context from which he or she cannot escape. Interpretation is not a choice but a necessity imposed by our limitations and possibilities as human beings. Reading emerges, in Gadamer's terms, from the encounter between the horizon of the reader and the horizon of the text, from the experience of a tension that interpretation must use instead of covering up (Gadamer 1960: 306). The tension moves from the 'text–author' (the reality behind discourse) to the 'reader–text' (the distance between researcher and discourse), and manifestations are not understood as an intersection between researcher and reality but as the point of departure for the construction of understandings. The research report does not 'describe' the world (or the discourses of the world), but is the result of a tension produced in the encounter between researcher and manifestation.

The acceptance of the 'death of the author', the possibility of reaching the mythical original point which accounts for present conditions and arrives at 'reality', brings out the question of politics. Without a reality to uncover there does not seem to be any justification for research. A perspective like critical realism considers it necessary to postulate an ontological reality that grounds emancipatory action. Not all conversations between 'reader' and 'text' are equally valid, so research is committed to uncovering underlying structures shaping social reality. Critical action depends upon the transformation of structures of oppression, so there is a need to develop an explanatory social theory that accounts for the transformations required (Bhaskar 1989: 178). Critical realism suggests tackling the epistemological lack of symmetry between reality and manifestation by making a distinction between 'a theory of knowledge' and 'a theory of being'. With this distinction, it is possible simultaneously to have a relativist epistemology and a realist ontology. Not being able to know reality does not mean it is not there, and so collapsing ontology into epistemology is inappropriate (Bhaskar 1989: 13). While knowledge depends on the procedures used to produce it, reality is independent of those procedures.

Despite the strength of this argument at the conceptual level, it encounters some difficulties in practice. Grounding emancipatory action in knowledge of reality simply leads to epistemological and ontological debate about the nature of the 'reality' uncovered by critical analysis. The epistemological debate assesses the adequacy of the methods used, while the ontological debate focuses on the nature and consequences of the 'being' defined by the research. Feminist perspectives, as political movements, have long acknowledged these complexities. While relativism permits patriarchal knowledge to be questioned, by demonstrating its historical and social specificity, it also diminishes the force of the analysis and its potential emancipatory value. On the other hand, realism allows the definition of a 'feminist standpoint' that grounds political action – at the expense of essentializing such notions as 'women' and 'oppression'. Haraway suggests that, in order to make political claims, one has to recognize the historical nature of knowledge claims, be aware of the technologies of meaning production and, at the same time, commit oneself to accounts of the 'real' world (Haraway 1991: 187). Critical realism aims to identify *the* underlying structures shaping social reality, leading to the dangerous claim 'that there is ever a single, foundationally proper "ideological position" from which any set of events *must* be read' (Stainton-Rogers and Stainton-Rogers 1997). A different approach would ground political action not in *the* knowledge of social reality but in a *local* knowledge, in terms of situated knowledge (Haraway 1991). Interpretation is about more than creating multiple versions of social reality: it has to consider the embodied, material and semiotic position of reader, interpreter or researcher.

Some concepts developed by Paul Ricoeur are helpful in concretising this issue. He advocates a hermeneutic interpretation where the 'fusion of horizons' draws a world that the reader could 'inhabit' (Ricoeur 1983: 93), moving from 'what the text says' to 'what can be said from the text'. The interpretive act explores not the text, but the world displayed by the text from the perspective of the author. It is not just a simple 'fusion of horizons', but a purposively constructed horizon suggesting a 'reality ahead' instead of a 'reality behind' (or a contemporary reality). The analyst takes an active role, far away from the metaphor of 'discovery', directed towards suggesting, producing and generating a world in which he or she could live (Ricoeur 1983: 112). The knowledge thus generated is a local knowledge conditioned by a network of material and semiotic positions.

As we have emphasized, interpretation is a necessity, not a luxury; it is the inevitable result of being-in-the-world. Research pursues what is 'absent and other than oneself', a theme present in the work of Jacques Lacan and Jacques Derrida. Derrida (in Kearney 1984) uses the metaphor of love to define the relationship between interpreter and text, making salient the notions of strangeness (that makes possible the pursuit of otherness) and familiarity (that makes possible the relationship between lovers). Both reader and text lose and gain from each other, and the reading is only activated because of the materiality of reader and text: 'To deconstruct a text is to disclose how it functions as desire, as a search for presence and fulfilment which is interminably deferred ... In every reading there is a *corps-à-corps* between reader and text, an incorporation of the reader's desire into the desire of the text' (Derrida in Kearney 1984: 126). From this perspective, interpretation results from the dialectical relationship between the reader and the strangeness/familiarity of the text, from the tectonics of the material position of the researcher and the object of research. 'To identify a discourse is to take a position, and the ability to step outside a discourse and to label it in a particular way is a function of both the accessing of dominant cultural meanings and the marginal (critical) position which the researcher takes (within or alongside another discourse or sub-culture or "common sense")' (Parker 1992: 33).

Conclusion

Because language is the legitimate tool for representing and communicating knowledge, it is difficult to negate its role as the primary human phenomena. Technologies of writing make the world knowable by processes of purification, but it is a mistake to reduce questions of ontology to epistemology, as critical realism points out, excluding issues such as materiality, embodiment or experience from our psychological repertoire. The discourse/ materiality debate is inscribed in a set of wider debates, including ontological, epistemological and political issues. It is important in this context to deploy new metaphors that address these issues, like the cyborg (Haraway 1991), or the 'reality-as-machine' in this chapter.

Taking into consideration the epistemological limits of our present technologies of knowledge, there is an inevitable gap between 'representation' and 'what is represented', between 'the expression of experience' and 'experience itself'. Therefore, there is no simple relationship between these two realms. Moreover, it is unfeasible to assume simple access to other people's understandings when the material and embodied dimensions are considered, since one cannot take someone else's material–semiotic position. Meaning does not pre-exist but is created in the process of interaction: the researcher constructs meanings through interaction with different material and symbolic positions. Interpretation is the outcome not of reflection by the researcher, but of the material/discursive interaction between researcher and researched. It is legitimized not by the accuracy of the representation produced, but by the value of the reading and the strategy of its construction. Understanding 'what is other than oneself' is an accomplishment forced by the needs and demands of interaction. Distance, embodiment and implication are preconditions for interpretation and not barriers to it: 'our understandings, being worldly (whether scientific or not), are inevitably partial, interested and located, and inevitably draw upon understandings already in place' (Stenner 1998: 68).

There are different ways to unravel the slippery Gordian knot that ties discourse and materiality together. Discursive psychology prioritizes the epistemological and language, while critical realism emphasizes the need for a non-discursive ontology that is rationally knowable. This chapter has developed a parallel perspective inspired by the work of Donna Haraway and actor–network theory, rejecting the segregation between discourse and materiality and considering the role of materiality and embodiment. The objects identified (discourses, interpretative repertoires etc.) are neither valid (*mis*)understandings of the world nor subjective apprehensions of it, but political actions forced by the interaction of the position of the researcher and of what is researched. Methodological guidelines must emphasize neither subjective proximity nor objective distance, but the subjective desire to overcome the difference from the object of research. Research needs to consider the position of the researcher in order to generate a productive 'strangeness' with a familiar object. The evaluation of the research has to pay attention not only to its formal aspects but also to the world opened by this research, for the possibilities and understandings offered to its recipients. Research is not about the reduction of the distance between the subject and object but about the dialogical impossibility of its relationship. Hybridity (as in the 'reality as machine' metaphor) offers a perspective where the dislocation of categories and, therefore, the production of new worlds is facilitated.

Acknowledgement

This work has been possible thanks to the scholarship Batista i Roca (Comissionat per a Universitats i Recerca de la Generalitat de Catalunya).

References

Antaki, C. (1994) *Explaining and Arguing: The Social Organization of Accounts.* London: Sage.

Ayer, A. J. (1953) Cogito, ergo sum, *Analysis*, 14(2): 27–31. Reprinted in G. J. D. Moyal (ed.) *René Descartes: Critical Assessments, Volume II*. London: Routledge (1991).

Bhaskar, R. (1989) *Reclaiming Reality: A Critical Introduction to Contemporary Philosophy*. London: Verso.

Bleicher, J. (1980) *Contemporary Hermeneutics: Hermeneutics as Method, Philosophy, and Critique*. London: Routledge and Kegan Paul.

Callon, M. (1986) The sociology of an actor-network: the case of the electric vehicle, in M. Callon, J. Law and A. Rip (eds) *Mapping the Dynamics of Science and Technology*. London: Macmillan.

Callon, M. and Latour, B. (1981) Unscrewing the big leviathan, in K. D. Knorr-Cetina and M. Mulkay (eds) *Advances in Social Theory and Methodology*. London: Routledge. 275–303.

Curt, B. C. (1994) *Textuality and Tectonics: Troubling Social and Psychological Science*. Buckingham: Open University Press.

Derrida, J. (1973) *Speech and Phenomena, and Other Essays on Husserl's Theory of Signs*. Evanston, IL: Northwestern University Press.

Descartes, R. (1641) *Meditations on First Philosophy*. London: Routledge (1991).

Edwards, D. (1996) *Discourse and Cognition*. London: Sage.

Edwards, D. and Potter, J. (1992) *Discursive Psychology*. London: Sage.

Gadamer, H. (1960) *Truth and Method*, 2nd edn. New York: Continuum.

Gergen, K. J. (1973) Social psychology as history, *Journal of Personality and Social Psychology*, 26: 309–20.

Gergen, K. J. (1982) *Toward Transformation in Social Knowledge*. New York: Springer-Verlag.

Gergen, K. J. (1985) Social constructionist inquiry: context and implications, in K. J. Gergen and K. E. Davis (eds) *The Social Construction of the Person*. New York: Springer-Verlag.

Giddens, A. (1984) *The Constitution of Society: Outline of the Theory of Structuration*. Cambridge: Polity Press.

Haraway, D. J. (1991) *Simians, Cyborgs and Women: The Reinvention of Nature*. London: Free Association Books.

Harré, R. (1995) Discursive psychology, in J. A. Smith, R. Harré and L. Van Langenhove (eds) *Rethinking Psychology*. London: Sage.

Herzberger, H. (1970) Paradoxes of grounding in semantics, *Journal of Philosophy*, 67(6): 145–67.

Hewstone, M., Stroebe, W. and Stephenson, G. M. (1996) *Introduction to Social Psychology*. Oxford: Blackwell.

Kearney, R. (1984) *Dialogues with Contemporary Continental Thinkers*. Manchester: Manchester University Press.

Knorr-Cetina, K. (1997) What scientists do, in T. Ibáñez and L. Íñiguez (eds) *Critical Social Psychology*. London: Sage.

Latour, B. (1987) *Science in Action: How to Follow Engineers in Society*. Milton Keynes: Open University Press.

Latour, B. (1991) Technology is society made durable, in J. Law (ed.) *A Sociology of Monsters: Essays on Power, Technology and Domination*. London: Routledge.

Leyden, W. von (1963) Cogito ergo sum, *Proceedings of the Aristotelian Society*, 63: 67–82. Reprinted in G. J. D. Moyal (ed.) *René Descartes: Critical Assessments, Volume II*. London: Routledge (1991).

Malcolm, N. (1965) Descartes' proof that his essence is thinking, *Philosophical Review*, 74: 315–338. Reprinted in G. J. D. Moyal (ed.) *René Descartes: Critical Assessments, Volume II*. London: Routledge (1991).

Michael, M. (1996) *Constructing Identities*. London: Sage.

Michael, M. (1997) Critical social psychology: identity and de-prioritization of the social, in T. Ibáñez and L. Íñiguez (eds) *Critical Social Psychology*. London: Sage.

Mulkay, M. (1984) The scientist talks back: a one-act play, with a moral, about replication in science and reflexivity in sociology, *Social Studies of Science*, 14: 265–8.

Nietzsche, F. (1887) On the genealogy of morality: a polemic, in K. Ansell-Pearson (ed.) *On the Genealogy of Morality*. Cambridge: Cambridge University Press (1994).

Parker, I. (1992) *Discourse Dynamics: Critical Analysis for Social and Individual Psychology*. London: Routledge.

Potter, J. (1996a) Attitudes, social representations and discursive psychology, in M. Wetherell (ed.) *Identities, Groups and Social Issues*. London: Sage.

Potter, J. (1996b) *Representing Reality: Discourse, Rhetoric and Social Construction.* London: Sage.

Potter, J. and Wetherell, M. (1987) *Discourse and Social Psychology.* London: Sage.

Ricoeur, P. (1983) *Hermeneutics and the Human Sciences.* Cambridge: Cambridge University Press.

Sampson, E. (1996) Establishing embodiment in psychology, *Theory and Psychology*, 6(4): 601–24.

Slezak, P. (1983) Descartes' diagonal deduction, *British Journal for the Philosophy of Science*, 34: 13–36. Reprinted in G. J. D. Moyal (ed.) *René Descartes: Critical Assessments, Volume II.* London: Routledge (1991).

Stainton-Rogers, W. and Stainton-Rogers, R. (1997) Does critical social psychology mean the end of the world?, in T. Ibáñez and L. Íñiguez (eds) *Critical Social Psychology.* London: Sage.

Stenner, P. (1998) Heidegger and the subject: questions concerning psychology, *Theory and Psychology*, 8(1): 59–77.

Stoppard, J. M. (1998) Dis-ordering depression in women: toward a materialist-discursive account, *Theory and Psychology*, 8(1): 79–99.

Wilkinson, S. (1997) Prioritizing the political: feminist psychology, in T. Ibáñez and L. Íñiguez (eds) *Critical Social Psychology.* London: Sage.

Yardley, L. (1996) Reconciling discursive and materialist perspectives on health and illness: a re-construction of the biopsychosocial approach, *Theory and Psychology*, 6: 485–508.

7 Discourse and the embodied person

ROM HARRÉ

Introduction

Ways of talking about people

Twenty years ago there were two shops in our village, a grocer's and a butcher's. Now there is only a village store, while the old grocery has become a centre for alternative medicine, the Iffley Clinic. Outside, signs read 'Body, Mind, Spirit', while the window offers a catalogue of the good things to be found within: Qi Gong ('acupuncture without needles'), Alexander technique, aromatherapy and many more. The striking thing about the list is that every item presupposes the unity of an embodied person. Treatment of the body *is* treatment of the mind and spirit.

The shop sign or motto is made up of three nouns. The grammar of nouns suggests that they refer to things or substances: in this case 'parts of a person'. There are the familiar 'Cartesian' pair, mind and body, the two substances at the core of Descartes's analysis of a human being. Then there is a third noun, 'spirit', suggestive of yet a third part or substance composing the complete human being. Are these separable parts, like the engine and chassis of a car? Descartes certainly thought that the mind not only could, but necessarily must, exist independently of the body with which it was linked so inextricably in life, so that he contrasted the intimacy of that relation with the way a captain is in his ship. The therapies on offer seem to invite us to enter a world seen as peopled. Yet it is a world in which the therapies make sense only if the people to which they are addressed are embodied, in such a way that the intimacy is more than Cartesian. It seems to be a world that is ordered in ways that are prior to the distinction upon which both materialism and social constructionism depend, that between chemistry and narrative. It is molecular, though not constituted wholly of molecules. It is a storied world, though it is not constituted wholly of narratives.

Although materialism and social constructionism both deny the reductive hegemony of the other, claiming it for itself, the intelligibility of either world view depends on the meaningfulness of its polar opposite. Each is partly defined by what the other is not. In just the same way, the startling claim that life is but a dream is intelligible and thrilling only if the contrast between dreaming and waking is sustained. 'Everything is a dream' fatally impales itself on the conditions of its own intelligibility.

Suppose we take the fundamental beings of our world to be people, and build out from there. Like the aromatherapists we might say something like this:

> People are embodied active beings, capable of intentional action and acting according to locally valid norms, constructing systems of symbols within which to live, devising projects and setting about their joint realization.

What about people? They live and die. They walk about, argue with one another. They fashion tools for various jobs, only some of which seem to be wholly utilitarian. They tell stories, only some of which are true and so on. People are also organisms of the species *Homo sapiens sapiens*, sharing 98 per cent of their DNA with a similar species, *Pan troglodytes*, though these relatives do not have the power of speech. Aristotle summed up peopleness in his famous phrase 'rational featherless bipeds'. That is close. Rationality is a *desirable* property of talk and it is bare bodies that walk about on two legs. Here we have in a phrase the troublesome duality of symbolic power sustained in an otherwise unremarkable organism.

Suppose we tidied things up by staking out the study of human symbol-using powers as the territory of a science of psychology, while leaving the organismic aspects to biologists. Would that do? Would that it were so simple. All sorts of things seem to be sayable about people in addition to those in Aristotle's short catalogue. Let us add to the list 'stupid', 'pretty', 'constipated', 'voluptuous', 'stingy', 'grubby', 'fat', 'upset', 'lost', 'legendary', 'self-sacrificing' and so on and so on. It is an immensely diverse list. Now let us look back at the slogan over the door of the alternative medicine shop. When we start on the road to a science of people by setting about building a classificatory scheme for these attributes, how shall we begin?

We might try to arrange the attributes in the list as properties of the three substances that seem to make up the tripartite human being: the body, the mind and the spirit. So bodies are fat, minds are stupid and souls are stingy. But very soon we run across such comments as 'Fat is a feminist issue', 'Only someone really stupid would go out without an umbrella' and 'He is so stingy he keeps all the apples for himself.' More puzzling yet, our doctor asks 'Where is the pain?' and expects an answer such as 'In my shoulder', even though we all agree that a pain is not a part of my body. It would not show up in a dissection.

The advent of the discursive turn

Some forty years ago the first intimations of another approach began to appear, mostly in the writings of philosophers,[1] but also in the works of psychologists, at that time almost isolated in the old Soviet Union. What if the nouns 'body', 'mind' and 'spirit' did not refer to parts of the person, one visible and two invisible, but to ways of talking about people? Each way of talking focused our attention on different attributes of people. And even more radically, what if these seeming attributes of the mind or the soul were attributes of what people did rather than of what they were; and the most important and characteristically human activity that people engaged in was talk? But what sort of talk? What do people mostly say to one another and to themselves? Broadly speaking, giving instructions, performing other social acts and telling stories make up the bulk of what people say. Exchanging matters of fact is very rare. Suppose that psychological phenomena like emotions, attitudes, memories, decisions and so on are not states of individual people, but attributes of the streams of joint action people create in interaction with one another, most of which are discursive. On this showing psychology should have a place within just such an account, namely as a form of interpersonal talking and writing. But it would differ from other forms of talk, in that it would aim at reporting matters of fact about the talking and writing through which the life of the everyday is brought into being.

There seem to be at least three main ways of talking about people. Each of these ways has its own vocabulary and preferred forms, while each has its own standards of propriety, its own 'grammar'. Each way of discussing people is grounded in its own preferred basic repertoire of unanalysable elements. In discussing people as bodies, the final element as we anatomize a body into organs and their constituents is the level of molecules. In discussing people as minds we anatomize the flow of symbolic representations into meaningful elements and the structures they coalesce into. In discussing people as spirits (which I take to be a discussion of people as moral beings) we anatomize the flow of interpersonal interaction into actions, intended public behaviour and acts, the meanings of those actions. Not only are these three discourse genres about people but they are also, in the two latter cases, discourses about discourses. This point needs to be stated with care. There are all kinds of symbolic activities, and there are many ways of performing social acts, other than by speaking or writing. But all symbolic and intentional activity has two leading characteristics. It is intentional – that is, meant by the actor – and does not just happen, nor is it just emitted as the effect of a cause, and it is normative – that is, it is always, in principle, subject to standards of correctness and propriety. For instance, not just any old recollection that strikes one as about the past is a memory. Only correct recollections *count* as rememberings. This is not something that has been discovered by psychologists, but is a feature of the grammar of the concept of memory.

In this situation two centrifugal tendencies have appeared, driving psychology towards yet another flirtation with incompatible polarities. Perhaps everything that can be said about the mental and spiritual aspects of people can also be said in the 'body' grammar, the discourse of molecules. But the alternative has been advocated with a great deal of enthusiasm. Perhaps everything that can be said about the material aspects of people could be said in the grammar appropriate to an account of symbolic activities. While the one camp would have it that symbolic exchanges are molecular interactions, the other camp would have it that the materiality of people is just a social construction. 'Weight' and 'loyalty' would be the same kind of attribute in the final analysis, for both camps! For the former the root science is biochemistry, for the latter it is socio-linguistics. Looked at from the point of view of strong social constructionism, both biochemistry and socio-linguistics are discourse genres, and their narratives are stories, which is itself a socio-linguistic claim.

How can we maintain the fundamental role of the person as the elementary being of our world, while acknowledging that people have a place in arrays of material things, some of which are not people, and have a place as speakers and listeners in an interpersonal conversation. People are born into both these worlds, which they find ready made. How can we do justice to the fact of human embodiment in a world of symbols? I shall try to show that there are three ways in which the symbolic world could not have the character it has were people not embodied. In other words, embodiment is a necessary condition for a symbolic world of the general character of ours.

Here we come to one of the great metaphors of the age, a metaphor briefly introduced above, that of a 'grammar'. A grammar, in this general sense, is a set of rules for the use of a symbolic system: for instance, a verbal repertoire. Although grammars are influenced by that which they are used to create discourses about, they are not determined by their subject matter. There are all sorts of grammars in use in our daily and professional lives. Psychology is a cluster of diverse discourses about human beings, and makes use of several grammars. Choice of grammar makes a difference to which aspects of the world stand out for us. Choosing a grammar is rather like choosing a particular dye to stain a bacterium. With one dye one set of microstructures becomes visible, with a different dye another stands out. Each is there in the bacterium, but is available to a human observer only, when stained. Similarly, when we talk about human beings using a people-based grammar, certain aspects of human life stand out, while the use of a molecule-based grammar highlights others. Some postmodernists have slipped into using such expressions as a 'world of people' or a 'world of molecules' to introduce the idea that what we can come to know is relative to our choice of instrument for exploring human life. This has led to some people denying that there is a common world, shared by all human beings. But what we have is the world seen as peopled and the world seen as molecular and so on. So whether a grammar is valuable or dysfunctional for the purpose at hand depends on whether the world affords aspects that would be available to a human observer did they exist.

What do grammars determine? A grammar can be expressed in the form of two hierarchies of terms, with the rules for their use. One of these hierarchies is used for classifications and the other for explanations. They both grow and develop in use, expanding in some directions and shrinking in others. But they are organized by quite different principles. Classificatory hierarchies are organized by relations among supertypes and subtypes, like species and genus. The genus *canine* includes such species as *dog* and *wolf*. But the concept *canine* has no explanatory role with respect to questions we might ask about dogs and wolves. Explanatory hierarchies are often organized on the basis of parts and wholes. In one common pattern the properties of wholes are explained by reference to the properties of parts, together with the structure that links aggregates of parts into wholes. For instance, the capabilities of a machine are explained by reference to the parts and how they are arranged. The size, number of teeth and their helical arrangement in the geartrain explains the behaviour of an automatic gearbox. There has been an alarming tendency for psychologists to treat classificatory hierarchies as if they were explanatory, particularly in the field of studies of personality and temperament. Why is Bill outgoing and cheerful? Because he is an extrovert. But the hierarchy within which outgoing and extrover-sion have a place is classificatory, not explanatory. Molière's famous jibe at the medical profession's explanation of the soporific powers of opium as due to its dormative virtue makes the same point. Of course there are proper explanations in terms of powers and dispositions. But the develop-ment of their workings is beyond the scope of this chapter.

I have suggested that there are at least three grammars in play in the discourses with which people, both lay and professional, deal with human life. They can be set out as a hierarchy (see Figure 1). How would a human being look if it were to be embedded in each of these grammars? In the grammar for discourses about 'people in relation to things', a human being

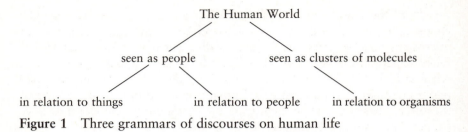

Figure 1 Three grammars of discourses on human life

would most naturally be seen in terms of activity and passivity, as actively engaging with material things to accomplish projects and from time to time being the recipient of usually unwanted causal assaults from them. In the grammar of 'people in relation to people', a human being would most naturally be seen in terms of the moral quality of those relations in relation to the networks of positions that constitute the local social order. But in the grammar of 'clusters of molecules', a human being is an organism, and in relation to material things and other organisms would be seen in causal relations. King Canute's famous attempt to cross these grammars at the behest of his courtiers simply led to his getting his feet wet.

The necessity of embodiment

Narrative and the person as narrator

Narratives are stories told by people, individuals positioned here and there in the social fabric. Stories are told about discernible persons and more often than not prefixed by 'I'.

What is the role of the first person singular? At first glance it might look as if 'I' was a queer kind of name, one that each person could use to refer to himself or herself. But already we can see that there is something odd about that suggestion. Unless the person addressed is aware of who is speaking, the self-referential function of 'I' is ineffective. So who is 'I' for the moment is discovered, so to say, by knowing who is speaking (or writing). In this way it is quite unlike a proper name. I know who is being referred to when someone uses the words 'Banjo Paterson', even though he is long since dead and gone and only his songs live on. I am addressed by my proper name, but never by 'I'. The pronoun of address is 'you'. If 'I' and 'you' were names why don't small children use 'you' rather than 'I' to prefix self-referential utterances?

One common use for the first person singular, in English, is to take responsibility, or to make a commitment. By using 'I' the speaker makes that commitment, as himself or herself. 'I'll look after the children' is very close to a promise in force. But one has to be there, or otherwise to know who is speaking to know where the responsibility lies. It can be done over the phone, so immediate physical presence is not necessary, either in space or in time.[2] So it seems that embodiment is not a necessary condition for this use of 'I'. I suppose commitments could be entered into via a ouija board.

However, there is another use of 'I', often going along with the one just described, in which the role of 'I' is to index the content of a report with the spatial position of the speaker. This is common in everyday life, but it is the core of autobiography. Telling about an event in the first person places the speaker at or near the event in question. 'I watched the planes circle and come in to drop their bombs on the bridge' carries at least the conversational implicature that 'I was there!' The archetypal autobiographical anecdote has both place and time indexes: 'When I was in Nevada . . .' Authority for myself as the author of the story is claimed just by the use of the first person. Compare the fairy tale opening 'Once upon a time there lived a King who had three sons' with the autobiographical 'I was one of three brothers.'

Places are locations in physical space. They are defined by relations between material things. Insofar as I have a place in space I have it by virtue of the fact of my embodiment. Insofar as the tenses of the verbs in my utterances relate what I am saying to the times of events as past or future, my utterances themselves must be events in the same time frame as those events. Insofar as those events are happenings in the material world, so must my utterances be. At least one aspect of myself must be a trajectory in space and time.

There is more. To be a person is to be a singularity, to be just one person. This is not a ubiquitous fact that students of human life have discovered. It is part of the grammar of the 'person' concept. Strawson (1964) pointed out that it is only as embodied beings that people are routinely identified and reidentified as the singularities they are. They share this metaphysical property with the material things among which they are embodied. As a grammatical remark about people it fits well with the observations I have made above about the indexical force of the first person singular in reports and autobiographical narratives. Personhood is so bounded by the singularity of each human being's embodiment that neither more nor less than one person per body is permitted to stand.

In summary, then, in order to understand a perceptual report I have to know *where* the speaker is in space. But that spatial position is fixed by the relations that the speaker bears to the things in the material environment. To have a place in such an array a speaker must be embodied, as a thing among things. The acts performed by the active person with whom we are engaged are embedded within sequences of events in the material environment, such as the risings and settings of the sun or the ticking of clocks. So a speaker's acts must be carried by events in the material world. To understand a perceptual report fully I must know how the event of making the report and the event reported are related in time. Both must be material events, and this again requires that the speaker be embodied. The general principle that acts must be sustained materially has long been accorded a place in social psychology and ethology in the act–action–behaviour distinction. Behaviours are material phenomena, actions are material phenomena seen as intended by the actor and acts are the social meanings of actions as they are seen within unfolding social episodes.

Once again the traditional 'mind/body' distinction is no longer required. Instead we are using such distinctions between events localized in space and time and those that are more diffuse. Singular embodiment, one person per body and one body per person, focuses our attention on that which is localized in space and time. People are many and history is rich in events. The emphasis I have placed on embodiment ought not to obscure the importance of studying cognitive phenomena that are generated in the symbolic interactions of crowds and in the historical unfolding of long-term 'conversations'.

Ethology and the language of feeling

We are out bird-watching and I want to draw your attention to a double breasted spatchcock. If it is very close I might tap your shoulder, point and catch your eye. Or if it is some distance away I might say, 'Look over there, to the left.' The gesture and the utterance can play the same role. In this and many other cases we see how gesture and utterance can be substituted for one another. In this case one might say that both gesture and utterance are within discourse. Perhaps both have to be learned and we are trained in the norms for their use. They are intentional and normatively constrained. We could indicate direction by pointing to the place from whence we have come, as we do with the wind direction. We could mime silence by some other gesture than the finger to the lips.

Bearing all this in mind, we shall find the body once more at the centre of our psychological studies when we tackle the question of how it is possible for people to discuss their private experiences – for example, bodily feelings – with one another. Why is this a problem? Suppose it is assumed that youngsters learn the meanings of words by having examples pointed out to them by someone already knowledgeable in the language. So one might have learned 'elephant', 'mauve', 'horizon' and so on. The exemplar must be able to be jointly attended to by both teacher and learner. What about 'itch', 'vanilla' and like words? While we can both see the ice cream, each experiences a wholly private taste. So we use the ice cream as a public vehicle for learning the taste word, and we never ask ourselves, unless prompted by philosophers, whether the taste as an experience is the same for both teacher and learner. It does not seem to matter, since we have the ice cream to go on. But 'itch' (and Wittgenstein's favourite 'pain') is not like this. Itches are not public either as experiences or in some matrix of causality. 'Tickle' is more like 'vanilla' than it is like 'pain'.

The psychological question came up incidentally for Wittgenstein, who was in hostile pursuit of the 'pointing to exemplar' theory of meaning into its farthest reaches. Incidentally, he gives a solution to the problem of how public discussion of private feeling is possible in almost an aside, of profound significance for psychology. One way a child might learn the word 'pain' would be as a verbal substitute for the natural expression of pain. Instead of crying and rubbing the spot the child would be taught to *say* 'That hurts', 'I've got a pain' and so on. Tightening and generalizing this insight, it seems that human ethology – inherited fixed action patterns – underwrites the possibility of acquiring and using a vocabulary of feeling, and indeed of much else that is of psychological importance.

There is a further step that can take us deeper into the grammar of feeling words. An implication of Wittgenstein's insight is that feeling and behavioural tendency are a unity, a psychological whole. If someone claimed to be in pain and had no tendency to cry out or to rub the spot and so on then whatever it was he or she was feeling it would not be pain: that is, not properly called 'pain'.

Tasks and tools

I read the instructions on the packet: 'Prepare a trench not more than 5 cm deep.' I could scoop out the earth with my hands, scraping a shallow trench to plant the peas. But I could use a spade for the same job. But I might also use the spade to pat down the earth, to carry some hot coals, and for a myriad other tasks. While I could use my hands for the former I would not, if I were wise, use them for the latter. In this example there is a bodily organ more or less adapted to a range of tasks, and there are prosthetic substitutes with which a person can carry out at least some of the same range of tasks. The same principle holds for cognitive as well as for practical jobs. I can tot up my income tax liabilities 'in my head', using only my brain for the job. I can keep a tally of the brain work by jotting down the steps on a piece of paper. But I can consign the whole job to a surrogate, my calculator. Of course there are some cognitive acts, such as recognizing the numbers in my employer's annual return which I will need to punch into the machine, but even these are close to being handed over to a prosthesis.

Once we drop the mind–body dichotomy, which now looks like a metaphysical illusion spawned by the nominative form of at least some traditional person discourse, we are free to bring other distinctions to bear. In the above paragraph the distinction at work is that between task and tool. Tasks are defined in a goal-setting or means–end discourse. It is clear that in practical matters I can use a bodily organ to carry them out or in many cases I can make or buy a suitable inorganic tool. The same is true for cognitive tasks, where the bodily organ is the brain and the surrogate a diary (instead of remembering), a calculator (instead of mental arithmetic), a map (instead of a mental picture of the countryside) and so on.

As referents of mentalistic discourse bodies and their organs are tools. Tasks are not reducible to tools, in the sense that there is no way that the task to be performed or that had been performed could be deduced from knowledge of the tool. The fit is too loose, the boundaries of possible employments too broad. Furthermore, a strictly physico-chemical description of a tool not only could not entail a task description, but would not include any criteria for good working. That is defined only relative to the task. I buy a ball-pein hammer and soon find the head becoming scored and pitted. Without reference to the tasks for which hammers are meant as tools that is just another fact about the hammer, like the shape of the back of the head. I find a brain clogged up with tangled skeins of dendrites. By what criterion can I decide whether or not that is how it is meant to be, except by reference to a task. Not the task of being unable to recognize one's relatives, but the task of remembering one's mother tongue. But why shouldn't the task be 'Try not to recognize your relatives', as, say, the advice given by the leader of the resistance in some small French village during the Second World War? Because it runs counter to some of our deepest social norms.

The way in which bodily organs serve as tools for tasks can be illustrated in more detail by returning for a closer look at remembering. The work of memory is a socio-linguistic practice, something we learn to do. I know of no major study of the acquisition of the concept of memory, a yawning gap in our understanding of human development. We can imagine all sorts of things and we can say all sorts of things. Which are acts of remembering? We cannot learn the distinction by comparing what happened with what we think or say happened. The past is gone beyond recall, and for the most part leaves hardly any traces. The distinction must be learned from others of superior memorial power.

What does memorial power mean? Does it mean a more accurate recall? But how could the person who claims memorial power establish that his or her recollections were indeed more accurate portrayals of the past than someone else's. Plainly there is no way. Of course, the moment we think about real cases of remembering we realize that, like many other claims to authority, it rests in prior acts of positioning. Relative to someone who is positioned as authoritative someone else is positioned as in need of instruction. When the former is Mum and the latter is Baby we have the usual Vygtoskian set-up, in which Baby can appropriate the distinction between imagining something happened and remembering something happened from situations in which Mother makes the distinction for Baby, long before Baby can make it for itself. This is a complex distinction, since not only does it require a monitoring of larger coherences but also each pole of the distinction is embedded in different criteria of excellence. The ideas of 'accurate imagining' or 'correct day-dreaming' make no sense.

Remembering is a discursive practice in origin. Does it preserve this character as people become more and more individualized in their mental activity as they grow older? It seems that in one important respect it does. Recently, two major research projects have shown the importance of conversations in the course of which remembering is achieved: that is, in which putative recollections are negotiated and eventually certified as memories. In one study (Middleton and Edwards 1990), a group of young people were asked to remember a film. The creation of the memories was tracked though a sequence of negotiations, not only as to what had occurred in the film, but also as to who was to serve as the arbiter of 'correctness'. It is important to bear in mind that the concept of correctness as it is used in this discussion cannot be defined as the degree of good fit between the recollection and the event remembered, since the event remembered is available only as recollections of various people, which is the situation of everyday life.[3]

Another more recent study that illustrates the same point was based on a comparative analysis of people recollecting events individually and recollecting them in the course of a memorial conversation (Dixon 1996). To sum up an extensive programme of research, it turned out that older and younger married couples remembered the same amount of information about a story, but that the difference between individual recollections and collaborative remembering were greater for the older people than for the younger. Importantly, the social relations between the collaborators had a marked influence on the efficacy of conversational remembering, so that doing memory work with a long-term partner was more effective than doing it with a stranger. It also turned out that in younger couples the greater memorial rights went to the women. Unlike real life, the story that each couple were asked to remember survived from past to future, to serve as a yardstick of memorial correctness for the psychologists, but not of course for the participants, since they had no access to it to check their recollections.

It should be abundantly clear that the concept of 'memory', or better of 'remembering', has a place in the 'world-seen-as-people' grammar, a world the substance of which is conversation. As many have argued, the prime place for cognition is in public conversation rather than in individual mental activity. But at the same time the Dixon study, like Sabat's work on Alzheimer's sufferers, showed that, individually, elderly participants did less well on his tasks. At this point the discourse must undergo a radical shift from a 'world-seen-as-people' grammar to a 'world-seen-as-molecular-clusters' grammar. In the former world the brains of the participants are the tools with which they accomplish the tasks Dixon set them. But if the tools are not functioning according to the local norms, set by the performances of the younger people, there must be something amiss with the tool.

In the world seen as molecular clusters the biochemistry of the brain has a role to play: in relation to brain not as *objet trouvé*, but as tool. Otherwise, there is no basis for getting criteria for good and less good functioning. I show you a machine, and tell you it is a tool. Then I ask you whether it is working properly. It is certainly doing something, emitting buzzes and clicks and jumping up and down. But unless I let on what it is for you have no basis for assessing its performance. The idea that memory could be the subject of a study couched wholly in the grammar of the world seen as molecular clusters is completely astray. Remembering is not something brains do. It is something people do using their brains. To see this let us remind ourselves of the instructive role of prostheses. Instead of relying on the remembering tool in my skull I have my Psion Series 3A organizer, which I treat in much the same way. I switch it on and press a few buttons, and lo and behold I read off the screen that my daughter's fax number is so and so. Asked my Danish Person Number, I pause a moment and then recite 1812272213, to the amazement of my friends. Asked my UK Social Security number, I go back chagrined to my Psion.

The body as toolkit lies partly in the world seen as persons and partly in the world seen as molecular clusters. It shifts from one to the other as different issues come into play, but it never resides wholly in the one or the other.

The interrelations of the grammars

Let us now look more carefully at the three grammars that have intersected in this discussion. There is person-talk, in which concepts like tool and task, skill, means and ends and so on have a natural place. There is matter-talk, in which concepts like cause and effect, tensile strength, mass and so on have a natural place. In the former there is a key role for concepts like 'skilful', 'incorrect' and so on, while these have no place at all in the latter. In the former, material things are tools, while there is no place for that concept in the latter. Is there a place for the concept of 'person' in the grammar of matter-talk? People initiate action, they have projects, they are constrained by norms of many sorts. None of these crucial person-defining aspects has a place in matter-talk. So the word 'person' cannot find a place. Of course, 'human body' is well established in matter-talk. More is known about bodies than is known about persons.[4] Where is the third grammar in all this?

The norms that I have cited here and there in the past couple of paragraphs have been more or less practical requirements for managing lives in this or that environment. But there is no doubt that no culture has rested content with that. Just living is possible, but a tempest of talk of a very different kind swirls around us. It is the discourse of 'living well'. Once the preserve of the soul, it has come to be the dominant discourse in the domain of the body, but in a very different way from the discourse in which the body figures as a toolkit.

Halting the slide into idealism

How has social constructionism shaded over into idealism? How has it lost the materiality and intransigence of the body? There seem to be at least two mistakes that have led to the collapse.

The role of prior knowledge

It is true that for something to be perceptible as something of a certain sort depends on one's prior knowledge and beliefs about what there could be in the world, and in particular on the type-hierarchy or classification scheme that one has picked up for identifying things in their kinds. When I worked as the assistant to an expert wool judge as a lad, I never matched his capacity to identify 120 categories, but I could pick out about 40 different types and grades of fleece. I am quite sure the majority of the readers of this fragment of autobiography would be lucky to distinguish two or three. Other distinctions among fleeces were possible too, but the one in commercial use could not have evolved had fleece not differed in texture, staple, colour and so on, distinctions there to be found by the professionals. We did not make them, although they were visible only to us. It is all very well for feminists to assert that male/female is a categorial distinction in a humanly forged taxonomy, but although there are other ways of classifying human beings, that distinction does focus attention on distinguishing characteristics that are materially there. The realization that there are many ways of classifying things into kinds does not entail that any of them are arbitrary. They may all be based upon material distinctions.

The variety of explanation formats

The sciences are also in demand to furnish explanations of phenomena. However, there are a variety of legitimate explanation formats, one of which has become the standard for explanations in the physical sciences. That is the technique of imagining unobservable mechanisms – for example, molecular exchanges – as the causes of observable phenomena. In these sciences there is usually a further search for independent evidence for the existence of the imagined process and its material grounding. But there are two other explanation formats that play a central role in everyday life, especially where it is human behaviour that seems to be in need of explanation.

One such format is based on the thesis that people generally try to act in a proper or correct fashion, or at least to seem to do so. There are norms for skilled work in the carpenter's shop, just as there are norms for how one treats one's mother-in-law. Normative explanations fall into a space defined by two pairs of distinctions. There are cases where a person or a group of people attend to a rule, and treat it as an instruction, which they follow. There are also cases where behaviour that was once rule-following in the explicit sense becomes habitual. The latter case tends to mimic causal constraints on action. To break a habit may be difficult, but it involves regressing to the learning situation in that one used the rule as an explicit instruction. The second dimension runs between cases where a rule or instruction is transcendent to the action, capable of being explicitly formulated and commented upon without any relevant action having taken place. Then there are norms that are immanent in the action, ways of doing things that are learned by imitation perhaps.

The third format is historical. It stands in contrast to genetic explanations, a species of causality. If one's performance is a fixed action pattern, brought into being by a neural process in a structure that has been inherited through Darwinian selection, then although the past is cited in the explanation, it is hardly historical. By historical explanation I mean one that refers to some past discursive activity out of which a decision arises, or some other way by which a practice becomes a settled custom. The Mormons, with many war widows to find support for, turned to polygamy. Their adoption of this marriage mode was not the result of a fixed action pattern caused by a 'selfish gene'. Americans drive on the right because Lafayette convinced the town government of Philadelphia that it was the proper republican way to organize the traffic. Aristocrats, as right-handed swordsmen, rode on the left of the path.

Turning now to our three cases in which embodiment is a necessary condition for the possibility of discourse, the most developed aspect of the world seen-as-symbolic, we can relate each to the distinctions in explanatory formats. The narrator's location in a space of things and a time of events is a purely formal feature of first person claims. There is no room for causal explanations of how the narrator unfolds the tale. Narrative genres are conventions that quickly become local story-telling habits. Why do we tell stories in the way we do? Perhaps only a historical explanation will do.

Causal explanations do play a part in the genesis of a psychological vocabulary, since without the natural expression of feeling, and certain thoughts, the crucial substitutions of verbal for ethological expressions would have no starting point.

The task/tool metaphor also involves causal and normative explanations. How tools work calls for a causal account. Mechanics explains how a ball is returned by impact with a racquet. But what they are used for, and which ways of so using them are correct, must make use of explanations that invoke rules, conventions and cultural history.

The postmodern extravaganza

It has become clear over the past hundred years or so that the rules of formal logic do not suffice to account for the acceptance or rejection of explanations among the scientific community, even for those that are not of the standard unobservable mechanism sort. Logic cannot justify the use of local evidence to support the truth of universe-wide laws of nature; nor has logic the means to distinguish between two theories from each of which the known facts can be deduced. Yet we do find ourselves convinced of the truth of Ohm's Law and of the truth of the electrochemical account of the architecture of molecules. One of the ways of trying to account for historically given decisions on these has profound consequences for psychology. Some have argued that the deficit between the limits of logic and historically recorded decisions is made up by a social negotiation among interested parties and not by the results of experiments or observations. These, it is alleged, only count when drawn into such a negotiation and legitimated by the social power of those who cite them. So each theory creates, via selective attention, its own repertoire of supporting evidence. That this amazing doctrine is not a fantasy I can illustrate in the following quotation: 'the confirmations (or disconfirmations) of hypotheses through research findings are achieved through social consensus, not through observation of the "facts". The "empirical test" is possible because the conventions of linguistic indexing are so fully shared ("so commonsensical") that they appear to "reflect" reality' (Gergen and Gergen 1991: 81–2).

Of course, science is not and never has been the preserve of formal logic. Those who take the fall of logic as an invitation to unreason do not realize how the natural sciences work within a fairly tight rational frame. The standards of good work in science are based on model building, on simulation of nature, and not on logical operations other than as secondary ways of maintaining the consistency of a discourse. Once one looks closely at how a picture of nature is built up and legitimated, the gap that seems to yawn between evidence and hypothesis, when logic is our only tool of analysis, rapidly closes. The rift is healed, though it existed only in the imaginations of philosophers ill-informed about the historical process of gathering knowledge of material nature.

The turn to discourse is not an invitation to knowledge brokering by social consensus. Instead it involves a huge enrichment of the repertoire of models to which we might turn to reveal this or that aspect of social and psychological reality.

Notes

1 One must remind oneself that Bartlett, writing in the 1930s, had anticipated a good deal of what was to come.

2 'I hereby will and bequeath . . .' is effective long after the time of writing.
3 On this matter the otherwise admirable science journalist Bruce Bower got it wrong. In commenting on a letter to the editor of *Science News*, he accepted the letter writer's suggestion that the reason why people remembered better in groups was that each corrected the other. This cannot be 'corrected' in the ordinary sense, since no one had access to the past.
4 This obvious but somewhat startling truth is, in part, a consequence of the huge waste of manpower and resources on research projects into the symbolic world of persons using methods and philosophies of science that are at home in the study of the material world of molecules and natural mechanisms. Imagine trying to investigate the machines of a bygone culture using only physics!

References

Bruner, J. S. (1986) *Actual Minds, Possible Worlds*. Cambridge, MA: Harvard University Press.

Dixon, R. A. (1996) *Interactive Minds*. New York: Cambridge University Press.

Gergen, K. J. and Gergen, M. (1991) Towards reflexive methodologies, in F. Steier (ed.) *Research and Reflexivity*. London: Sage.

Middleton, D. and Edwards, D. (1990) *Collective Remembering*. London: Sage.

Strawson, P. F. (1964) *Individuals: An Essay in Descriptive Metaphysics*. London: Methuen.

8 The extra-discursive in social constructionism

VIVIEN BURR

Introduction

My aim is first to explain why I agree with the main tenets of social constructionism, and then to point out what I see as its areas of weakness. For the purposes of this chapter, the weaknesses that I shall focus on are the status of personal experience and the role of embodiment in producing that experience. I shall argue that, largely owing to constructionism's focus upon language as the primary constructive force behind social and psychological phenomena, the person as an experiencing subject has been exorcised from our understanding of human life. I do not wish to deny the legitimacy of this view of language (as constructive rather than descriptive of the world). However, drawing on the phenomenology of Merleau-Ponty, I shall argue that important aspects of human experience are located outside of language, in the 'extra-discursive'. This is a realm of experience primarily constructed in and expressed through embodiment, rather than through language, and relatively resistant to translation into it. Extra-discursive modes of experience and expression include art, dance and music, and I shall draw on examples from these in making my argument.

Much of the benefit of the social constructionist view of language has been in the way it renders social and psychological phenomena political.

Discourses may be described as coherent systems of meaning which produce knowledge, and which serve particular power relations. I shall argue that to draw attention away from language towards the extra-discursive is not to neglect this issue, but to offer additional ways of responding to and resisting power. Such arguments regarding the expressiveness of the body and its political possibilities are not new in disciplines outside of psychology (see Benthall and Polhemus 1975) but psychology has largely ignored them.

The social constructionist challenge to psychology

Social constructionism is a term used predominantly by psychologists. Most sociologists, by contrast, would broadly consider themselves to be social constructionists, since most sociological theories argue that our experience of the world is produced by social forces. To sociologists, the term 'social constructionism' fails to signify anything meaningfully different from what they already know and do. But for psychologists the term refers to a body of theory and practice which is radically different from what is normally thought of as psychology.

My own position is one that is broadly sympathetic to the claims and intentions of social constructionism. In particular, there are three features of social constructionist thinking that I welcome. First, as a form of critical psychology (see Fox and Prilleltensky 1997), it claims that all knowledge is historically and culturally specific and advocates a sceptical approach to things that present themselves as 'fact' or 'truth'. It therefore exhorts us to view the received wisdoms of psychology as temporary social constructions which bear the marks of the assumptions and concerns of their society of origin. Psychology, like other forms of knowledge, is embedded in and produced by a system of values and power relations. It can therefore never be apolitical, and 'objective science' becomes an ideology serving to mask this state of affairs.

Second, social constructionism challenges the essentialism and individualism that are central to Western psychology. In the move to explain more and more phenomena (alcoholism, criminality and mental distress among others) in terms of properties of individual persons, such things are readily pathologized and left at the door of problematic individuals who must endeavour to 'cure' themselves. Social constructionism has an important role in reframing such phenomena as constructed in the social realm within a particular system of social structures and power relations. Such an analysis reveals the way in which the individual is made to carry the responsibility for social ills, while the social conditions and vested interests which form their breeding ground remain invisible. Social constructionism is therefore suffused with an anti-cognitivism that refuses to locate psychological phenomena inside the minds of individuals.

Third, social constructionism has revolutionized the role of language in psychology. Within traditional psychology, language is simply the tool with which people communicate private ideas and states to others. In itself, language is seen as passive and unproblematic; a device for describing and externalizing pre-existing objects and events. By contrast, social constructionism places language centre-stage and gives it a highly constructive role. It is language that allows people who share a common tongue to generate a common currency of concepts and meanings. It is through their dealings in this common currency that people fabricate their world. But social constructionism also claims an intimate relation between language and power, so that the concepts and constructions that we build through language bear the hallmark of the structural and power relations in our society. Language is therefore never indifferent to power; power, and resistance to it, are constantly played out in our uses of language.

But what happened to the person?

'The person', the traditional focus of Western psychology, has become a problematic concept for social constructionism. All the features which we had taken for granted as the things that make us unique individuals – personality traits, motivations, drives, attitudes, thoughts and so on – become reframed as social constructions. They are effects of discourse which give us the illusion of selfhood as we live them out in our daily lives. The thoughts and ideas that we had previously owned and cherished as the solid foundation of our personal decisions and choices become reworked as manifestations of discourses speaking through us. No longer the originator or author of its own ideas, the self becomes turned into a text, a complex narrative accomplishment suffused with discourses. It is a text written and rewritten from moment to moment according to the demands of a multitude of social contexts.

The status of our personal experience thus becomes questionable. If our experience is the outcome of our subject positions in discourse, then our accounts of it are only further texts to be 'read' in order to find clues to the operation of prevailing discourses. This has led to a curious about-turn in the approach to research taken by those who have been critical of the power relations embedded in traditional social psychological research. The 'crisis' in social psychology (Harré and Secord 1972; Brown 1973; Armistead 1974) had led some writers to argue that the 'voice' of research subjects should be heard; that what people have to say about their own experience is as important as, if not more important than, the observations of experimental social psychologists. This concern led to a move towards a greater use of qualitative methods, where participants' accounts of their lives are treated as valid data. However, although social constructionists are often just as concerned about this power relation, they cannot take at face value accounts of personal experience.

Some writers, myself included, are keen to retain some notion of choice and agency, and see the person as one who can take up or resist positions within discourse (Butt *et al.* 1997; Burr 1998). Gavey (1997: 54) writes: 'Individuals . . . are active and have "choice" when positioning themselves in relation to various discourses. For example, women can identify and conform to traditional discursive constructions of femininity or they can resist, reject and challenge them (to a greater or lesser extent).' Hollway (1995) too responds to the need to account for a person's capacity to negotiate their position within discourses, albeit with a psychodynamic account which many social constructionists would regard as inevitably essentialist.

If we do not allow for some notion of choice and agency, and in particular for the capacity of persons to challenge and resist positions within discourse, then it is difficult to see the point of academic (or any other) debate and argumentation.

And what happened to the body?

A second weakness of current social constructionist writing concerns the banishing of the body from our accounts of the person and its reintroduction as a form of textuality. The body has long been absent from traditional psychology, which has primarily seen its task as describing and explaining mental events and behaviour. The body has thus been regarded as simply the physiological and neurological substrate which allows or produces such mental and behavioural events. Psychoanalysis, which was overtaken by behaviourism and then cognitive science as the dominant psychology, is perhaps alone in its concern with the psychological meaningfulness of the body. Within traditional psychology an entrenched mind–body dualism has located the phenomena of psychology firmly within the mental realm, with the bodily realm explored as a source of possible explanations of the mental.

Within disciplines such as sociology and cultural theory the body has led a rather different life. Here, it is a signifier made to carry social meanings that can be 'read off' from a person's appearance or from visual representations (Barthes 1972; Goffman 1976; Easthope 1986). The social meaning of the body as discussed by Foucault (1976, 1977) has also been taken up with enthusiasm in recent times. Foucault went beyond a semiotic analysis of the body – that is, how it may be 'read' for signs of social relations such as gender and class – to an analysis which located the body as a prime site of power relations. The body thus conceptualized is a plastic, malleable object which has become a powerful instrument of social control. Those behaviours and bodily processes that so deeply concern and bother us – for example, the acts of eating, drinking and excreting and especially sexual behaviour – and the body parts involved in these functions have assumed the status of major problems for us precisely because the body has been discursively produced as a tool of widespread social control (Foucault 1976). For Foucault, the body is thus a prime instrument of 'disciplinary power' (Foucault 1977). Through our worries about sexual normality and perversion in both our own and others' behaviour, through our desires and fantasies, and through what have come to be regarded as and experienced as the insistent but dangerous demands of the body, we have come to regulate our thoughts and behaviours, to take part in a wholesale process of 'self-discipline'. By our own efforts, we bring our behaviour and desires into line with what is necessary to maintain major social institutions such as marriage and the family, which in turn are crucial to the maintenance of the dominant social order. Society is thus effectively controlled, through all of us becoming willing volunteers to discipline our own bodies.

This analysis of the body has been enthusiastically taken up by those sociologists, social constructionist psychologists and others who have been particularly interested in power relations where the body appears central, such as in gender and sexuality. For example, Featherstone (1991) analyses body image and the search for self-realization through an ever more beautiful, healthy, pleasurable and disciplined body. Gavey (1997) analyses women's experiences of sexual coercion within heterosexual relationships, showing how their experience is produced and 'read' through prevailing discourses of heterosexuality, and Sawicki (1991) uses the Foucauldian concept of 'biopower' to show how new reproductive technologies control women's bodies through the incitement of desires and the creation of identities (for example, as infertile or surrogate mothers).

Although some, like Sawicki, have been keen to explore the possibilities for resistance that may be present in 'subjugated knowledges' (in her case, women's own accounts of their experiences), the power of discourse and social practice to define and produce bodily experience is highlighted. The explicit aim of a recent edited collection (Ussher 1997) is to recover the 'material body' and to examine how it is experienced as a material, corporeal reality rather than as a product of discourse (often through interviews about the bodily experience of things such as pre-menstrual syndrome (PMS) or anorexia). However, even with this explicit aim in mind, discourse is repeatedly described as a realm in which bodily experience is produced. Despite the claim to validate both the discursive and materiality, the emphasis seems to be upon how experience is shaped through available discourses. For example, Swann, writing on PMS, argues that 'Discourses of femininity and biology frame women's experience' (Swann 1997: 192), and Malson, in the same volume, sees discourses as involving both language and social practices, both of which produce our bodily experience.

This move to bring back the material and embodied world from the margins and to give it equal status with textuality is important. However, we are still left with embodied experience as the outcome of discourse and social practices. Malson (1997) boldly suggests that the physical properties of bodies impose limitations upon and provide possibilities for what can be discursively 'made' of them. But the view that 'Just as discourses constitute and regulate the body, so they also lean on the physical body to support their "truths"' (Malson 1997: 231) may be seen by some social constructionists as foundationalist. Grosz (1994: 156), however, also supports this view: 'I am suggesting that, in feminist terms at least, it is problematic to see the body as a blank, passive page, a neutral "medium" or signifier for the inscription of a text . . . one and the same message, inscribed on a female or male body, does not always or even usually mean the same thing or result in the same text.' Again, while this is an important move towards recognizing that discourses are not entirely autonomous, the body's power to carry meaning is once more confined to the discursive realm. Bodies may exert a strong 'pull' on the meanings they can carry, but these meanings exist only in the discursive realm. The body thus remains subjugated to discourse and can only gain meaning through it.

The meaningful body

According to Radley (1995: 5), social theory's approach to the body has been limited to 'explaining the control of its functions on the one hand, or its appearances on the other, as if these constituted it entirely.' He evocatively claims that 'physical existence is brought, bound and gagged, on to the centre stage of social theory in order to indicate the primary role of discourse' (Radley 1995: 6) and that 'Such a position renders the body so docile, so pliable as to be nothing more than a passive mirror in which to catch the reflections of social action' (Radley 1995: 7). He claims that the body is an important expressive medium and that the 'lived body' has been marginalized by social constructionism. The use of the term 'expressive' here should not be taken to mean that there is some internal cognitive or emotional state which we attempt to externalize through the use of our bodies, a position that is not compatible with social constructionism. This would be a slide back into a traditional essentialism which sees cognitions and emotions as originating within the individual before being 'communicated' to others. Rather, it refers to the body's power to display or illustrate ways of being, to conjure them up rather than to represent them.

Drawing upon the phenomenology of Merleau-Ponty, Radley goes on to argue for a recognition of the body's expressive power – that is, its capacity to mean, to configure alternative ways of being – and for a conception of the body which focuses upon lived experience and embodiment. Such a conception places at least some of human meaning-making outside of language and discourse. It also brings with it interesting questions about the workings of power and its resistance. A key concept in Radley's argument is the 'dumb insolence' of the body's expressiveness, which 'incenses because it cannot be directly countered, because it is not of the same order as the power that it subverts' (Radley 1995: 18–19). The implication here is that power which operates discursively may be resisted through the expressive capacities of the body. The meanings expressed by the 'mute' or 'dumb' body cannot be countered from within discourse. It is precisely because the body does not 'speak the same language' as discursive power that it is able to resist it.

The extra-discursive nature of bodily expressiveness is well illustrated in the case of dance. Bateson (1987; cited in Radley 1995: 13) quotes the dancer Isadora Duncan, who, on being asked what her dance meant, replied 'If I could tell you what it meant, there would be no point in dancing it.' That there exist parts of our experience as human beings of which we find it difficult, if not impossible, literally to 'speak' is by no means a new idea. Freud invented the unconscious precisely for this reason, and Kelly (1955), in his theory of personal constructs, talks of the existence of 'pre-verbal constructs', which profoundly affect our view of ourselves and our world but which are very difficult to access through the verbal and written methods of repertory grids and self-characterization sketches. However, my argument, following Radley, is that much of what we 'know but cannot tell' is unavailable to us in language simply because it originates, exists and therefore is only or primarily accessible in the realm of the extra-discursive, in the lived world of embodiment. For example, when we reflect upon the experience of sexual excitement, we recognize immediately and 'know' with certainty what we find exciting and arousing. That is to say, our bodies do this recognizing and knowing, for we are frequently struck dumb in our attempts to capture this knowledge in language and thus to explain the experience to anyone else (or even to ourselves). I do not mean that we are unable to tell someone what we find pleasurable. But pleasure lies in the meaning that gestures, actions and caresses carry for us, and it is in our attempts to articulate these meanings that we are often confounded. A kiss is like an improvised *pas de deux*, in which bodies take their cues from each other and weave an exciting conversation, a sequence of question and answer, in which both partners recognize and 'know' exactly the meaning of each invitation and response. But although our bodies may readily 'talk to' each other and exchange these meanings with relative ease, our attempts to 'translate' these meanings into language often leave us literally lost for words.

Embodied 'knowing' is a feature of other art forms too. Davidson and Scripp (1992) place importance on kinaesthetic activity in the development of musical performance. Using the concept of 'knowledge-in-performance', they argue that 'musical understanding is embedded in the action itself' (Davidson and Scripp 1992: 396). The psychology of music has been dominated by a cognitive approach, which has seen the listener as a processor of information. However, recent research has investigated the role of the body in the production of music. Davidson (1993) demonstrated that when musicians were instructed to deliver a performance in either a 'deadpan' or an 'expressive' way, differences in the expressiveness of their performance were most readily noticed by an audience when the performer was seen rather than just heard. That the meaning of such expressivity lies outside of language is suggested by McNeil (1996, 1997), who interviewed music teachers about the characteristics of a good musical performance. The teachers often made use of the term 'musicality', and McNeil reports that although they felt that they 'knew' what this meant they were often unable to explain this meaning in language.

Current psychologies, including social constructionism, do not help us to understand such things. If the body does indeed play a central role in creating meaning, then we need a theory that can accommodate this and that will enable social constructionists to conceptualize the relationship of the body to discourse in a new way. In the remainder of this chapter, I shall further explore the possibilities of the phenomenology of Merleau-Ponty for achieving this aim.

A phenomenological account of embodiment

Without doubt, Merleau-Ponty regarded the body, or rather embodiment, as the origin of experience. The phrase 'being-in-the-world' (a term borrowed from Heidegger) is used to indicate how he thought of the relationship between embodied persons and the world they inhabit. But in fact to talk of a 'relationship' in this way is precisely what Merleau-Ponty was rejecting. Persons and the world they inhabit are not separable entities that interact with each other. Our relation to what we call the 'outside' world is misconceived, and he was critical of the positivist/empiricist notion that people (subjects) come to know a world external to them (objects) by mentalistic and disembodied perceptual processes. Merleau-Ponty draws our attention to the way in which we apprehend our world always and inevitably through our bodies. Our bodies are our only means of knowing the world; our experience is given to us through our bodies. We inhabit the material world, we live *in* it and are not observers *of* it. The haptic sense (the sense of touch), relatively ignored by psychologists, who have instead primarily studied the senses of vision and audition, assumes a greater importance in this framework as it provides the raw data of our experience of the physical resistances and affordances of our material environment. Our physical relation to objects, our use of them, our movement around them all become part of the 'corporeal schema' or body image: 'The body therefore extends out beyond the boundaries of its own skin to incorporate the experienced, lived world: but because it [the body] moves itself and sees, it holds things in a circle around itself; they are encrusted into its flesh, they are part of its full definition; the world is made of the same stuff as the body' (Merleau-Ponty 1964: 163). Merleau-Ponty thus dissolves the subject/object dichotomy and so discredits the question of how we can acquire mental representations of the world. Because we are embodied, we simply have direct access to the world. The properties and qualities of the material world are co-terminous with our embodied experience.

Experience is therefore given primarily through the body and not through language. Merleau-Ponty wrote extensively about the perceptual means through which we apprehend the world, and focused in particular upon vision. However, he was keen to stress two things. First, vision, like all our perceptual processes, is an embodied activity rather than one of mentalistic representation; second, the perceptual processes cannot meaningfully be separated from each other. Our senses of vision, hearing, touch, smell and kinesis operate as one system in our lived experience, and our experience is therefore given to us through all our senses simultaneously. There is therefore a certain interchangeability between the senses, such that visual experience may come to us 'textured' by sounds, odours and movement, and 'The eye lives in this texture as a man lives in his house' (Merleau-Ponty 1964: 160). Vision, thus conceived, is much more than the translation of patterns of light into mental images, as described in psychology textbooks. It is the process which thrusts the body beyond the confines of its skin into the lived world. This is how the world we perceive has depth, volume, solidity and movement.

Art and the lived world

Merleau-Ponty's intense interest in vision led him to a study of how artists were able to use their skills in order to render this 'lived world' visually available to us in their paintings. He wrote: 'It is by lending his body to the world that the artist changes the world into paintings' (Merleau-Ponty 1964: 162) and:

'Nature is on the inside', says Cezanne. Quality, light, colour, depth, which are there before us, are there only because they awaken an echo in our body and because the body welcomes them. Things have an internal equivalent in me; they arouse in me a carnal formula of their presence. Why shouldn't these [correspondences] in their turn give rise to some [external] visible shape in which anyone else would recognise these motifs which support his own inspection of the world?

(Merleau-Ponty 1964: 164)

The painter is therefore able to recreate the lived word for us, to deliver it back to us for our inspection. Writing specifically on Merleau-Ponty's analysis of painting, Madison (1981: 73–4) states: 'What therefore a reflection on painting can teach us is the very relation which we entertain with the world ... painting illustrates nothing other than our bodily insertion in being. What is proper to painting is that it renders visible, in a work accessible to everyone, the world which we inhabit.'

Merleau-Ponty further argues that painting, like vision, does not strive to represent the world in images that have a one-to-one correspondence with their 'real' counterparts. In a telling example, he contrasts the world as it is rendered to us in painting with that rendered through photography:

> When a horse is photographed at that instant when he is completely off the ground, with his legs almost folded under him – an instant, therefore, when he must be moving – why does he look as though he were leaping in place? Then why do Gericault's horses really *run* on canvas, in a posture impossible for a real horse at the gallop? ... Rodin said very wisely 'It is the artist who is truthful, while the photograph is mendacious; for, in reality, time never stops cold.' The photograph keeps open the instants which the onrush of time closes up forthwith; it destroys the overtaking, the overlapping, the 'metamorphosis' [Rodin] of time. But this is what painting, in contrast, makes visible, because the horses have in them that 'leaving here, going there,' because they have a foot in each instant.
>
> (Merleau-Ponty 1964: 185–6)

Thus, painting does not deal in images, but in the experience of the lived world. Through painting (and, we may suppose, through other visual arts) experience which is extra-discursive can be articulated and presented back to us, its meaning appreciated and recognized by us through the same embodied perceptual processes through which the artist accesses them: 'The language of painting is a language which says without saying' (Madison 1981: 106). If the realm of embodiment, of the extra-discursive, is indeed relatively inaccessible to discourse, then we should not be surprised at the difficulty we experience in trying to articulate such things.

Embodiment and power

Writing from a postmodern perspective, Boyne (1991) makes some observations remarkably similar to those of Merleau-Ponty when discussing the work of painter Francis Bacon. Merleau-Ponty was careful to point out that even though all painting potentially captures some aspect of the lived world, no single painting ever captures its 'truth'. The 'plurality of interpretation' that Boyne (1991) sees as characteristic of postmodernity is fundamental to the phenomenological approach. Boyne further helps us to make the link between the phenomenology of Merleau-Ponty and postmodern, constructionist thinking by emphasizing that 'the postmodern sensibility involves a shift of emphasis from epistemology to ontology, if it is understood as a *deprivileging* shift from knowledge to experience, from theory to practice, from mind to body' (Boyne 1991: 281).

Boyne does not give a theoretical explanation of our embodied response to works of art, as Merleau-Ponty does, appearing to view its existence as self-evident. Interestingly, he notes that such embodied responding has been addressed by psychoanalysis, but warns that 'the theorisation of the psychic and sensual aspects of art can effect a withdrawal, into discourse, from those aspects' (Boyne 1991: 284). He therefore cautions against using text or narrative to accompany works of art, as this may interfere with the immediate bodily experience by intellectualizing it and turning it into a representation, something that must stand for something else and therefore cannot be experienced in its own right. The power of discourse to represent (literally to re-present) experience to us is important here. Using the example of madness, Boyne, drawing on Foucault, argues that the discourses of science and reason have systematically functioned to deny and invalidate the experience of madness. But, in earlier times, the paintings of Hieronymus Bosch were able to 'summon' madness without denying it, and he argues that today, in a society saturated with representation, it is even more important that we preserve our capacity to 'display' experience, and in particular experience that prevailing discourse would wish to exclude or deny.

Although Merleau-Ponty wrote extensively about painting, there seems no reason why the same analysis should not be extended to other art forms, such as dance and music, or to multimedia performances. Through the combined use of movement, music, set, lighting and costume, dance becomes a multimedia site of artistic expression where the divisions between movement, painting and music become blurred. The 'crossover' between art, dance and music is demonstrated by the dance troupe the Featherstonehoughs (pronounced Fanshaws), who gave performances in Britain based upon and powerfully evoking the drawings of Egon Schiele. Here, the audience is put in contact with Schiele's contorted images through a medium where drawings come to life and movement becomes pictorial as art and dance dissolve into each other.

For the social constructionist, one reason for recognizing the 'extra-discursive' and its expressive power is in the possibilities for resistance that lie in Radley's (1995) 'dumb insolence'. The body 'eludes discourse, not because of its physicality per se, but because it signifies in ways that discourse cannot adequately embrace' (Radley 1995: 12). Extra-discursive modes of expression therefore offer opportunities for 'speaking' of experience and social conditions, for depicting a world which cannot be invalidated through discourse. Radley is critical of the move to encourage those whose voices are marginalized to 'speak for themselves' through written and spoken texts:

> However, the serious charge against the move towards narrative as the privileged medium of enlightenment is that it attempts to render experience legitimate only when it is spoken. This cuts away the content of experience from the form (the body-subject) in which its meaning originated, and to which it must continue to be referred if others are to understand what it means to be sick or oppressed.
>
> (Radley 1995: 19)

Powerful institutions such as the state and the church at times condemn and outlaw forms of art, dance and music because of their perceived subversive power. A famous example is that of Girolamo Savonarola, a Dominican monk who, five hunded years ago, was responsible for the destruction of many works of art thought to be subversive. From the perspective of our current Cartesian investment in reason, thought and language, such concerns seem trivial. But in the light of the arguments put forward above they appear more justified. The 'dangerousness' of artistic forms, furthermore, lies not only in their power to evade discourse but also in their accessibility. While academic texts (such as this one) reach a limited audience (an audience which, it may convincingly be argued, is unlikely to be composed of members of marginalized groups), art, dance and music allow for a much wider dissemination of their messages. If we take a Foucauldian view of power as 'local', as 'micro-practices of power that . . . constitute a shared background of habits and dispositions that are rarely questioned' (Sawicki 1991: 98–9), then we can begin to understand the possibilities for resistance offered by forms of art.

Conclusion: implications for social constructionism

The capacity of the body to create and express meaning has largely been ignored by social constructionism. This has meant not only that important aspects of personal experience have been marginalized but also that opportunities for developing ways of resisting discursive power through the 'extra-discursive' have not been explored. The phenomenology of Merleau-Ponty offers a theoretical framework for understanding extra-discursive phenomena, and one that is compatible with the major tenets of social constructionism. Both of these theoretical approaches aim to deconstruct some fundamental dichotomies of Western philosophical thought, such as subject/object and self/other. Both reject a cognitivism which turns our experience of the world into mental representations, and both reject positivism, being rooted in a pluralism which acknowledges the impossibility of arriving at one 'true' account of the world. Furthermore, phenomenology allows a way of recognizing and legitimating personal experience without relegating its status to that of an effect of discourse.

In arguing that we take the body seriously as a site of meaning-making, I am not suggesting that language and discourse may be less important than social constructionists had supposed. Merleau-Ponty appeared to view the relationship between embodied experience and language as a dialectical process in which each depended on the other for its form of expression. Such formulations are promising, but are hard to grasp and spell out since they do not conform to the reductionist and causal accounts with which we have become so familiar in social science. The power of discourse to create 'knowledge' and to silence the voices of those who are in some way 'different' has been well documented in social constructionism. It is time for the body to have its say.

References

Armistead, N. (1974) *Reconstructing Social Psychology*. Harmondsworth: Penguin.

Barthes, R. (1972) *Mythologies*. New York: Hill and Wang.

Bateson, G. (1987) *Steps to an Ecology of Mind*. Northvale, NJ: Jason Aronson.

Benthall, J. and Polhemus, T. (eds) (1975) *The Body as a Medium of Expression*. London: Allen Lane.

Boyne, R. (1991) The art of the body in the discourse of postmodernity, in M. Featherstone, M. Hepworth and B. S. Turner (eds) *The Body: Social Process and Cultural Theory*. London: Sage.

Brown, P. (1973) *Radical Psychology*. London: Tavistock.

Burr, V. (1998) Realism, relativism, social constructionism and discourse, in I. Parker (ed.) *Social Constructionism, Discourse and Realism*. London: Sage.

Butt, T. W., Burr, V. and Epting, F. (1997) Core construing: self-discovery or self-invention?, in R. A. Neimeyer and G. Neimeyer (eds) *Advances in Personal Construct Psychology, Volume 4*. New York: Springer.

Davidson, J. (1993) Visual perception of performance manner in the movements of solo musicians, *Journal of Music and Music Education*, 21(2): 103–13.

Davidson, L. and Scripp, L. (1992) Surveying the coordinates of cognitive skills in music, in R. Colwell (ed.) *Handbook of Research on Music Teaching and Learning*. New York: Schirmer Books.

Easthope, A. (1986) *What a Man's Gotta Do*. London: Paladin.

Featherstone, M. (1991) The body in consumer culture, in M. Featherstone, M. Hepworth and B. S. Turner (eds) *The Body: Social Process and Cultural Theory*. London: Sage.

Foucault, M. (1976) *The History of Sexuality, Volume 1*. Harmondsworth: Penguin.

Foucault, M. (1977) *Discipline and Punish: The Birth of the Prison*. London: Allen Lane.

Fox, D. R. and Prilleltensky, I. (eds) (1997) *Critical Psychology: An Introduction*. London: Sage.

Gavey, N. (1997) Feminist poststructuralism and discourse analysis, in M. M. Gergen and S. N. Davis (eds) *Toward a New Psychology of Gender: A Reader*. London: Routledge.

Goffman, E. (1976) *Gender Advertisements*. New York and London: Harper and Row.

Grosz, E. (1994) *Volatile Bodies: Toward a Corporeal Feminism*. Bloomington and Indianapolis: Indiana University Press.

Harré, R. and Secord, P. F. (1972) *The Explanation of Social Behaviour*. Oxford: Basil Blackwell.

Hollway, W. (1995) A second bite at the heterosexual cherry, *Feminism and Psychology*, 5(1): 126–30.

Kelly, G. (1955) *The Psychology of Personal Constructs*. New York and London: W. W. Norton and Co.

McNeil, A. (1996) Conference review. Paper presented at the Fourth International Conference on Music Perception and Cognition, McGill University, Montreal, Canada.

McNeil, A. (1997) How to assess aural ability within the performing musician: proposals. Paper presented to the Third Triennial Conference of the European Society for the Cognitive Sciences of Music, Uppsala, Sweden.

Madison, G. B. (1981) *The Phenomenology of Merleau-Ponty*. Athens: Ohio University Press.

Malson, H. M. (1997) Anorexic bodies and the discursive production of feminine excess, in J. M. Ussher (ed.) *Body Talk: The Material and Discursive Regulation of Sexuality, Madness and Reproduction*. London: Routledge.

Merleau-Ponty, M. (1964) Eye and mind, in J. Edie (ed.) *The Primacy of Perception*. Evanston, IL: Northwestern University Press.

Radley, A. (1995) The elusory body and social constructionist theory, *Body and Society*, 1(2): 3–23.

Sawicki, J. (1991) *Disciplining Foucault: Feminism, Power and the Body*. London: Routledge.

Swann, C. (1997) Reading the bleeding body: discourses of premenstrual syndrome, in J. M. Ussher (ed.) *Body Talk: The Material and Discursive Regulation of Sexuality, Madness and Reproduction*. London: Routledge.

Ussher, J. M. (ed.) (1997) *Body Talk: The Material and Discursive Regulation of Sexuality, Madness and Reproduction*. London: Routledge.

9 Realism, constructionism and phenomenology

TREVOR BUTT

Introduction

Whether we adopt a realist or a constructionist approach in social psychology has many implications for how we understand psychological issues that arise in everyday life. In this chapter, I focus on emotional experience and emotional talk as an example. In recent times we have often been encouraged to 'get in touch with our feelings'. How should we understand this advice?

If some people were to have fallen asleep fifty years ago, and woken up in the Britain or America of today, what changes would they notice? Of course, they would be amazed at the technological advances around them, but I suspect they would be almost equally surprised at the proliferation of 'feeling talk' as well. The way that Gulf War pilots disclosed their anxiety after sorties, the outpouring of grief at Princess Diana's death, the elaboration of the effects of stress and abuse might all seem astonishing – even embarrassing – to the time traveller from the 1940s. They might find the proliferation of sexual stories (Plummer 1995) particularly perplexing – stories of recovery and desire in the media and popular press. Up to fifteen million Americans participate in half a million self-help and recovery groups, at the forefront of which are recoverers from sexual suffering (Plummer 1995). In Britain, the recovery industry may be less well developed, but the psychology section of any bookshop will have several shelves devoted to self-help, counselling and recovery.

It looks as though people experience themselves differently now from how they did in the recent past. They appear to be reflecting more on their emotions. Is this because they have at last recognized hitherto buried feelings that were once denied and repressed, or is it that we have collectively conjured up an extended vocabulary of emotion which we mistakenly believe refers to inner states that we are encouraged to 'get in touch with'? Are these experiences found or made, discovered or invented? And is this reflection on ourselves a useful exercise? Orthodox psychology has traditionally adopted a realist position, positing a real world of events in some way 'inside' individuals, whether they are cognitive structures, ego states, selves or emotions, which it is the job of psychology to describe and explain. The expanding counselling profession has promoted this realist philosophy, which has now become accepted as common sense.

However, in the past decade, we have seen the advent of a movement which is described by the umbrella term of social constructionism (Burr 1995). This takes the opposite view, that individual experience is largely determined and regulated by the social world, particularly through the medium of language. Different forms of social constructionism vary in their formulation of personal agency. However, they all see agency as overestimated in psychology, and often prefer to talk of the 'subject' rather than the 'person' to code this. Personal experience is downplayed. Subjects may be mistaken in thinking that talking about their feelings is helpful; indeed, the proliferation of discourse about emotion may serve to elaborate and amplify feeling. Foucault's (1981) contention was that individuals have been increasingly encouraged in the confessional of psychotherapy to enlarge on the peculiarities of their experience (particularly of a sexual nature). This has had the effect not of freeing them, but of binding them more tightly to the normative order as this discursive practice creates rather than discovers pathology.

In this chapter, I argue that both these approaches misrepresent emotional experience. I see the constructionist position as an important advance on that of realism, in that it focuses on what is going on between people rather than within them. However, in my view it fails to do justice to our experience of emotion. It seems to imply that experience is thoroughly malleable: we could experience things totally differently in a different linguistic community. Although language shapes our experience, it is also shaped by it. Each of us is born into a linguistic community that predates us, but language has evolved from speech, which is a form of expression. I will address this realism/constructionism debate from the perspective of existential phenomenology, which has been largely ignored by contemporary psychologists. I will begin by summarizing what we may call a realist view of emotional experience, before describing the constructionist critique of it. I will then argue that this critique focuses too much on language; that emotions dissolve in discursive practices. Finally, I will develop an existential-phenomenological view, which recognizes the power of the constructionist critique while preserving the intentionality of the lived experience of emotions.

Realism and emotions

The current debate in orthodox psychology centres on whether emotions are 'hardwired' adaptations to the environment or post-cognitive internal states which follow from the individual's appraisal of a particular situation.

At one end of the spectrum, Zajonc (1984) argues that empirical evidence demonstrates that the existence of emotions predates cognition. Non-human animals and babies both show emotions that are intelligible in terms of environmental conditions. Brain stimulation and ablation studies show the 'hardwired' primitive biological basis of emotion. Evolution 'programmes in' a series of primary emotions which help the species to deal with events. Consciousness of emotional reaction is an epiphenomenon. The alternative view, that emotion depends on cognitive appraisal, is advocated by Lazarus (1984). In the same cognitive tradition, cognitive-behaviour therapists like Beck (1976) and Ellis (1962) see emotional reactions as following what we say to ourselves about the world. We do not have hidden emotions that we need to get in touch with; instead, emotions are synthesized by rational or irrational cognitive processes.

Safran and Greenberg (1988) argue that there is a truth in both positions. There are a limited number of primary emotions (such as fear and anger) that are 'hardwired' responses to the environment. Insults naturally produce anger, as danger does fear. There are also post-cognitive self-appraisal emotions. The problem for the clinician is how to tell one from the other (and there are also emotions that are strategically used, either to defend us from worse emotions or to manipulate other people).

All these approaches have in common the view that emotions do indeed exist; they inhabit the person, frequently causing 'maladaptive' behaviour as well as the experience of distress (itself an emotion?). As Sarbin (1986) points out, both Zajonc and Lazarus are trying to answer the question 'What *is* emotion?' The research programme within this realist framework is to identify separate primary emotions. Tomkins (cited in Kaufman 1993) identifies nine, while Plutchik (cited in Harré 1986) offers eight. The spirit of this project is nicely captured in the following text on counselling:

> All affects must be distinguished ... and labelled separately ... The widespread lack of precision in our scientific language has seriously

hindered both theoretical and therapeutic progress in psychology. To borrow an analogy from a sister science, if an electron were interchangeably called a neutron or a positron by physicists adhering to different schools of thought, imagine the confusion that would result.

(Kaufman 1993: 161)

Perhaps this approach is more like mental chemistry than physics. The psychologist's job is to carry out a qualitative analysis of a complex chemical compound in order to identify the constituting elements. Presumably by watching and listening to the client, the psychologist will be able to identify the constituent parts of a particular emotion. The role of language is as a transparent medium, to describe ever more accurately these internal states.

Kaufman (1993: 4–5) believes that the primary emotion of shame is responsible for many of the new syndromes that seem to plague contemporary life. Shame is seen as crucial in the formation of identity and a sense of self, and it lies at the root of addictive, eating, sexual, compulsive, narcissistic and borderline disorders. His contention is that shame produces such painful experience that sufferers develop a range of strategies, or defending scripts, to deal with it. Shame is caused in infants by a sense of abandonment; the rupturing of the bond with the parent. The discipline invoked by some parents can depend heavily on shaming and humiliation. This is particularly true when the child is subject to physical abuse. Sexual abuse also produces feelings of exposure, powerlessness and humiliation. Memories of abuse may be 'seared into the victim's imagination'. Alternatively, they may be 'Banished from awareness, fully disowned' (1993: 124).

This realist view of knowledge was called 'accumulative fragmentalism' by George Kelly (1955). In this positivist framework, the disinterested researcher gathers together a series of 'facts', and proceeds to piece them together to find the pattern they will reveal. But of course the scientist is never disinterested, never able to adopt a god-like perspective outside his or her existence in the culture in which he or she happens to be thrown. This applies perhaps most of all to the psychologist, whose subject matter is humankind. As times and perspectives change, so too does what is obvious, and what constitutes a fact. One only has to consult psychologists' advice on how to raise children fifty years ago to recognize this. The world affords many viable interpretations, and the realist culture that leads psychologists to claim 'we now know that . . .' has been challenged most successfully by the social constructionists.

Social construction and emotions

Constructionists have questioned what we previously took to be natural, seeing it instead as the product of societal and cultural factors. They attempt to stand back and call into question that which we take for granted. They have drawn to our attention the social context of psychological knowledge, and questioned its truths and taken-for-granted assumptions. The climate within which psychology has grown, they claim, is one of 'possessive individualism' (Shotter 1989; Sampson 1993). This arises in Western democracies, where universal franchise has replaced rights based on property-owning as the criterion for participating in public life.

'Possessive individualism first tells us that in order to vote one must be free; and second, in order to be free – that is, independent from another's will – one must be the owner of oneself' (Sampson 1993: 33). For Shotter (1989), we are the prisoners of this text of possessive individualism; we are born into it, and cannot see beyond it. This accounts for the common-sense nature of individualism for us. It then seems obvious that individuals 'have' emotions, and that psychologists need to develop ways of looking inside them to describe, explain and clarify what they are experiencing.

Instead of joining the 'rush under the skull' to find explanations of action within individuals, social constructionism has focused on the interpersonal domain, what goes on between people, in its search for the understanding of human experience. Harré (1989), Gergen (1992), Sampson (1993) and Shotter (1993) all stress interaction and conversational realities that precede the individual, and from which the individual is forged. So we cannot understand emotional talk without reference to the social context within which the individual is situated. Safran and Greenberg's (1988) listing of anger as a primary emotion, the natural response to an insult or injury, may provide the clinician with a useful heuristic device, but it surely will not stand up theoretically. What counts as an insult or injury in one society does not in another. Perhaps 'road rage' is best understood in terms not of individual experience, but of the extended vocabulary of rights which individuals may construe as being violated.

Harré (1986) notes that psychology takes for granted the existence of emotions within individuals, which are the proper objects of study. From angry people, grieving rituals and shameful episodes, psychologists abstracted anger, grief and shame. In our climate of possessive individualism, there is a drift from the social to the personal, where the properties of social contexts and practices become the property of individuals. So 'cosiness' once referred to huddling in a warm shelter; it now refers to a feeling. 'Shaming' once referred to a social process where someone was exposed as having morally transgressed. Now it denotes a feeling of embarrassed self-consciousness.

Emotions, as Harré writes, are intentional – they centre on the person's relationship with the world, and are always about something. An emotional display is a powerful judgement (Harré 1995), an avowal (Warner 1986), and decidedly not a reflection of some inner state. Constructionists have convincingly argued that we cannot consider language to be a transparent medium through which we can perceive an emotional reality (Harré 1986). Following Wittgenstein (1972), they have pointed out that description is only one of many 'language games', and that emotional talk cannot constitute the description of inner states. The reification of internal states has certainly bedevilled psychology, which has looked inside people for traits, intelligence, cognitions and feelings that do not exist in the way that brains do.

Emotions and the 'discursive turn'

The social constructionist critique provides a long-overdue correction to an individualistic and positivistic psychology which looked inside us to find motives and emotions. It enables us to stand back from the common-sense position and to question our taken-for-granted assumptions about inner states. However, it has concentrated mainly on one aspect of interpersonal life: language. In their review of the trends in post-positive psychology, Smith *et al.* (1995) recognize the existence of 'old voices' such as phenomenology and interactionism, as well as the appearance of 'new voices' – cultural psychology, social representations and feminism. But they reserve a special section describing 'the turn to discourse'. In this section, discursive psychology, dialogical psychology and narratology testify to the new psychology's rediscovery of language and its vital role in the construction of social reality.

Until a decade ago, the average psychologist's knowledge of language issues could be caricatured (not too unfairly!) as comprising a nodding acquaintance with the Skinner/Chomsky debate and a vague recollection that someone had commented that Eskimos had seven words for snow. There was no appreciation of the performative as well as the descriptive aspects of speech (Austin 1962), that we do things as well as describe things with our speech. Until Potter and Wetherell's work (1987), language was seen largely by psychologists as a transparent medium through which we could glimpse a real external and even an internal world. Social constructionism has pointed to the constitutive aspects of language, its role not just in shaping, but in constituting, thought. Discursive psychology focuses on what we are doing with emotional talk – on the performative aspect of language (Edwards 1997).

Discursive psychology sees people as 'active users of sign systems, and of course, the bodily equipment necessary to employ them' (Harré 1995: 146). Emotional displays are discursive acts, 'judgements on matters of morality, aesthetics and prudence, they must occupy their place in unfolding episodes, to be analysed something like conversations' (Harré and Gillett 1994: 153–4). The discursive psychologist is concerned with the rules governing the emotional vocabulary used in a particular culture.

Harré points out that emotional displays constitute complex judgements and statements. So embarrassment simultaneously shows an acknowledgement that one has been inept, a recognition of the local moral order and an apology (Harré 1995: 154). Emotional displays also embody a powerful judgement that has more force than language could employ. Harré does not ignore embodiment; indeed, discursive psychology is an attempt to get beyond Cartesian mind/body dualism. Yet this body seems to be that of physiology and chemistry; it belongs in the physical world and obeys causal laws. Discursive psychology, on the other hand, is 'located in arrays of people, and is concerned with speech acts and rule-following' (Harré and Gillett 1994: 29). The task of (discursive) psychology, Harré (1989: 34) tells us, 'is to lay bare our system of norms and representations and to compare and contrast the enormous variety of systems; the rest is physiology.' In other words, discursive psychology's terrain is largely the same as that of sociology. The person is divided up between the physical and socio-linguistic realms.

Instead of overcoming the Cartesian dualism that it sets out to confront, social constructionism appears to give up the body to the dictates of mechanism, so that it can concentrate on the rule-governed world of texts and ideas. The text shapes, even constitutes, the person, fashioning it out of the material of the body. Rorty (1982) asserts that twentieth-century textualism is the heir of nineteenth-century idealism. Both take their starting point as opposition to natural science, and both insist that reality is always mediated, through either ideas or language. The textualist sees everything as language-relative, the product of our use of a particular vocabulary and language game.

Constructionists have had little to say about the proliferation of 'feeling talk' in contemporary society. Certainly it cannot be taken as being caused by underlying internal states like shame, and is more likely to be accounted for in terms of societal conditions which facilitate the telling of such stories (Plummer 1995). Even so, Plummer notes that recovery tales do invariably follow a similar structure. They tell of movement from a secret shameful world to a more public one. The recovery is from shame into a world of acceptance. Sociological accounts like Plummer's focus mainly on the societal conditions that encourage the making of the private public. But he acknowledges a development from private pain to public discourse; the discursive realm does not generate private experience, but gives voice to it. Personal experience is for him the primary datum, out of which individuals forge themselves through stories of identity. It is ironical that Plummer's sociological account gives more weight to personal experience than does social constructionism. For the social constructionist, the person is little more than a rule-follower, using emotions in the same way as language.

So what is the status of emotions in realism and constructionism? At the realist end of the spectrum, emotions are to be found inside the person.

People are talking more about their feelings nowadays because they have a vocabulary to hand that enables them to describe what they is going on inside them. They are in a better position to tell us what hurts them and what they want, and to be more honest with themselves. For the social constructionist, there is no prelinguistic experience to describe, to get 'in touch' with. All individuals are born into a world of language which pre-dates them, and they acquire discursive skills which come to seem natural to them. In the same way, they absorb rules about emotional display and experience. Their emotional talk therefore speaks not of their experience, but of the discourses that surround them.

Merleau-Ponty's phenomenology

The realism/constructionism debate that now exercises social psychologists was essentially Merleau-Ponty's prime target in *Phenomenology of Perception* (1962). Merleau-Ponty's contention was that both realism and idealism are based on 'objective thought', which separates the subject from the objective world, positing an objective world of discrete and definable objects in which causal relationships apply. Objective thought underpins work in both the natural and social sciences, and informs what we now-adays take to be 'common sense'. Realism overemphasizes humankind's passivity in the face of 'stimuli' that impinge on it in the form of sensations. Idealism overemphasizes humankind's interpretive and construction-ist power.

Merleau-Ponty attempted to show that neither empiricism nor intellec-tualism, the research programmes of realism and idealism respectively, can succeed in understanding human beings. He saw the psychology of his day as having been captured by realism. Here humankind is seen as part of an objective world, and scientific inquiry, a privileged form of knowledge, has the job of working out what makes us tick – of providing causal explana-tions of our behaviour and perception. This is what Merleau-Ponty terms 'empiricism'. He was clearly opposed to this 'scientific' approach to the person, believing that it cannot succeed in appreciating the life-worlds of people. 'Science manipulates things and gives up living in them' (Merleau-Ponty 1964: 159). Here we see a convergence with Harré's view. Empiri-cism has abstracted emotions from the lived world: it has attempted to define and distil them from the contexts in which they have meaning.

However, in his rejection of empiricism, Merleau-Ponty is keen to point out that his position is not idealism (and by implication, constructionism). Idealism sees the world as being constituted by the subject, a sort of dis-embodied entity that uses its cognitive powers to constitute the world. Phenomenology is not mentalistic, it does not posit an inner world that imposes itself on an outer world. I cannot decide to see an ambiguous figure in any way that I want to. Neither can I decide not to be angry or ashamed.

Merleau-Ponty takes perception as the reality which should be privileged in psychology. This is because our perception cannot be doubted; it is not open to dispute. I see a keyboard in front of me, and this is indisputable. Of course, I could be wrong about what exactly I see, and my perception might change. But that I perceive something is self-evident, and not evidenced by other data. My body synthesizes perceptions, and they are given to me – this process is pre-reflective. The emphasis on perception places psychology's focus *between* the person and the world rather than within either. This therefore avoids the errors of empiricism and intellectualism.

Perception, then, is not imposed, either by an external real world or by a construction of it. It is instead a questioning process, an inquiry into a world which exhibits a resistance to our constructions. We cannot be driven by the discourses that surround us any more than we can be driven by ideas. The world of events is presented to us in our perception in a way that is relevant to our projects. I know I feel shame, or anger, just as I know I have a headache. I might not be able or willing to articulate it, but it is not a matter of evidence convincing me.

In Merleau-Ponty's view, a study of perception can return us to the 'lived world' of experience, and phenomenology's aim is the description (and not the analysis or explanation) of this experience. The 'lived world' is his alternative construction to objective thought. What objective thought has overlooked is the extraordinary properties of the human body, and that it is inextricably part of external world. Merleau-Ponty's contention is that an appreciation of our corporeal subjectivity promotes the realization that our bodies are part of a world system: 'Our own body is in the world as the heart is in the organism: it keeps the visible spectacle constantly alive, it breathes life into it and sustains it inwardly, and with it forms a system' (Merleau-Ponty 1962: 203). Thus the lived world is always perceived from within this system. It is structured in terms of its relevance to our body, our body's hold on it. Consciousness is primarily a matter of 'I can' rather than 'I know', and the world that we perceive is one which responds to our interests and capabilities.

A reader consulting *Phenomenology of Perception* will find no specific reference to emotion throughout the book. This is because Merleau-Ponty does not see the person as having separate faculties of reason, emotion and action. There is no rationality behind emotion or behaviour as there is for the intellectualist. Our cognitions and thoughts are the *result* of reflection on our intention, and our intention, our relationship with the world and other body-subjects, is infused throughout with emotion. Anger, shame, anxiety, jealousy, love – all show a particular colour of a pre-reflective engagement with our interpersonal world. Whereas objective thought sees 'external' causal relationships in phenomena, it is 'internal' relationships that characterize the lived world (Hammond *et al.* 1991). When a person feels shame under the gaze of a critical other, it is not a question of a feeling leading to his or her facial expression, blushing and excuses. Neither does their behaviour cause the feeling. Shame *is* this multiple expression – this conduct is what it means to be shameful. It is a communication to others, intentional conduct.

Emotions and intersubjectivity

The aspect of our interaction that is inevitably infused with emotion is our interaction with others. Our interactions with others are always 'mooded' (Crossley 1996: 45). Our perceptions are always coloured by an emotional hue. When one person reacts to another, she does not normally infer the other's intention from his behaviour, and then act accordingly. There is no internal cognitive process, no judgement, no intellectual assessment. It is in the nature of embodied human subjects to read each other's intention directly.

Merleau-Ponty's evidence for this view comes from the observation of infants. He notes that when an adult playfully prepares to bite one of a baby's fingers, the baby spontaneously mimics a biting action with its mouth. It also naturally responds to a smiling face with a smile of its own. How can an infant who has not yet acquired a visual image of itself copy the actions of another? How does it translate the intentions and movements of another into actions it makes? Merleau-Ponty contends that the dualist argument by analogy – 'I feel this when I do such and such so he or she must as well' – in fact has to assume a common world, that it is attempting to explain. We take for granted the commonality that comes with embodiment. There is a primitive commonality between us, and not a primitive individuality. There could be no communication between people if they did not share the same horizons. We only feel shame under the gaze of other people because they are human like us. 'A dog's gaze directed towards me causes me no embarrassment' (Merleau-Ponty 1962: 361).

We appear to live in the experience of others, or at least in what we take to be their experience. Emotional display is central to this conversation of gestures, which predates our participation in discourse (Mead 1934). We show our intentionality to others in it. Of course, as we develop, we gain access to language and then thought, and with it the ability to pretend feeling, to hide it and to mislead others. We can reflect on our experience, and try to deny others access to it. To say that we have a primitive intersubjectivity is to say that we naturally display our intentional relation with the world, that this is something that may have to be hidden or controlled. When people are not concerned to monitor their expression, they show their feeling in this gestural form. If you catch a glimpse of people's faces when they watch television, it is not uncommon to see them mirroring emotion in the same way that infants mirror the intention of others.

Emotional display is a invaluable guide to intention – it is essentially there as a communication. Reflecting on our own emotional experience also tells us something about our own intention, the way we are connecting to the world. When it is said that people have an 'aura' about them, what is often meant is that they express something we cannot define, but none the less feel the weight of. In the company of one person, we may feel unaccountably elated, optimistic; in that of another, curiously tense, despite his or her apparent friendliness. People may be 'doing' something that they may not have reflected on, but they are doing it none the less.

If we are asked to describe how we feel, we can only draw on prevailing social constructions in the discursive field to do this. The phenomenologist would agree with the social constructionist that we cannot go inside ourselves and describe an inner feeling. Merleau-Ponty was insistent that there exists no 'inner world'. But our prereflective engagement with others is not a private affair, and may well not be captured adequately in any language that we have to hand. For one thing, the lived world is ambiguous, open to a range of alternative constructions. This ambiguity may be experienced simultaneously, when, say, our complicated engagement with a parent, child or partner cannot be separated into affection, irritation, protectiveness or resentment. The phenomenologist is not proposing the sort of mental chemistry that is advocated by the realist; it is not a matter of mixing primary emotions into a particular hue that is made up of a number of components. One emotion is not diluted or balanced by another. We can feel love and hate at the same time; can be excited by shame, thrilled by danger and curiously comforted by melancholy. It is of course impossible to say what we 'really feel' – the discursive turn can stand in the way of an understanding of the lived world.

Getting in touch with our feelings

From a phenomenological perspective, then, it does make sense to talk about 'getting in touch with one's feelings'. However, the feeling we get in touch with is not inside us, it is not a private well of emotions that we can draw on and describe. When we touch an object, the feeling is not inside us, nor is it 'in' the object; it is a component of the perception that occurs between us and the object. Similarly, emotions are between us and the world, a feeling that tells us something about our connection with it. They are vital clues about our intention that we might otherwise miss. Since our engagement with the world is prereflective, we are frequently not aware of the meaning of our conduct. This can be either because we do not have the words to spell it out, or because we would rather not recognize it. We may choose not to look at what we are doing, how we are hurting others, being vengeful, acting cruelly. This may be because this picture does not fit into our self-theory. For the social constructionists, the self may be merely a self-theory (Harré 1989), but for phenomenologists, it is a theory that the bearer takes seriously – it will be harder to acknowledge action that we see as inconsistent with it (Butt *et al.* 1997). Often, our engagement is obvious to others long before we care to recognize it. Indeed, the more absorbed we are in an emotional attitude, the more it is unrealized background, rather than figure, in our perception (Crossley 1996).

So our emotional engagement is not just made in language; it is a reality that is constructed between the person and his or her world. This engagement is often ambiguous, and our feelings are often ambivalent. They cannot be reduced to simple description of what we really want, or feel. There is no internal meter to be read, as the realist would have us believe. A counsellor, friend, TV programme or newspaper article might convince me that I have been abused, am a victim, have been shamed. Here we see a socially constructed aspect of emotion. An extended vocabulary of emotion, plus a local moral order that accentuates individual rights, enables a telling of abuse stories, as well as a community into which they are received. However, this construction of events has to be afforded by the events themselves – that is, by the person's prereflective experience – and constitutes one possible construction of events that is viable. Following Merleau-Ponty, Madison sums up the relationship between speech and pre-reflective experience: 'If what I say has a meaning, it is because it finds a confirmation in the unspoken experience which I am attempting to formulate. Truth is not a free invention, but the deliverance of "what wanted to be said" . . . Expression must be viewed as a *response* to a solicitation coming to it from below' (Madison 1981: 138).

Today's insight is not a truth that cancels previous constructions. Our histories afford a finite variety of constructions. Yet we cannot project any meaning at all on to events. Shotter (1992) argues that, paradoxically, we must accept that we both make *and* find our worlds. Social constructionism has provided a vital antithesis to the naive realism that has for so long dominated orthodox psychology. It offers a way of conceptualizing the person that escapes the intrapsychic empiricism of cognitive psychology. However, the 'discursive turn' threatens to leave us with no psychology at all. It can overemphasize the making at the expense of the finding. It does not seem to do justice to our personal experience. The elaboration of personal experience is a matter of both discovery and construction.

References

Austin, J. (1962) *How to Do Things with Words*. Oxford: Oxford University Press.
Beck, A. (1976) *Cognitive Therapy and the Emotional Disorders*. Harmondsworth: Penguin.

Burr, V. (1995) *Introduction to Social Constructionism*. London: Routledge.

Butt, T. W., Burr, V. and Epting, F. (1997) Core construing: discovery or invention? in R. A. Neimeyer and G. Neimeyer (eds) *Advances in Personal Construct Theory, Volume 4*. New York: Springer.

Crossley, N. (1996) *Intersubjectivity*. London: Sage.

Edwards, D. (1997) *Discourse and Cognition*. London: Sage.

Ellis, A. (1962) *Reason and Emotion in Psychotherapy*. New York: Lyle Stuart.

Foucault, M. (1981) *The History of Sexuality: Part 1*. Harmondsworth: Penguin

Gergen, K. (1992) Towards a postmodern psychology, in S. Kvale (ed.) *Psychology and Postmodernism*. London: Sage.

Hammond, M., Howarth, J. and Keat, R. (1991) *Understanding Phenomenology*. Oxford: Blackwell.

Harré, R. (1986) An outline of the social constructionist viewpoint, in R. Harré (ed.) *The Social Construction of Emotions*. Oxford: Blackwell.

Harré, R. (1989) Language games and the texts of identity, in J. Shotter and K. Gergen (eds) *Texts of Identity*. London: Sage.

Harré, R. (1995) Discursive psychology, in J. A. Smith, R. Harré and L. Van Langenhove (eds) *Rethinking Psychology*. London: Sage.

Harré, R. and Gillett, G. (1994) *The Discursive Mind*. London: Sage.

Kaufman, G. (1993) *The Psychology of Shame*. London: Routledge.

Kelly, G. (1955) *The Psychology of Personal Constructs*. New York: Norton.

Kvale, S. (1992) Postmodern psychology: a contradiction in terms? in S. Kvale (ed.) *Psychology and Postmodernism*. London: Sage.

Lazarus, R. (1984) On the primacy of cognition. *American Psychologist*, 39: 124–9.

Madison, G. (1981) *The Phenomenology of Merleau-Ponty*. Athens: Ohio University Press.

Matthews, E. (1996) *Twentieth Century French Philosophy*. Oxford: Oxford University Press.

Mead, G. (1934) *Mind, Self and Society*. Chicago: University of Chicago Press.

Merleau-Ponty, M. (1962) *Phenomenology of Perception*. London: Routledge.

Merleau-Ponty, M. (1964) The child's relations with others, in J. Edie (ed.) *The Primacy of Perception*. Evanston, IL: Northwestern University Press.

Plummer, K. (1995) *Telling Sexual Stories*. London: Routledge.

Potter, J. and Wetherell, M. (1987) *Discourse and Social Psychology*. London: Sage.

Rorty, R. (1982) *Consequences of Pragmatism*. New York and London: Harvester Wheatsheaf.

Safran, J. and Greenberg, L. (1988) Feeling, thinking and acting: a cognitive framework for psychotherapy integration, *Journal of Cognitive Psychotherapy*, 2(2): 109–31.

Sampson, E. (1989) The deconstruction of the self, in J. Shotter and K. Gergen (eds) *Texts of Identity*. London: Sage.

Sampson, E. (1993) *Celebrating the Other: A Dialogic Account of Human Nature*. New York: Harvester Wheatsheaf.

Sarbin, T. (1986) Emotion and act: roles and rhetoric, in R. Harré (ed.) *The Social Construction of Emotions*. Oxford: Blackwell.

Shotter, J. (1989) Social accountability and the social construction of 'you', in J. Shotter and K. Gergen (eds) *Texts of Identity*. London: Sage.

Shotter, J. (1992) Getting in touch, in S. Kvale (ed.) *Psychology and Postmodernism*. London: Sage.

Shotter, J. (1993) *Cultural Politics of Everyday Life*. Buckingham: Open University Press

Smith, J., Harré, R. and Van Langenhove, L. (1995) *Rethinking Psychology*. London: Sage.

Warner, C. T. (1986) Anger and similar delusions, in R. Harré (ed.) *The Social Construction of Emotions*. Oxford: Blackwell.

Wittgenstein, L. (1972) *Philosophical Investigations*. Oxford: Blackwell.

Zajonc, R. (1984) On the primacy of affect, *American Psychologist*, 39: 117–23.

10 Taking our selves seriously

JOHN CROMBY AND
PENNY STANDEN

In this chapter we argue that social constructionism needs explicitly to adopt some conception of the self if it is to continue developing in a theoretically coherent, progressive manner. By this, we do not just mean that a theory of the self should be endorsed or acknowledged as suitably constructionist and commended to those with an interest; we also mean that constructionism now needs a notion of self thoroughly integrated into its research and practice.

In our view, there are many reasons why this is necessary. First, to overcome the loss of ecological validity incurred by current, dominant trends in constructionism, which theorize and carry out research with no recourse to subjectivity or selfhood. Second, to ground analyses with reference to the material factors and personal–social histories that constrain the identities and subject positions which individuals might plausibly take up. Third, to enable us better to understand continuity as well as variability in people's experience, since structures of meaning and social practices are not the only sources of coherence and stability of identity; most aspects of embodiment, for example, typically change quite slowly (if at all). Fourth, to facilitate critical constructionist work, which must often refer to individual's subjective experiences, their awareness of their own oppression or exploitation and their desire for a better world. And fifth, because there are both costs and dangers for constructionism itself in proceeding without an integral notion of the self; we describe some of these costs and dangers later.

Of course, we are aware that some constructionists already address the self (e.g. Harré 1983; Hollway 1984; Sarbin 1986; Gergen 1991; Wetherell and Maybin 1996). Nevertheless, there remains an influential strand of constructionist work which proceeds with discursive analyses as though selves were simply a non-issue, arguing that what such an analysis does is 'break down the idea that there are certain classes of utterance whose interest is primarily in their relation to some putative reality, and other classes of ascriptive, confessional or revelatory utterances whose interest is in what they reveal about self, motivation or cognition' (Edwards and Potter 1992: 142). A focus on discourse does indeed break down the distinction between 'world-making and self-making' (ibid.), but this does not mean that personal–social history, subjectivity and embodiment can then be ignored, or dismissively reduced to transient, epiphenomenal effects of discourse. The need for social constructionism to address the extra-discursive has been discussed already (Cromby and Nightingale, this volume, Chapter 1). The self not only brings this need into sharp focus, it also reveals many of the problems and pitfalls that accompany any attempt to transcend the exclusively discursive.

Before proceeding further, we must briefly discuss our choice of terminology. We are aware that our use of the word 'self' may be considered suspect, steeped as it is in an influential history of humanistic psychology and liberal individualism. The term usually preferred by constructionists is 'subjectivity', but 'self' has been retained by some (e.g. Craig 1997) who are attempting to learn from postmodern critiques of the subject while nevertheless retaining some notion of the embodied person. We are aware that 'self' is not an ideal term, but it is at least one whose limitations and general meaning are widely known. We hope that its familiarity will facilitate the critical analysis with which we have associated it.

The chapter is structured as follows. First, we very briefly outline some critiques of mainstream psychology's typical conception of the self. Second, we look at some principal objections to notions of the self, and suggest how they might be addressed. Third, we describe some of the costs and dangers for constructionism of theorizing without any notion of the self. Finally, we indicate some possible directions for the development of future constructionist work in this area.

Critiques of mainstream psychology's self

We want to make it clear that when we say that social constructionism must adopt a notion of the self, we are definitely not recommending the resurrection of mainstream psychology's self, the notion of the person as a 'bounded, unique, more-or-less integrated motivational and cognitive universe, a dynamic centre of awareness, emotion, judgement and action, organized into a distinctive whole and set contrastively against other such wholes and against a social and natural background' (Geertz 1979: 229). The inaccuracy and inadequacy of this notion of the self, which Sampson (1983) calls 'self contained individualism', has been demonstrated on both empirical and conceptual grounds.

Empirical evidence comes from history, anthropology and cross-cultural psychology. Historical studies show that both selves and the societies that produce and maintain them have changed greatly over time. Some of these changes concern the relative weight attached to those core moments of mainstream psychology's self, the 'I' and the 'Me' (Logan 1987). Other historical changes concern the acceptable contents of the self, and point to marked variation in the kinds of self it is legitimate to be in different epochs (Burkitt 1991: 167–78). The specificity of the self with relation to historic-ally variable social and institutional practices was also a major focus of Foucault's later work (Foucault 1988). Anthropologists, similarly, are critical of Western psychology's ethnocentric bias (e.g. Shweder and Levine 1984). Studies in cross-cultural and folk psychology have also revealed significant differences, even between neighbouring countries, in both the content of the self and socially shared understandings of experiences such as emotion (e.g. Heelas and Lock 1981; Marsella *et al.* 1985; Harré 1986). Feminists and critical psychologists have provided conceptual arguments against mainstream psychology's conception of the self. Both have noted how accepted notions of self fit neatly with the demands of the social order (for example, how women's traditional roles as mothers and homemakers are neatly congruent with their supposed 'naturally' dominant characteristics: acceptance, caring, passivity and dependence), suggesting that the self typic-ally has an ideological component (e.g. Marcuse 1969; Held 1980; Henriques *et al.* 1984; Weisstein 1993).

In addition, recent social constructionist work has mounted both implicit and explicit challenges to psychology's notion of the self. Implicit challenges have come from attempts to show how processes and properties usually considered to be facets of individuals, and typically studied within cognitive or neuro-psychology, are in fact equally social in nature and origin and so amenable to a constructionist analysis. Substantive foci of this work include memory (Edwards and Middleton 1986; Middleton and Edwards 1990) and thought itself (Billig 1987). Explicit social constructionist chal-lenges to traditional notions of the self include both empirical studies which question the notion that individuals are the owners of relatively stable and distinct personalities (e.g. Edwards and Potter 1992), and a range of conceptual critiques which highlight both the conceptual shortcomings and ideological effects of self theory in psychology (e.g. Shotter and Gergen 1989).

These various studies and critiques strongly suggest that Western psychology's notion of the self as a unitary, rational, unique, self-contained individual is deeply flawed. We accept the general thrust of these critiques, if not all of their fine detail, and agree that the self as psychology typically conceives of it must be jettisoned. But at the same time, we are unhappy with the tendency within constructionism to theorize and research as though selves were a non-issue. While mainstream psychology's self is deeply flawed and must be rejected, it is our view that social constructionist psychology nevertheless requires some notion of the self as a process embodied within individuals. By this, we mean that constructionism needs to acknowledge that both personal–social history and embodiment are influences upon what we do and what we say. This might sound reasonable enough, but many objections to this proposal have been raised. We will now discuss some of them, and begin to suggest ways in which they might be refuted.

Objections to notions of the self

First, it is sometimes claimed that theories of the self must posit the *a priori* existence of an asocial individual, on to whom a social veneer is later grafted. Hence, such theories may pave the way for both Cartesian and self/society, agency/structure dualisms.

The objection that theories of the self give rise to Cartesian dualism seems to confuse arguments about the existence or possibility of human mental activity with arguments about its nature. It is the *embodied* character of thought ('I *think*, therefore I am') that produces the problem of Cartesian dualism, and whether there is also a trans-situational patterning of thought that we might describe as the activity of a 'self' is surely a separate issue. The argument that the thoughts of individuals may be patterned in characteristic ways that would lead us to recognize them as the product of a particular 'self' is entirely distinct from the contention that there is any such thing as thought in the first place. Note that we are not claiming here to have 'solved' the problem of Cartesian dualism, we are merely questioning whether it is a necessary consequence of theories of the self.

In any case, constructionism's failure to integrate a theory of the self has not rid psychology of Cartesian dualism. The individualistic, biologistic and essentialist selves promoted by other areas of psychology are still alive and well. Instead of addressing the phenomena which these versions of the self are made to account for, social constructionism erects an arbitrary boundary between itself and the rest of psychology based in part upon this issue; in this way the Cartesian dualism it aims to transcend is in fact kept alive, reproduced within the discipline at a macro level by the creation of a Stygian abyss between the social and the biological or organic components of psychology. Nor, it must be emphasized, has Cartesian dualism been removed from social constructionism. Questioning the status of talk about bodily factors and inner experience, by ignoring their embodied origins and reducing them to performative discourse, does not remove dualism. Dualism is concealed by this strategy, not addressed, and its proponents have little choice but to re-enact a (suitably ironic) parody of 1960s behaviourism whenever issues to do with the self threaten to become relevant.

The related objection, that by theorizing the self we bring into psychology the agency/structure dualism which has handicapped social theory for many years, is similarly misconceived. In our view, this objection actually presupposes the very problem it professes to identify. Far from being a rejection of mainstream psychology's self, it suggests instead a failure to transcend it adequately. There is evidence that both the contents and the processes of thought (which must be central to any conception of the self) are largely social in both origin and nature. Vygotsky (1978) provides examples which show how both the contents and the skills of thinking may be acquired in social interaction, and Harré (1987) suggests that the Vygotskian argument can be extended to provide an outline of the sociogenesis of the self. More fundamentally, Holzkamp provides an evolutionary argument which suggests that a social organization capable of meeting individuals' immediate, material survival needs was a necessary evolutionary precondition for the development of consciousness. Moreover, Holzkamp argues that the subjective possibilities afforded by the material, economic organization of society are an ongoing, structuring influence on individual experience (see Tolman 1994: 86–114). These and other similar analyses suggest that selves are already thoroughly social products, the living embodiment of aspects of their culture. As Burkitt (1991: 189) says, 'This makes the idea that there is a basic division between society and the individual into a nonsense. All efforts to find the "relationship" between the "two" are wasted, for when we look at society and the individual we are viewing exactly the same thing – social being – from two different angles.' As with Cartesian dualism, it must also be emphasized that those strands of constructionism which proceed without theorizing the self only avoid the self/society, agency/structure dichotomy by this omission. This smacks of flat-earthism, especially for an approach that is ostensibly focused upon the activities and interests of people going about the business of everyday life, and is a substantial barrier to ecological validity.

Constructionists sometimes advance ethical or political arguments against self theory. Sometimes it is claimed that relativism and anti-essentialism are as politically progressive as, if not more so, critical realist or dialectical approaches (e.g. Edwards *et al.* 1995). With specific reference to the self, some draw on Foucault to argue that refusing to theorize the self is politically progressive because it draws attention to and delegitimates the power relationships and institutional practices by which individuals are made subjects (e.g. Widdicombe 1992). Although it is entirely possible to read Foucault as supporting the deletion of the subject from philosophy and psychology, Callinicos (1989) is one of numerous commentators who observe that Foucault is inconsistent on this issue. Foucault wanted to see subjectivity as the product of power, yet he also wanted to leave space for resistance and change. But it is difficult to see how a subjectivity forged purely through power can then bite the hand that made it and fight back. Limitations of space preclude a thorough discussion of this issue, but it is our view that an accurate assessment of Foucault's entire corpus of work actually reveals it as a sustained effort to understand and critique the ways in which individuals become subjects or acquire selves, rather than a naive denial that selves exist. Foucault's critical analyses of ethics, sexuality and disciplinary power do not imply that we reject selves *per se*. Rather, his work urges us to challenge and reject the particular configuration of self and society that the dominant social order currently imposes.

Foucault aside, refusing to theorize the self offers an implausible basis for political activity. 'No masters, no selves' is an unconvincing rallying cry, and outside of academia it seems unlikely that many people could be persuaded for long that the selves they fondly imagine themselves to be are no more than tricks of language. From the perspective of the present, at least, it is hard to imagine such a proposal forming part of any successful programme for social change. The negative impact upon political activity of such post-structuralist ideas has been described by Lynne Segal, who writes:

> The absorption of Althusser, Lacan, and later of Foucault, into marxist and academic feminist theory increased this distance [between political activists and academic theorists]. Academic feminists who were influenced by these developments began to reject the importance of women's testimonies of their own lives and experience on which the feminist practice of 'consciousness raising' in small groups of women as a central part of the movement was based.
>
> (Segal 1987: 52)

We would add to this the mundane observation that, at a moment in history when much radical political activity is focused on the material world and the impact of our species upon its ecology, a psychology which ignores the embodied materiality of human existence will inevitably be insulated from this political activity, and as a consequence is likely to be liberal at best and deeply conservative at worst.

It could be argued that empirical studies using discourse analysis demonstrate the irrelevance of self theory. Discourse analysts have shown how varying constructions of the self are deployed in everyday interaction to bring off immediate social goals such as excusing or blaming, or to bolster one account against other competing versions. Such studies seem to demonstrate that the self as a 'thing' or 'process' within individuals is an unnecessary component in the understanding of social interaction, a misleading distraction from the processes which the discursive analysis reveals. But, in our view, this apparent proof that notions of the self are redundant is illusory. The illusion occurs through the imposition of a false horizon of immediate discursive opportunities, within which core issues to do with the self simply never arise. For example, discourse analysts are easily able to differentiate between various possible responses to an accusation, such as a denial, a justification or an excuse. At the same time, they are wholly unable even to speculate as to why on a particular occasion the response to a specific accusation was a denial, rather than a justification or an excuse. Moreover, showing how self-related discourse can be functional in social interaction, and even accepting that talk, all talk, always has a functional component, cannot exclude the possibility that on occasion it may *also* be expressive or representative.

The costs and dangers of ignoring the self

The principal cost of constructionism's failure to theorize the self is a missed opportunity to study the self as a real product of social practices. Webster (1995) argues that psychology has at its core a cryptotheologistic attitude which has led it to prioritize the rational and mental and ignore or downplay the embodied, the desiring and the carnal. This attitude, rooted in the evolutionary origins of the discipline as a secular continuation of Christian doctrines, blinds us to evidence concerning both the extent of biological influences upon human action (embodiment) and the thoroughly intertwined constitution of self and society (personal–social history). Constructionists, to the extent that they focus on discourse and disregard bodies and selves, maintain this same attitude and in so doing greatly impoverish their approach.

The extent of this impoverishment can be demonstrated by discussing both personal–social histories and embodiment. Since embodiment has been discussed at length elsewhere (see Chapters 8 and 9, this volume), we shall say little about it here, except to comment that its full significance becomes apparent if we consider the lives of people for whom their embodied nature is a particular issue. There are many people whose physical impairments are a defining factor in their experiences and relationships, yet social psychology typically understands this almost exclusively in terms of labelling, prejudice and discrimination, as though this was the whole of having a physical impairment. Social constructionism is more sophisticated, identifying the discourses within which impairments are located and analysing their deployment in fields such as medicine and social policy. However, both constructionism and mainstream social psychology explore only a small part of this experience, because the significance of these impairments, for those who have them, is not just a matter of language. Rather, the impairments enter into and influence the range of social practices and interactions of which their bearers are a part, making a purely discursive analysis strikingly inadequate. Wendell (1996: 31–2) states that what North American people with disabilities have in common includes:

> verbal, medical and physical abuse; neglect of the most basic educational needs; sexual abuse and exploitation; enforced poverty; harassment by public and private sector bureaucracies; job discrimination; segregation in schools, housing and workshops; inaccessibility of buildings, transportation and other public facilities; social isolation due to prejudice and ignorant fear; erasure as a sexual being.

Constructionism's focus on discourse makes many of these experiences invisible – or, alternatively, may 'ironize' them (Potter and Wetherell 1987) by implicitly suggesting that talk about them is just that, and no more. We should also recall that there are many people entirely without language, and constructionism's almost exclusive focus upon discourse may be understood as one more element in the constellation of views and practices that treat them as somehow less than human.

To show how the study of personal–social histories might enrich constructionism we will discuss power; more specifically, the abuse of power and its consequences. Our focus here is not high profile, spectacular abuses of power (wars, genocide, terrorism, mass murderers and serial killers), but the more mundane, 'everyday' abuses of power and their consequences. There is now a widespread perception that such abuses are more common in our culture than we previously cared to admit. Domestic violence and child physical and sexual abuse, for example, are much more widely recognized than they were previously (although whether they actually occur more often is difficult to establish, because reliable prevalence data are notoriously difficult to obtain). Moreover, evidence has been accumulating for some time that in many cases those who abuse others are themselves the victims of prior abuse (e.g. Gebhard *et al.* 1965; Groth and Burgess 1979; Abel *et al.* 1984; Elliot *et al.* 1995; NCH 1995). While there is not an inevitable connection between childhood trauma and later acts of violence (Briggs *et al.* 1998), there is often an association. Child sexual abuse studies show that up to 40 per cent of abusers were themselves abused, and Araji and Finkelhor (1986: 104) describe this as 'one of the most consistent findings of the research'. So, many of those who abuse power may themselves have been *socialized* into doing so, albeit inadvertently; they grew up learning a language of abuse which they then articulate in their relationships with others. A clinical psychologist describing his work with the predominantly female inmates of Rampton Special Hospital (the majority of whom have carried out acts of violence) observed that 'almost without exception, the women who had been detained had experienced traumatic and absolutely tragic lives. Experiences of sexual abuse, physical violence and emotional maltreatment were the norm rather than the exception for these women' (Godsi 1996: 261). Godsi uses the case history of a black woman, 'Lynn', to illustrate this, and argues that commonplace diagnostic labels such as post-traumatic stress disorder are inadequate here, since in Lynn's case 'her whole life was traumatic, there was hardly any respite, no breathing space. "Trauma" was in a profound sense almost all that she has known, it was the very air that she breathed' (Godsi 1996: 264). Rather than her 'faulty brain' or her 'mental illness', Godsi emphasizes that it is Lynn's personal–social history, the cumulative impact of years of degradation and abuse (much of it carried out by men, including the male psychiatrists who gave her electro-convulsive therapy), that is the key to understanding her violent actions. His paper shows how, far from lapsing into cognitivism or individualism, the study of personal–social histories actually highlights both the effects of power and their embodied consequences.

The writings of David Smail (e.g. 1984, 1993, 1996) similarly highlight abuses of power that impact negatively upon individuals and have consequences for their experience and conduct. Describing the recent history and current state of the 'helping professions', he writes:

> Official psychology and psychiatry barely took societal issues into account in their approaches to the understanding and treatment of 'mental illness', and certainly nowhere were they made central to the field of enquiry. We had simply overlooked those factors that give society its dynamic force and most closely affect its members: the distribution, maintenance and embodied effects of *power*. What caused people distress was not so much their own mistakes, inadequacies and illnesses as the powers and influences that bore down upon them from the world beyond their skin.
>
> (Smail 1996: 12)

Smail's focus is not so much on abusive upbringings that would be considered cruel and unusual by any conceivable community standards. He concentrates on the effects of unemployment, poor housing and poverty, and socio-cultural transformations such as the fragmentation of communities, changed gender roles and the pervasive influence of the 'business culture' of the 1980s. He uses his extensive clinical experience to show how symptoms of 'mental illness' (such as depression, anxiety, panic attacks, feelings of being out of control or unmotivated), far from being mysterious or pathological, are actually rooted in the concrete, lived circumstances of people's lives – circumstances defined largely through the operation of economic forces and socio-cultural shifts. Such so-called 'symptoms' are not at all bizarre and abnormal, but are in fact perfectly ordinary responses to distressing situations. However, for a variety of reasons people typically fail to realize this, and attribute their difficulties to personal failings and proximal situations, rather than to more distal socio-economic or cultural forces, as in this example:

> Having been a housewife for fifteen years can be tantamount to spending time in a total institution, cut off from the changes and developments taking place in the outside world, gradually losing confidence in one's ability to cope with them. However sensitive to the situation the male partner may be, his greater access to and freedom in the outside world are almost certain to inject into the relationship elements of isolation, envy and resentment on the one side, and frustration, impatience and incomprehension on the other. What is in fact the inevitable consequence of occupancy of different worlds (a pattern imposed by distal socio-economic factors well beyond individuals' control) is likely to be proximally interpreted by those involved as a purely personal predicament.
>
> (Smail 1996: 77–8)

Smail highlights our culture's encouragement of economic exploitation and dependence upon structures of hierarchical power, showing that these economic and structural forces impact directly upon experience. His approach illustrates how power and exploitation mould personal–social histories, with unwanted consequences that reverberate on down through people's lives. His work strongly suggests that the social structures we have created are rather less benign than many people typically assume. Not only do they do damage to individuals (making it possible that they will inflict related damage upon children and others they may be responsible for), they also predispose them to view such damage as their own fault.

These examples suggest that the constructionist study of personal–social histories might illuminate our understanding of 'psychopathology', so countering the individualistic, mentalistic and biological reductionist approaches which dominate this field (Parker *et al.* 1995). They also show how the study of personal–social histories has a critical force, and might provide valuable pointers to the social construction of more caring and wholesome ways of relating and being. It is through the loss of these alternative understandings of experiences such as distress, and the critical force these understandings carry, that constructionism impoverishes itself without a notion of the self.

We will now discuss some of the dangers facing social constructionism unless it integrates some notion of the self into its theory and practice. These dangers are best exemplified by the Human Genome Project, an international research project which aims to map the sequence of nucleotide bases that are strung along the DNA molecules of the human genome, the sequence that gives the human species its distinct identity. However, the majority of researchers are less interested in this medium-term goal (the Project is aiming for completion by 2005) than in practical outcomes such as the identification of specific sequences which cause or predispose individuals to illness or disease (Friedman *et al.* 1992). The pace of this research is continually accelerating as each new discovery makes the overall picture slightly clearer and so facilitates further advances. When medical genetics became a recognized medical specialism in the USA in 1991, the number of identifiable disorders which specialists had to be familiar with was approximately 3000; just four years later, this number had already increased to 4000 (Brock 1995).

The Human Genome Project highlights two distinct dangers for a social constructionism which, because it permits no notion of the embodied person, is incapable of thorough integration with other forms of knowledge. First, there is the intellectual impoverishment and increasing marginalization that constructionism is likely to undergo as the practical ability of gene mapping to provide embodied explanations for human activity continues. Constructionism's reduction of other disciplines to 'discourses of . . .' makes it incapable of integration with them, and if sustained may leave it isolated and disrespected. Second, and more dangerous still, constructionists will remain unable to contest the worst excesses of biological determinism, which have accompanied genetic approaches in the past and undoubtedly will do so again. These dangers interact with, and add a special weight to, the loss of ecological validity constructionists incur when they ignore the self. Expressions such as 'he has His Father's eyes' (Levin 1968: 198) have been common currency for many years, and serve as points of ballast which anchor biologistic and individualistic notions of self firmly in the fabric of everyday life.

None of this is to suggest that we capitulate to the eugenicists and sociobiologists by granting primacy to the genetic machinery of reproduction in the creation of our lived social world. Murphy (1995) suggests that constructionists typically fail to look at biological and genetic research, because of the understandable revulsion and repulsion that biological determinism causes and because they prefer to keep their approach 'pure'. But genetic research and theories do not themselves make people into reactionaries: as with all science, it is the ideological consensus of society that gives this work its predominant political complexion. So, taking the Genome Project seriously does not require us already to surrender the ideological battle we have identified. On the contrary, our argument is that we can only properly engage with it by developing a mature social constructionism which includes an integral notion of the self. We suggested above that personal–social histories might explain far more 'psychopathology' and individual difference than is typically assumed. A substantial body of social constructionist research directed at this issue might provide valuable evidence to help counter the tide of biological determinism that the Genome Project is already creating. In its absence, however, we suspect that social constructionism will find itself unable to rebut convincingly the geneticists' claims.

Reconstructing the self

Social constructionism emphasizes the constitutive potential of social processes. Thus far, it has theorized and described some of those processes (e.g. in discourse, or in Shotter's notion of 'joint action'), but has for the most part maintained the individual/society, agency/structure dichotomy by not simultaneously theorizing the individual who is both product and user of these social processes. Some recent constructionist work seems to acknowledge this need (Bayer and Shotter 1998), but we still do not have a description of the person from a constructionist perspective. This, we believe, is the task now facing us.

Below we describe some hesitant first steps towards this goal, but first we need to emphasize again that the simple inclusion of mainstream psychology's self will not suffice. In this model of the self, the distinction between 'I' (self as agent) and 'Me' (self as object) ushers in and mirrors the dualisms between mind and body, individual and society. The separation of agency and conscious awareness ('I') from its own contents and goals ('Me') actually replicates – in miniature, within the individual – the disciplinary divide that erroneously separates psychology from the other social and human sciences. In this way, the 'I/Me' distinction of mainstream psychology's self places that division at the heart of psychology and, by making it appear as an inevitable consequence of our species-being, helps to naturalize it. This is how mainstream psychology's self inevitably produces dualisms, and so must be rejected by constructionists. The question facing us, then, is what to put in its place.

In this chapter we have emphasized the significance of both personal–social histories and embodiment. We have argued that these influential aspects of existence, which are typically subsumed under the heading 'self', cannot be adequately understood as mere discourse and its epiphenomena. To begin to understand how they might be studied within a constructionist framework, we will now briefly discuss each in turn.

The study of personal–social histories both requires and facilitates a focus on power, and so from Foucault (e.g. 1977, 1988) we can take the notion of power relationships as constitutive and productive of selves. The study of the various 'technologies of the self' that characterize a given culture, and that may be identified within bureaucratic procedures, education, assessments, training and therapy (as well as in other, more distal sites such as the 'Dear Marje' columns of newspapers and magazines), is relevant here. However, we would wish to supplement the Foucauldian view with the understanding that consciousness is also structured by material possibilities and constraints (Tolman 1994). Personal–social histories are the outcome, then, not just of a totalizing and abstract power; they are played out as embodied activity in a material world which actually gives power its grounding and force. Narrative approaches (e.g. Freeman 1993) may be useful in uncovering some of the processes of social construction that occur here. Haug's (1987) method of 'memory-work', which potentially reveals how we construct our selves but are always constrained in this activity by the social and material resources that are available to us, might also be applied to the study of personal–social histories.

Turning now to embodiment, there are again numerous possibilities. The chapters in this volume by Butt and Burr advocate a phenomenological approach to the constructionist study of embodiment. Detailed study of discourses and discursive practices concerning the body and its (dys)functions may be valuable (e.g. Ussher 1997; Young 1997). However, in our view constructionism also needs an understanding of the body as more than mere metaphor, symbol or discursive arena. We need to include within our constructionist framework the influence of phenomenal, hormonal, anatomical and physiological factors, but to do so without falling prey to either deterministic essentialism or Cartesian dualism. We do not imagine that this is an easy task, but it is one that is not without precedent: there is a sense in which psychoanalysis, in its earliest formulations, attempted to do precisely this. The integration of current work in neurology with constructionist insights into the socio-cultural determination of subjective experience may provide us with a non-speculative basis for this immensely difficult project (Harré and Gillett 1994; see also Nightingale and Cromby, this volume, Chapter 14).

Conclusion

In this chapter we have given reasons why constructionism needs to integrate a notion of the self into its research and practices, and shown how failing to do so may give rise to both costs and dangers. We have also tried to show how objections which are commonly raised to this proposal are misguided or fallacious. We have suggested that in both implicitly ceding the body to medicine and failing adequately to consider the personal–social histories that might provide social (as opposed to biological or psychiatric) explanations for patterns of human activity, constructionists actually entrench the dualisms which their approach strives to overcome. We believe that the benefits to constructionism of continuing without an integral notion of the self are largely illusory, and are in any case outweighed by the costs and dangers incurred. It is time for constructionists to take our selves seriously.

References

Abel, G., Becker, J. and Skinner, L. (1984) Complications, consent and cognitions in sex between children and adults, *International Journal of Law and Psychiatry*, 7: 89–103.

Araji, S. and Finkelhor, D. (1986) Abusers: a review of the research, in D. Finkelhor *et al.* (eds) *A Coursebook in Child Sexual Abuse.* London: Sage.

Bayer, B. M. and Shotter, J. (1998) *Reconstructing the Psychological Subject: Bodies Practices and Technologies.* London: Sage.

Billig, M. (1987) *Arguing and Thinking: A Rhetorical Approach to Social Psychology.* Cambridge: Cambridge University Press.

Briggs, D., Doyle, P., Gooch, T. and Kennington, R. (1998) *Assessing Men Who Sexually Abuse: A Practice Guide.* London: Jessica Kingsley.

Brock, S. C. (1995) Narrative and medical genetics: on ethics and therapeutics, *Qualitative Health Research*, 5(2): 150–68.

Burkitt, I. (1991) *Social Selves: Theories of the Social Formation of Personality.* London: Sage.

Callinicos, A. (1989) *Against Postmodernism: A Marxist Critique.* Cambridge: Polity Press.

Craig, A. (1997) Postmodern pluralism and our selves, *Theory and Psychology*, 7(4): 505–27.

Edwards, D., Ashmore, M. and Potter, J. (1995) Death and furniture: the rhetoric, politics and theology of bottom-line arguments against relativism, *History of the Human Sciences*, 8(2): 25–49.

Edwards, D. and Middleton, D. (1986) Joint remembering: constructing an account of shared experience through conversational discourse, *Discourse Processes*, 9(4): 91–104.

Edwards, D. and Potter, J. (1992) *Discursive Psychology.* London: Sage.

Elliot, M., Browne, K. and Kilcoyne, J. (1995) What child sex offenders tell us, *Child Abuse and Neglect*, 19(5): 579–94.

Foucault, M. (1977) *Discipline and Punish.* Harmondsworth: Penguin.

Foucault, M. (1988) Technologies of the self, in L. H. Martin, H. Guttman and P. H. Hutton (eds) *Technologies of the Self.* London: Tavistock Publications.

Freeman, M. (1993) *Rewriting the Self: History, Memory, Narrative.* London: Routledge.

Friedman, G., Reichlet, R. and Shera, K. (1992) *Los Alamos Science No. 20: The Human Genome Project.* Los Alamos, NM: Los Alamos National Laboratory.

Gebhard, P., Gagnon, J., Pomeroy, W. and Christenson, C. (1965) *Sex Offenders: An Analysis of Types.* New York: Harper & Row.

Geertz, C. (1979) From the native's point of view: on the nature of anthropological understanding, in P. Rabinow and W. M. Sullivan (eds) *Interpretive Social Science.* Berkeley: University of California Press.

Gergen, K. J. (1991) *The Saturated Self.* New York: Basic Books.

Godsi, E. (1996) Life as trauma, *Changes: International Journal of Psychology and Psychotherapy*, 13(4): 261–9.

Groth, N. and Burgess, A. (1979) Sexual trauma in the life histories of rapists and child molesters, *Victimology: An International Journal*, 4: 10–16.

Harré, R. (1983) *Personal Being: A Theory for Individual Psychology.* Oxford: Basil Blackwell.

Harré, R. (ed.) (1986) *The Social Construction of Emotions.* Oxford: Basil Blackwell.

Harré, R. (1987) The social construction of selves, in K. Yardley and T. Honess (eds) *Self and Identity: Psychosocial Perspectives.* Chichester: John Wiley & Sons.

Harré, R. and Gillett, G. (1994) *The Discursive Mind*. London: Sage.

Haug, F. (1987) *Female Sexualisation*. London: Verso.

Heelas, P. and Lock, A. (eds) (1981) *Indigenous Psychologies: The Anthropology of the Self*. London: Academic Press.

Held, D. (1980) *Introduction to Critical Theory*. Berkeley: University of California Press.

Henriques, J., Hollway, W., Urwin, C., Venn, C. and Walkerdine, V. (1984) *Changing the Subject: Psychology, Social Regulation and Subjectivity*. London: Methuen.

Hollway, W. (1984) Gender difference and the production of subjectivity, in J. Henriques, W. Hollway, C. Urwin, C. Venn and V. Walkerdine (eds) *Changing the Subject: Psychology, Social Regulation and Subjectivity*. London: Methuen.

Levin, I. (1968) *Rosemary's Baby*. London: Pan Books.

Logan, R. D. (1987) Historical change in prevailing sense of self, in K. Yardley and T. Honess (eds) *Self and Identity: Psychosocial Perspectives*. Chichester: John Wiley & Sons.

Marcuse, H. (1969) *Eros and Civilisation*. London: Sphere Books.

Marsella, A. J., Devos, G. and Hsu, F. K. L. (eds) (1985) *Culture and Self: Asian and Western Perspectives*. New York: Tavistock Publications.

Middleton, D. and Edwards, D. (eds) (1990) *Collective Remembering*. London: Sage.

Murphy, R. (1995) Sociology as if nature did not matter: an ecological critique, *British Journal of Sociology*, 46(4): 688–707.

NCH (1995) Action for children: report on joint project (with NSPCC and the Tavistock Clinic) to treat sexually abusive children, *Community Care*, 6–12 April.

Parker, I., Georgaca, E., Harper, D., McLaughlin, T. and Stowell-Smith, M. (1995) *Deconstructing Psychopathology*. London: Sage.

Potter, J. and Wetherell, M. (1987) *Discourse and Social Psychology: Beyond Attitudes and Behaviour*. London: Sage.

Sampson, E. E. (1983) *Justice and the Critique of Pure Psychology*. New York: Plenum Press.

Sarbin, T. R. (1986) The narrative as root metaphor for psychology, in T. R. Sarbin (ed.) *Narrative Psychology: The Storied Nature of Human Conduct*. New York: Praeger.

Shweder, R. A. and Levine, R. A. (eds) (1984) *Culture Theory: Essays on Mind, Self and Emotion*. Cambridge: Cambridge University Press.

Segal, L. (1987) *Is the Future Female? Troubled Thoughts on Contemporary Feminism*. London: Virago Press.

Shotter, J. and Gergen, K. J. (eds) (1989) *Texts of Identity*. London: Sage.

Smail, D. (1984) *Illusion and Reality: The Meaning of Anxiety*. London: J. M. Dent & Sons.

Smail, D. (1993) *The Origins of Unhappiness*. London: HarperCollins.

Smail, D. (1996) *How to Survive without Psychotherapy*. London: Constable & Co.

Tolman, C. W. (1994) *Psychology, Society and Subjectivity: An Introduction to German Critical Psychology*. London: Routledge.

Ussher, J. M. (1997) *Body Talk: The Material and Discursive Regulation of Sexuality, Madness and Reproduction*. London: Sage.

Vygotsky, L. (1978) *Mind in Society: The Development of Higher Psychological Processes*. Cambridge, MA: Harvard University Press.

Webster, R. (1995) *Why Freud Was Wrong: Sin, Science and Psychoanalysis*. London: Fontana.

Weisstein, N. (1993) Psychology constructs the female, or the fantasy life of the male psychologist (with some attention to the fantasies of his friends, the male biologist and the male anthropologist), *Feminism and Psychology*, 3(2): 195–210 (originally published in 1968).

Wendell, S. (1996) *The Rejected Body: Feminist Philosophical Reflections on Disability*. London: Routledge.

Wetherell, M. and Maybin, J. (1996) The distributed self: a social constructionist perspective, in R. Stevens (ed.) *Understanding the Self*. London: Sage.

Widdicombe, S. M. (1992) Subjectivity, power and the practice of psychology: a review of W. Hollway, 'Subjectivity and Method in Psychology', *Theory and Psychology*, 2(4): 487–99.

Young, K. (1997) *Presence in the Flesh: The Body in Medicine*. Harvard, MA: Harvard University Press.

PART III

A critical analysis of practice

11 Whose construction?
Points from a feminist perspective

ERICA BURMAN

What is at stake in the move from social construction to deconstruction, and thence to reconstruction in psychology? How is it that the project of ten years ago to deconstruct psychology (e.g. Parker and Shotter 1990), which a decade or more before was preceded by one of constructing – a better – psychology (Armistead 1974; Gillham 1978), is now once again transmuting into calls for reconstruction of new varieties of – discursive or critical – psychology? Whose, as well as which, constructions threaten to be maintained in these enterprises, and why might feminist psychologists be wary of wholeheartedly siding with any of these camps?

These questions indicate the guiding concerns of this chapter, as a contribution to and commentary on this text on social constructionism within psychology. Since I aim to make several 'pointed' comments about the limits of, or unhelpful tendencies within, this enterprise, I should clarify that my own starting point here is one of cautious but critical alliance with the social constructionist impulses that give rise to this volume. My focus, like that of this book, is practices of psychology that are largely Anglo-US, and in some cases specifically British. To acknowledge this is to recognize its cultural limits as well as location. Through this disciplinary and cultural–historical focus, I argue that academic practice exemplifies the simultaneous impossibility and permanent transgression of the purported oppositions of theory/practice and form/content. Indeed, my focus on academic *practice* is intended precisely to destabilize those oppositions by highlighting the embodied and institutional character of academia. That is, upholding such oppositions works to deny practices of exclusion that define the content and work of the academy. Such meaningful misattributions can be read as forms of government and regulation of the discipline. Taking feminist work in psychology as a case study, I argue that while some of the institutional and conceptual forms this takes in psychology can be problematized, the marginality of other feminist work should be regarded as an underestimated resource for social constructionists and perhaps as modelling a disciplinary survival strategy.

This focus on academic practice therefore provides the strong case for what can be demonstrated more easily and clearly in the domain of so-called 'applied' psychology (a – gendered – false opposition if ever there was one). I want to claim that feminist interventions remain at the critical edge of psychology (see, for example, the two issues of *Psychology of Women Quarterly* edited by Crawford and Kimmell 1999). I will do this by commenting on how those more general themes and absences are exhibited by discourses of social constructionism. I will move from analysing how these are instantiated by equivalent debates within feminist work in psychology to consider what this indicates for social constructionist interventions in psychology, including this volume.

I start by highlighting the relevance for the politics of social constructionism in psychology of debates within feminism and women's studies. I make these comments from an understanding of the reciprocal relations between feminist debates and social constructionism in psychology, as sharing some theoretical–political reference points (hence the significance of Henriques *et al.* 1984), and some common organizational bases (for example, in organizations such as the Psychology and Psychotherapy Association, and from cohorts of postgraduate psychology conferences). Notwithstanding their different theoretical and political presuppositions, what critical realist and perspectivist readings of social constructionism offer to feminists are analytics connecting the acknowledgement of power relations with the aim to transform or to destabilize them respectively. However, I will suggest that feminists might be right to be as cautious of subscribing to the project of reconstruction that seems implied by social constructionism as they were of deconstruction; and right to be more cautious still of reconstructing some new improved variety of social constructionism, social psychology or even feminism for that matter.

Bodies of knowledge

The importance of situating knowledge within bodies of knowledge that are disciplinary as well as culturally and historically specific forms a key theme within social constructionist work in psychology. That such knowledge is embodied, or situated within specific bodies that carry markers of gender, 'race' and sexuality, is similarly reflected as a recurrent theme of this book. Yet notwithstanding its centrality, this book is largely sadly unreflexive about this assertion. Bodies remain abstract rhetorical entities within these chapters: embodiment is discussed as a topic, but specificities of inhabiting bodies – such as ascriptions of gender and sexuality – rarely figure. As such, 'social constructionism' is in danger of reproducing the ideal-typical subject of psychology as unitary, rational and culturally masculine. Calls to reconstruct 'the self' in psychology invite the question of *which* self: waving the banner for embodiment requires an analysis of specifically located bodies (see also Kitzinger 1992).

Here debates in women's studies have something to offer more seemingly parochial concerns within psychology. The 'crisis' in psychology that ushered in humanist-inspired interpretive approaches to challenge the instrumentalism of behaviourism (e.g. Reason and Rowan 1981) was paralleled by a general cultural shift towards concerns of 'self-help' and identity. The 1970s feminist slogan 'the personal is political' was informed by both varieties of psychology (and anti-psychology) and popular culture, and over the years has been reinterpreted (or appropriated) as a personalization of politics. While the general drift towards therapy, lifestyle and the culture of the body included those disillusioned with or exhausted by politics because of the intransigence of patriarchy and capitalism, this broader context of identity politics, celebration of (biological) motherhood and the family, and new age religion/magic also entered feminism (e.g. Bondi 1993; Nicholson and Seidman 1995).

It has also entered psychology. Notwithstanding claims that the notion of identity has been deconstructed, identity politics remains rife with ideologically loaded debates about the evils of qualitative (or alternatively, depending on the debater's preference, quantitative) research, about families or schools of discourse analysis and allegiances to particular (usually male) theorists (Lacan, Derrida, Foucault, Sachs, Kelly, Merleau-Ponty?). If it seems strange that feelings run so high when identities are these days supposedly so diffused, and cognitions supposedly so distributed, perhaps we would do well to recall that pay packets are not; and that ideas are embodied, and investments (in more senses than one) are high.

Just as capitalism's production of demand relies on the targeting or profiling of consumers (often with multilayered messages that address more than one segment of social stratification simultaneously – as doubtless this book will be marketed), so psychology's (critical) producers (and I include myself here) are fixed and labelled with institutional and career-inflected positions on particular methodologies or forms of interpretive analysis. It is worth recalling that the neo-liberalism of the global market that makes postmodernist accounts possible (Lyotard's *The Postmodern Condition* (1992) was written as a consultation document for the Canadian government) and popular goes hand in hand with fundamentalism; one produces the other, and perhaps in some senses requires it.

Similarly in psychology, there is an institutional drive towards an adversarial style of theory/method franchising and battling around vested interests. Paradoxically, whether committed to models of fragmented subjects or not, social constructionists are divided by academic conventions that require and thereby impose essentialized identities on 'authors' and insist on constructing opposing camps. Still worse, these conventions encourage a misrecognition or recasting of tactics for principles that work towards a coding of politics as method. Thus in psychology methods are essentialized as topics that can be taught in their 57 varieties, as if their value could be evaluated outside the particular research questions or contexts of study. Once they are so abstracted into technical fetishes, the further risk of technical fundamentalism arises, whereby a particular form of analysis or transcription can be invested with the capacity to generate the 'true' account, rather than another, particular, story.

Hence, once divided from each other, even subversive developments in theory and method can become sites for appropriation by psychology. Like the market for new methods, new forms of subjectivity can be incorporated (brought into the body of psychology). So the flexible selves of social constructionism, like our flexible credit cards (flexible in material, but not in signification – a seductive conflation that benefits capitalism at, and materially by virtue of, our expense), may not so much transgress psychology as open up more arenas for its penetration.

In this regard the varieties of social constructionism that continue to harbour (or champion) notions of 'self' may always be more attractive to psychology than those that refuse it. On the other hand, a repudiation of some integrated subject is so antithetical to mainstream psychology as to be beyond engagement, unlike those varieties that argue for its retention, who thereby become more of a target for psychology's most virulent efforts to recuperate them. By such means psychology and capitalism, through their common practices of reification and commodification, work to deradicalize critiques of research. They reconfigure such interventions as new techniques for the improvement of an even more broadly 'applicable' psychology, and in so doing assimilate and neutralize them.

Changing subjects: from deconstruction to reconstruction?

One of the tensions structuring both this book and the purported distinction between 'social constructionism' and 'deconstruction' is the different 'takes' they are seen to have on the conceptualization of a political subject capable of agency, responsibility and changing the world. Social constructionists and feminists shared some caution/hostility in their response to postmodern ideas (e.g. Brodribb 1992).

Current discussions in women's studies take up the challenge to the notion of sisterhood that was so central to the second wave feminism of the 1970s, in addressing the claims of black women and lesbians that the 'feminist movement' did not speak for their interests, or their oppression (e.g. Amos and Parmar 1984; Carby 1987). The unitary political category 'woman' has thus fragmented into many differently positioned and inter-pellated women, with varying political interests. This poses the urgent political question of how, or whether, alliances can be made between women across differences of class, 'race', sexuality and (dis)ability, to name but a few. The historical project of theorizing the complicity of early European and US feminism with colonialism (e.g. McClintock 1995), alongside tracing the interwoven origins of feminist and anti-slavery movements (Ware 1992), has challenged the homogeneity and abstraction of 'women' and 'feminism' and highlighted how gendered identifications always also intersect with subject positions organized around 'race', class and sexuality (Brah 1996). By situating the emergence of feminism within specific cultural and historical conditions, it has been possible to acknowledge how, like the nascent discipline of psychology, in its founding moments it was shot through with racist, anti working-class and heterosexist assumptions.

However, the problems of the exclusionary feminist subject (by virtue of its previous over-inclusivity) are not resolved by its deconstruction. Moving from a singular 'woman' to multiple varieties of women, or, even further, refusing to privilege gender as a relevant axis of subjectivity around which to organize, seems to offer no prospect of political agency or collective action. From a principled engagement with deconstructionist and post-modernist debates around the inevitability and significance of 'difference', a number of feminist responses have emerged. While these include some politicized women who would refuse to call themselves feminist because of the exclusionary legacies this term bears (see Brooks 1997), others (and I would include myself here) seek ways of rearticulating notions of political practice for and with women that are no longer based on notions of common (or correlatively irrecoverably separate) identities but on alliances or coalitions across differences that are both structural and open to some local contingent reconfiguration (e.g. Haraway 1991; Yuval-Davis 1993, 1997).

It is important to note that the alternative to deconstruction offered by these accounts is not the reconstruction of some new purged and squeaky clean feminist position. Rather than repeating the same problems (of exclusion and corresponding marginalization) that attend grand theory-building, it is possible to retain the broader political project of general social transformation by destabilizing (feminist) identities and positions. Instead, current feminist approaches highlight how knowledges are local and situated and can thereby be amenable to intervention or disruption in diverse, equally local and contingent, ways. Alliances between disparate political constituencies are negotiated on a provisional and tactical basis, rather than common political goals being presumed to flow in an unmediated way from some spuriously imposed shared identity.

Similarly, the hotly debated opposition between realism and relativism, while having its own trajectory within feminist discussions (Lovibund 1989; Soper 1991; Fraser 1992; Elam 1994; and in psychology see Gill 1995), also finds some resolution. Whether conceived of in terms of standpoint (Harding 1993) or the privilege of partial perspective (Haraway 1991), these feminist frameworks espouse a diversity of perspectives alongside their subscription to an analysis of power, oppression and exploitation. The relevance of these discussions to feminist interventions within and identifications with psychology was discussed by Hollway (1989), Squire (1989) and more recently Henwood *et al.* (1998).

Displacing or disciplining ourselves?

Perhaps like those women who can no longer identify themselves with feminism because of its sins of inception, I have noticed (within myself as well as others) some reticence about owning up to an institutional location in psychology. It is as if the move to social construction not only (correctly) dissolves disciplinary boundaries (for how – within 'post' debates – can the division between psychology and sociology or anthropology, for example, be sustained?), but seems also to offer backdoor routes to slip out of psychology's intellectual wastelands into more exciting and welcoming territories. Yet once there I find that I lack an object of reference – psychology – or else that my critical interventions within the discipline are more easily marginalized because they do not issue from a 'psychological' base.

It is certainly historically the case in the UK that many 'critical' psychologists have a biographical career trajectory that takes them out of psychology and into sociology or even management departments; or out of academic or 'professional' practice altogether.[1] Others have managed to remain 'within' psychology, some committed to retaining a (perhaps utopian) place for improving psychology, others to using their position strategically to undermine the power and knowledge claims from a position that is less easy to dismiss as outside and therefore irrelevant (although still being told by hostile students and colleagues that this work is history, philosophy, sociology, politics . . . anything but psychology).

Drawing on current theoretical perspectives, this situation could be seen not so much as a matter of identity – to be or not to be a 'psychologist' – as of speaking position. Perhaps the existential insecurity of social constructionist or critical psychologists expresses a necessary ambivalence about the privilege such a position wields, alongside vilification and suspicion from other, more critically 'developed' disciplines (but we should beware the progressivist discourse here). After all, to be comfortable with our 'selves' within psychology would be not only to be complicit with its oppressive practices but also – like good self-regulating subjects – to have produced our subjectivities within its own image (with, for example, high self-esteem and robust self-concepts?).

This ambivalence of identification does, I think, give rise to some lack of specification in the remit of the terminology used. I am in agreement with Viv Burr (this volume, Chapter 8), who notes that the term 'social constructionism' has meaning primarily only in relation to psychology, since elsewhere within the social and human sciences its theses are more or less presumed. Hence claims about the construction (e.g. of subjectivity) and deconstruction (e.g. of oppressive or banal psychological theories and practices) function within psychological models of knowledge production that are premised on obscuring (in the name of objective 'natural' science) precisely those traces of human embodiment and specificity that need to be recovered in order to expose their partiality (in the double sense of being incomplete and being ideological).

Here the very existence of the prefix 'social', used to qualify constructionism, by its very redundancy – for what de/construction is not social? – already concedes the point at issue in its intervention within psychology. The social is not grafted upon a thereby prior, original (structural, biological?) construction: the point is that all constructions occur within historical, geographical and cultural conditions that inform, permit and promote what is constructed, and how. 'Social constructionism' in psychology is heir to an equivalent history of historical and cultural contingencies, and multiple affiliations: but it originates and functions in relation to the discipline of *psychology*. As such, it mirrors, and thereby can better help us to reflect upon, some of the problems within psychology that it set out to address.

Let's talk about sex

I have already signposted my focus on gender issues, and made a case for the value of debates in feminist and women's studies for social constructionism in psychology. Given the above ambiguities of the relations between social constructionist critiques and psychology, I want now to consider resonances between the latter two domains in the framing and acknowledgement of gender issues.

First, let us note that I topicalized 'gender' rather than 'women' in my gloss above. This already invokes a hornet's nest of contested discourses. For it is something of a tender issue whether 'gender' codes for 'women' in psychology, or, alternatively, whether the ambiguity of referent is what warrants the trooping in of the men who had hitherto involved themselves in the 'sex difference' industry, and who are only kept out of this burgeoning academic/support space for women by virtue of its being named for/about women (see Wilkinson and Burns 1990).

Courses on gender in psychology are often seen as synonymous with courses on the (the?) 'psychology of women'. Why? Because women in psychology not only have gender, they *are* gender; they are marked with gender in the same way as black people are positioned as bearing 'race': in deconstructionist language, the subordinate group is attributed with a negative identity that is actually the outcome of a binary *relationship*. The deconstructive move is to attend to the covert norms (of whiteness, maleness) that maintain the objectifying and pathologizing gaze on women and black people. Thus, it would follow that the critical/constructionist agenda should be to refuse all stabilization of marginal identities as collusive within prevailing arrangements.

It is just such a stance that motivates the shift in course titles from 'women's' to 'gender' studies. But this is where calls for deconstruction meet resistance from some feminists (e.g. Jackson 1992), who note how claims for the fictive character of 'woman' coincide with women just beginning to gain some societal power and recognition. Even though they may appear to be reinforcing rather than transcending the traditional gender binary, and in danger of implying a spurious homogeneity of identity and commitment between women, feminists, including feminist psychologists (Haraway 1991; Henwood *et al.* 1998; Kitzinger 1998; Wilkinson 1997) have argued for the importance of retaining a speaking position for and as women within dominant discourses. This position may claim a common identity for women, but this is as a strategic, political intervention and not as ontological description (see Evans 1990; Kremer 1990; and for psychology see Burman 1998a).

Thus the conventional gendering of models and methods is one that feminists alternatively engage with and challenge. It is sometimes useful to draw attention to the ways the mainstream models reproduce dominant gendered values: that is, are malestream. In particular, modern psychology's project of formulating general, unilinear, presumed universal theories that are usually regarded as holding for all times and places can be helpfully challenged by highlighting its correspondence with prevailing forms of cultural masculinity.

At other times, it is important to ward off the equation between sexed bodies and bodies of knowledge, for these do not necessarily equate. So, for example, there is no reason why a theory formulated or espoused by a woman should – given the context in which women are taught and practise – be expected to be any freer of cultural masculinity than that expressed by a man (although such expectations, and the feelings associated with them, are themselves full of material warranting analysis). Equally, it is important to challenge the gendering of methods that occurs both explicitly (as in the equation between feminist and qualitative research – both by feminists until moderately recently and by non-feminists) and implicitly (as where quantitative research is 'hard' and manipulative while qualitative is seen as 'soft' and person-friendly: Burman 1997, 1998b). There is now an emerging set of debates about research approaches that draws the distinction between method or technique, methodological framework and epistemological position (Harding 1987), such that the relation between method and model becomes a complex articulation of politics and contextual relevance, rather than essential or automatic. This means that no method can be regarded as either quintessentially pro- or anti-feminist, for example. Qualitative methods can be as (or more?) intrusive and exploitative as qualitative approaches. There are moves afoot to queer the quantitative–qualitative dichotomy further by elaborating qualitative ways of using quantitative material, as in (the perhaps aptly named) Q methodology, as well as initiatives that reverse the presumed direction of contingency between gender and sexuality (Gordo-Lopez and Aitken in preparation).

Does talking make it worse?

It would seem that the project of highlighting the covert sexing and gendering of psychological theories and practices is useful. Perhaps this indicates a humanist/enlightenment-inflected variety of social constructionism – if we can know our sins, we can avoid them – thus presupposing a model of subjectivity capable of intention and agency. Yet there is another – more Foucauldian – reading of such practices that would emphasize its productive and collusive character.[2]

In the spirit of destabilizing this seeming opposition – between subject as actor and as discursive effect (or between textuality and techtonics: Curt 1994) – I want now to consider four examples where talking (about gender) is said to make matters worse. I will argue how paradoxically talking about gender can work to retain existing structures of exclusion and marginalization, but equally how this indicates the need to disrupt the traditional gatekeeping that excludes political concerns from psychological discussions. If, as British Telecom would have us believe, it's good to talk, then who benefits, and where does ownership of the medium of communication (or definition of the domain of discourse) come into it?

Talking gender in psychology

Talking gender in psychology has certainly created more publishing outlets for women and created more jobs in the academy for women like me.

There are, however, some limitations in gaining access to such arenas, for places of privilege create their own blindspots (compare how Harding (1993) retains a place within her postmodernist account for the more oppressed to have closer access to the – situated – truth of a situation). Feminists, including feminist psychologists, like other critical academics, need arenas of accountability not only to each other (rather than non-feminist psychologists) but also to feminists outside psychology, and outside academic/ professional practice. As many critics have pointed out (e.g. Carrigan *et al*. 1987; Crawford 1998; Unger 1998), the discourse of gender is liberal, in the sense of being (a) committed to an individualist and voluntarist model of social change. It thus is vulnerable to (b) a victim-blaming and asocial account of oppression and disadvantage; it (c) implies fixed positions and identities that are antithetical to current constructionist accounts, and (d) fails to offer any convincing account of how such positions could come to be different. Most importantly, it (e) fails to address real power relations by assuming that the two categories of gender (and are there really only two?) are symmetrical. In abstracting and condensing relationships between/ within men and women into a single contest, it thereby (f) reproduces as some natural, essential constant that which it apparently challenges; thus the very act of identifying gender can work to reinstate the very bipolar division it aims to transform.

In sum, the discourse of gender implies that the inequalities it describes are dispensable, symmetrical and mutually maintained. If we need any further evidence, it should be noted that gender is a domain that men can, and do, claim equal share of, and any apparent advantage occupied by women (which was in any case a token recognition of centuries of disadvantage) is easily turned around. As a specific example of the dangers of claiming *not* to talk gender specificity, the discourse of gender neutrality (a discourse which denies the specificity it performs), which was introduced to surpass the primary caretaker rule in child custody legislation in many European countries, disadvantages women as mothers (Smart and Sevenhuijsen 1989), while organizations like Families Need Fathers mobilize traditional patriarchal moralities of control and censure of women.

Naming feminism puts women/people off

It is often said to, and sometimes by, feminists that naming the work as 'feminist' alienates the very constituency that needs to hear the arguments. (Interestingly, this is typically said by someone who does not identify with this 'need', but who – as a classic form of mitigating disclaimer – seems happy to attribute this to others as long as they are elsewhere.) The rest, so it is said, is 'preaching to the converted'. This implies that the feminist teacher should hide her political affiliations but should, through skilful crafting of the classroom experience and persuasive argument, inveigle the sceptical but open-minded student to her political agenda. There is a curious sleight of hand here. On the one hand the audience is accorded political knowledge, or at least sufficient political understanding to be hostile (that is, it is accorded agency); on the other, the audience is positioned within a liberal educational discourse that subscribes to an empty vessel and rationalist model of the subject.

It is sadly all too frequent that men, and women, fed by the mass media, talk of feminism as a movement that is no longer relevant; saying that feminism has achieved its goals; that discrimination on the basis of gender is not an issue any more; and that (in more sophisticated forms) anyway surely 'race' and class are just as important, and as important in constructing 'race'- and class-specific forms of gendered experience. I think that precisely because of feminism's proclaimed irrelevance and continuing bad press (as in the yawn-generating stereotype of the hairy, dungaree-sporting lesbian) it is important that those who would position themselves as feminist teachers (in the broadest sense; after all, all the world's a classroom) own up to their political agendas. To do otherwise is to collude in their/our own ghettoization and marginalization. Moreover, the 'acceptable', 'reasonable' (or for that matter appropriately passionate and angry) critiques become precisely those that do not emanate from the mouths of so-called 'feminists', and so the cycle repeats itself, including the maintenance of the male-centred criteria for reason and logic.

Feminist psychology

This has now arisen as an intervention within what is otherwise non- or anti-feminist psychology. Moreover, the epithet of feminist psychology, or even feminist psychologists, has arisen as a successor to and comment upon the limits of work within the psychology of women, which seemingly could be done equivalently well by men or women, according to the British Psychological Society rules of membership of the section of that name. (This is not to question that many men do good work in this area, but that the institutional structures of representations would not countenance women organizing *as women*, but only in the name of a 'scientific' area of study.) Here we run directly into dynamics of institutionalization that attend any theory-building (or politics masquerading as theory) enterprise in academia, especially psychology, with the corresponding dangers of de-radicalization, containment of critique and (re)construction of a new orthodoxy (see Burman 1998c).

A further consequence of the elaboration of the domain of 'feminist' psychology is that it sets up precisely the separations between theory/politics and theory/practice that it aims to repair. Feminist psychology may be an excuse, or a space, to bring feminist debates into psychology, but it inevitably enacts its own demarcations, in this case between feminism(s) and feminist psychology. This occurs in part through having to subscribe to the 'normal' academic activities of the ownership/authorship and promotion of ideas.

In this sense feminist psychology looks like a restorative impulse that threatens to become as coercive and singular in its vision as the psychology it set out to critique/supplant. The answer would seem to be that feminists in/around psychology should avoid participating in such an enterprise. Or is it? Could this account for the relative silence around feminist work within social constructionism? A double bind seems to be operating here: on the one hand to talk gender ushers in a liberal discourse that makes women/feminists responsible for their own oppression within oppressive institutions (including psychology); on the other, not talking gender colludes in the institutional failure to acknowledge just how much critical movements in psychology owe to feminist work.

Who talks for whom?

Once such a disciplinary division between inside and outside is made, an abstraction of privilege of the authors' own perspectives takes place that in turn generates a corresponding need to engage in sometimes bizarre and complex contortions to claim deference to 'other' points of view. Having woken up to their own privilege, feminist academics now compulsively try to get those with whom we/they research who have lesser power (but of course only relatively) to tell us whether that is OK. The current concern in women's studies, echoed in feminist psychology with the politics and ethics of 'representing others' (see Opie 1992; Reay 1996; Wilkinson and Kitzinger 1996), can be viewed as an awakening to the fact not only that feminists – like women – are not unitary, but that feminist academics are increasingly privileged in relation to other women (and many men).[3]

The much vaunted move in post-structuralist thinking from time to space, from history to geography, is not only from depth to surface, but also from explicit hierarchy to diverse networks and distributions of power. What comes after the recognition that practices of representation are not transparent? Moreover, are such representational activities political or pictorial (or both)? Are we claiming to speak on behalf of others, or are we resignifying or translating into another medium configurations whose forms and relationships remain in some sense parallel to their 'other' site of enunciation? The problem for feminist and critical psychologists is that the projects are inextricably linked, because we are both inside and outside. Hence these representational surfaces are curved rather than flat, and not discussing ambiguities and complexities of their contours can produce practices of power that are the more terrorizing for being implicit.

Specificities and strategies in identifications and recognition

Throughout this chapter I have discussed the convergence of market pressures and psychologization within the reification of radical and critical currents within psychology, in which I would include social constructionism. In particular I have focused on dilemmas, strategies and trajectories of feminist interventions in psychology, since I would see feminist work as a key contributor to, and exponent of, critical and social constructionist work in psychology. While feminist work is not unique in its political and interpretive resources (perhaps especially in psychology), the fact that it is derivative (as is pretty well all of psychology) is not a reason for failing to acknowledge the energy, creativity and commitment that characterizes this body of work.

It is certainly the case that feminists do not occupy a distinct position within the schools of social constructionism or discourse work. We need to consider why this might be, what this indicates about the discipline, and what aspects of the discipline social constructionism in psychology is thereby reproducing.

While feminism is clearly not immune from transformation into a consumer item, feminist psychologists notably do not fit into the available categories and affiliations currently available within social constructionist/ postmodernist currents in (and out of) psychology. Yet the drive to categorize seems irresistible. I have read draft theses written by (feminist) research students (including ones I have supervised) who, in feeling obliged to offer some account of the social history of the currents in social constructionism and discourse work that inform their research, have produced a representation that wrote out all women, including feminists working around the area of discourse,[4] or else assimilated them into male-led 'schools' or movements.[5] These (repeated) experiences have led me to wonder what covert institutional discourses are being articulated by these students. While I would certainly not want to make claims of conspiracies (and not only because a postmodernist position would disallow such a fundamentalist intentionalist account), such phenomena demand interrogation and reflection.

Reiterated within social constructionism, then, is the past and continuing failure to acknowledge the contribution of feminists to the debates around the need for, and the limits of, constructionist accounts. This in itself would seem to speak to the need both for retaining feminist psychology as a separate space and for demanding recognition of feminist work in supporting other critical initiatives in or in relation to psychology. Thus, my focus on feminist work here is performative as well as instructional. I want to see feminist work acknowledged as a vital resource and component of critical currents in psychology.

I want to end by suggesting that there may be important institutional reasons why feminist work remains relatively peripheral within social constructionist work, as with most psychology. The fact that this is a general feature of women's treatment by the discipline is no excuse for those claiming to be its critics to maintain this. Nor am I suggesting that the answer is only to acknowledge and incorporate this work, for I am not sure that this is entirely possible (although some efforts towards acknowledgement would be a good thing).

The periphery is not a place to romanticize, but it does offer some important vantage points. The lesson may be that this work is important precisely because it does not lend itself to commodification and assimilation into any specific current or area of psychology. This could be regarded as a strategy of inscrutability that preserves the knowledge and networks of a subordinate group from being exposed to and thereby rendered docile by the discipline (Parpart 1995). At any rate it speaks to allegiances outside the discipline that maintain the capacity for critique, but also ensure that the discipline does not define its intellectual–political horizons – a problem to which, as I have discussed here, projects such as 'psychology of women' and 'feminist psychology', as with social constructionism and 'critical psychology', are always vulnerable. My final 'point', therefore, is that feminist work offers an example of a critical current in psychology struggling to resist disciplinary dynamics of incorporation, which merits the attention, if not emulation, of social constructionists.

Notes

1 The move of some into 'clinical' work is currently exercising other critical psychologists.
2 Here I am reluctant to subscribe to the opposition between dark and light forms of social constructionism identified by Danziger (1997) and discussed elsewhere in this book (Chapters 1 and 5). However useful the broad distinctions made may be, the terminology of light and dark constructionism carries inflections of Enlightenment discourse, which itself is inscribed by histories of racism and colonialism that are always evoked by discourses of vision and colour.
3 I reserve the term academic feminist for those women whose feminist politics were generated by and are confined to academic sites of struggle.
4 It would seem invidious to name such women, for I am, by the terms of my own argument, likely to 'miss out' important figures, and in any case can really only comment from the British scene, but as indicative examples I am thinking here of women such as Ros Gill, Chris Griffin, Karen Henwood, Wendy Hollway, Celia Kitzinger, Ann Phoenix, Corinne Squire and Sue Wilkinson.
5 Thus Margaret Wetherell and I get a look in because we have co-written or co-edited with men.

References

Amos, V. and Parmar, P. (1984) Challenging imperial feminism, *Feminist Review*, 17: 3–19.

Armistead, N. (ed.) (1974) *Reconstructing Social Psychology*. Harmondsworth: Penguin.

Brah, A. (1996) *Cartographies of Diaspora: Contesting Identities*. London: Routledge.

Bondi, L. (1993) Locating identity politics, in M. Keith and S. Pile (eds) *Place and the Politics of Identity*. London: Routledge.

Brodribb, S. (1992) *Nothing Mat(t)ers: A Feminist Critique of Postmodernism*. Melbourne: Spinifex.

Brooks, A. (ed.) (1997) *Postfeminisms: Feminism, Cultural Theory and Cultural Forms*. London: Routledge.

Burman, E. (1997) Minding the gap: positivism, psychology and the politics of qualitative methods, *Journal of Social Issues*, 53(4): 785–802.

Burman, E. (1998a) Deconstructing feminist psychology, in E. Burman (ed.) *Deconstructing Feminist Psychology*. London: Sage.

Burman, E. (1998b) Disciplinary apprentices: 'qualitative methods' in student psychological research, *International Journal of Social Research Methodology*, 1(1): 25–45.

Burman, E. (ed.) (1998c) *Deconstructing Feminist Psychology*. London: Sage.

Carby, H. (1987) Black feminism and the boundaries of sisterhood, in M. Arnot and G. Weiner (eds) *Gender and the Politics of Schooling*. Basingstoke: Hutchinson.

Carrigan, T., Connell, B. and Lee, J. (1987) The sex role framework and the sociology of masculinity, in G. Weinder and M. Arnot (eds) *Gender Under Scrutiny*. Basingstoke: Hutchinson.

Crawford, M. (1998) The reciprocity of psychology and popular culture, in E. Burman (ed.) *Deconstructing Feminist Psychology*. London: Sage.

Crawford, M. and Kimmell, E. (eds) (1999) *Psychology of Women Quarterly* (special issues on innovative methods in feminist research).

Curt, B. (1994) *Textuality and Tectonics*. Buckingham: Open University Press.

Danziger, K. (1997) Review essay: the varieties of social construction, *Theory and Psychology*, 7(3): 399–416.

Elam, D. (1994) *Feminism and Deconstruction: Ms en Abyme*. London: Routledge.

Evans, M. (1990) The problem of gender for women's studies, *Women's Studies International Forum*, 13(5): 457–63.

Fraser, N. (1992) The uses and abuses of French discourse theories for feminist politics, *Theory, Culture and Society*, 9: 51–71.

Gill, R. (1995) Relativism, reflexivity and politics: interrogating discourse analysis from a feminist perspective, in S. Wilkinson and C. Kitzinger (eds) *Feminism and Discourse*. London: Sage.

Gillham, B. (ed.) (1978) *Reconstructing Educational Psychology*. London: Macmillan.

Gordo-Lopez, A. and Aitken, G. (in press) *Queer Andtherness*. London: Cambridge University Press.

Haraway, D. (1991) Situated knowledges: feminist epistemology and the privilege of partial perspective, in *Simians, Cyborgs and Women*. London: Verso.

Harding, S. (ed.) (1987) *Feminism and Methodology*: Milton Keynes: Open University Press.

Harding, S. (1993) Rethinking feminist standpoint epistemology: what is strong objectivity?, in L. Alcott and E. Potter (eds) *Feminist Epistemologies*. London: Routledge.

Henriques, J., Hollway, W., Urwin, C., Venn, C. and Walkerdine, V. (1984) *Changing the Subject: Psychology, Social Regulation and Subjectivity*. London: Methuen.

Henwood, K., Griffin, C. and Phoenix, A. (eds) (1998) *Standpoints and Differences: Essays in the Practice of Feminist Psychology*. London: Sage.

Hollway, W. (1989) *Subjectivity and Method in Psychology*. London: Sage.

Jackson, S. (1992) The amazing deconstructing woman, *Trouble and Strife*, 25: 25–31.

Kitzinger, C. (1992) The individuated self concept: a critical analysis of social-constructionist writing on individualism, in G. Breakwell (ed.) *The Social Psychology of Identity and the Self Concept*. London: Academic Press and Surrey University Press.

Kitzinger, C. (1998) The token lesbian chapter, in S. Wilkinson (ed.) *Feminist Social Psychologies*. Buckingham: Open University Press.

Kremer, M. (1990) On saying no: keeping feminism for ourselves, *Women's Studies International Forum*, 13(5): 463–8.

Lovibund, S. (1989) Feminism and postmodernism, *New Left Review*, 78: 5–28.

Lyotard, J. (1992) *The Postmodern Condition: A Report on Knowledge*. Manchester: Manchester University Press.

McClintock, A. (1995) *Imperial Leather: Race, Gender and Sexuality in the Colonial Contest*. London: Routledge.

Nicholson, L. and Seidman, S. (eds) (1995) *Social Postmodernism: Beyond Identity Politics*. Cambridge: Cambridge University Press.

Opie, A. (1992) Qualitative research: appropriation of the 'Other' and empowerment, *Feminist Review*, 40: 52–69.

Parker, I. and Shotter, J. (eds) (1990) *Deconstructing Social Psychology*. London: Routledge.

Parpart, J. (1995) Deconstructing the development 'Expert': gender, development and the 'Vulnerable Groups', in H. Marchand and J. Parpart (eds) *Feminism/Postmodernism/Development*. London: Routledge.

Reay, D. (1996) Insider perspectives or stealing the words out of women's mouths: interpretation in the research process, *Feminist Review*, 53: 57–73.

Reason, P. and Rowan, J. (eds) (1981) *Human Inquiry: A Sourcebook of New Paradigm Research*. Chichester: Wiley.

Smart, C. and Sevenhuijsen, S. (eds) (1989) *Child Custody and the Politics of Gender*. London: Routledge.

Soper, K. (1991) Posmodernism and its discontents, *Feminist Review*, 37: 1–22.

Squire, C. (1989) *Significant Differences: Feminisms in Psychology*. London: Routledge.

Unger, R. (1998) *Resisting Gender*. London: Sage.

Ware, V. (1992) *Beyond the Pale: White Women, Racism and History*. London: Verso.

Wilkinson, S. and Burns, J. (1990) Women organising in psychology, in E. Burman (ed.) *Feminists and Psychological Practice*. London: Sage.

Wilkinson, S. (1997) Still seeking transformation: feminist challenges to psychology, in L. Stanley (ed.) *Knowing Feminisms*. London: Sage.

Wilkinson, S. (1998) Feminist social psychologies: a decade of development, in S. Wilkinson (ed.) *Feminist Social Psychologies*. Buckingham: Open University Press.

Wilkinson, S. and Burns, J. (1990) Women organising within psychology, in E. Burman (ed.) *Feminists and Psychological Practice*. London: Sage.

Wilkinson, S. and Kitzinger, C. (eds) (1996) *Representing the Other: A Feminism and Psychology Reader*. London: Sage.

Yuval-Davis, N. (1993) Beyond difference: women and coalition politics, in M. Kennedy, C. Lubelska and V. Walsh (eds) *Making Connections: Women's Studies, Women's Movements, Women's Lives*. London: Taylor and Francis.

Yuval-Davis, N. (1997) *Gender and Nation*. London: Routledge.

12 Social constructionism: implications for psychotherapeutic practice

CHRISTINE KENWOOD[1]

The emergence of social constructionism in the recent history of psychology presents practitioners with a significant alternative to traditional mechanistic and individualistic modes of thought. While the numbers of psychologists who identify with the social constructionist programme are increasing and the critique of mainstream psychology in areas such as cognition, teaching and personality is proceeding apace, the bulk of that psychology remains unaffected. Traditional psychologists, it seems, have constructed for themselves – that is, socially constructed – a fairly impenetrable fortress. However, if the proliferation of books, articles and practitioners is a good indicator, then it is in the area of psychotherapy that social constructionists appear to have had the greatest influence.

Granting the benefits and improvements provided by social constructionist-oriented therapies (some of which are outlined below) over the traditional biomedical approach, it seems that there may be little to criticize in either social constructionism or the therapeutic strategies it has nurtured. Even among sympathizers, however, serious concerns have been expressed about still unresolved problems in social constructionist theories. For example, Terwee (1995: 188–94) argues that social constructionism leads to relativistic consequences and that has failed in its attempt to escape empiricist traditions despite claims to having done so. Bhaskar (1979: 117–20) has expressed concerns with social constructionist characterizations of the relationship between the individual and society and Parrott (1992: 217) notes that social constructionism's claims to there being 'vagueness and mystery at the heart of our epistemological and moral worlds' and uncertainty about reality should suggest doubts about the theory itself.

It is important to ascertain whether social constructionist-influenced therapies may have incorporated some of social constructionism's unresolved problems along with its strengths. The intention here is twofold. Some of the considerable benefits of social constructionism and therapies influenced by this theory are outlined but, as well, some of the problems incurred in present versions of social constructionism are confronted. Particular attention is paid to how these problems may affect therapeutic practice.

Achievements of social constructionism

It has been a significant achievement of social constructionism to have criticized mainstream psychological approaches regarding the treatment of so-called 'mental illnesses' and to have described a viable alternative. Gergen (1990: 353; 1991: 13–16) has shown that traditional approaches are highly problematic in the way in which they tend actually to create and perpetuate the very 'illnesses' that they were devised to alleviate.

The biomedical approach to mental illness, among other things, fits out every 'patient' with a diagnosis. The diagnosis locates the source of the problem firmly inside the person, or, more specifically, inside the person's head. One important consequence is that the 'patient' becomes steeped in the destructive 'totalizing' and 'pathologizing' jargon that accompanies each diagnostic label. That is, the diagnosis brands people with mental deficits that come to characterize the essential nature of the person. The deficits associated with the diagnosis are not limited to a certain time or space (Gergen 1990: 359–60) but are seen to permeate the person's life so totally that past and present functioning as well as the future prognosis become saturated by the pathology.

Social constructionists criticize the assumption underlying the biomedical model that insists that since some problems are related to organic causes then all problems must be. As Gergen (1990: 363) has pointed out, the problematizing of behaviour has become ubiquitous, having spread outside of psychology into the broader world. He notes, for example, that what was once valued as 'active ambition' can now be reconstructed as 'workaholic', and he comments wryly that when therapists 'furnish the population with hammers of mental deficit . . . the whole world needs pounding' (*ibid.*).

What is the social constructionist alternative to the traditional approaches to 'mental illness'? Constructionist therapists maintain that most problems do not originate in an individual's brain (as in the traditional view of organic disorders), nor are they mere manifestations of any other kind of semi-permanent environmentally instigated modification of the organism (such as in the traditional view of functional disorders). Social constructionists seek the location of the problem elsewhere. They shift the locus of the problem from the space between the ears to the social space between people, a space in which the relations are mediated by language and dialogue.

It is crucial to establish that the source of the problem is correctly located, since the proposed solutions are radically different depending on the location of the problem. There would be something very wrong-headed, for example, in a doctor prescribing a lifetime of painkillers and antibiotics to treat a person who stood on a rusty nail. Obviously, removing the rusty nail altogether is preferable to living with lifelong drug therapy and the nail left embedded in one's foot.

Following a similar line of reasoning, social constructionist-oriented therapists would, for instance, in the case of depression, want to treat the 'interpersonal and social processes and dynamics that maintain the symptoms' (Fruggeri 1992: 48) rather than treating only the biological changes. The depressed symptoms, like pain and infection, are undeniable indicators that a problem exists; however, merely to assuage them at the biological level, without an attempt to address the actual external problem, is, social constructionists feel, fundamentally wrong. It is wrong because, as Gergen (1991: 158–9) explains, people's problems are 'only the by-products of troubled relations with others', and it is not people who are 'sick' but the social networks in which they participate.

Anderson and Goolishian (1992: 31) explain how the social space between people can be addressed:

> People live in and through the ever-changing narrative identities that they develop in conversation with one another. Individuals derive their sense of social agency for action from these dialogically derived narratives. Narratives permit (or inhibit) a personal perception of freedom or competency to make sense and to act (agency). The 'problems' dealt with in therapy can be thought of as emanating from social narratives and self-definitions that do not yield an agency that is effective for the tasks implicit in their self-narratives. Therapy provides opportunity for the development of new and different narratives that permit an expanded range of alternative agency for 'problem' dis-solution.

The shift in the location of the problem from inside the individual's head to the space of social relations and narratives reflects an important difference in beliefs about the nature of reality between social constructionists and mainstream psychologists. Mainstream psychologists, along with other natural scientists, share a conviction that the truth, once found, will correctly reflect objective reality and that the discovered knowledge will be universally true for all people. Alternately, as Shotter (1992: 202) explains, 'Social constructionists, rather than assuming that reality has an as yet undiscovered order, recognize that, as a matter of present, contingent fact, none of the social or mental forms of which we currently speak has an objective nature.'

Gergen (1988: 31–40) points out that the problem with objective reality is a problem of interpretation. To illustrate what he feels to be interpretive difficulties, he often resorts to a story about his friends Ross and Laura. Gergen notes that when Ross reaches out and touches Laura's hair, neither the observers of this event nor Ross himself know the true meaning of the action. Subsequently, he leads the reader through several 'contextual indicators' (e.g. Ross madly loves Laura, Ross is trying change Laura's perception that he is cold and unaffectionate) that Gergen feels are, in the end, unhelpful. They are unhelpful because, while each is supposedly a version of the truth about why Ross touched Laura's hair, the 'interpretation of any given action is subject to infinite revision' (Gergen 1988: 33). Gergen concludes that 'we find ourselves with no viable account of validity in interpretation' (Gergen 1988: 39), as each new piece of information disproves the validity of the last piece, and he sees no end to the process.

For social constructionists, the wholesale rejection of truth has a yet further implication. They argue that, since it is impossible to know what is actually true, it is reasonable and necessary to respect all points of view equally. The therapists Epston et al. (1992: 96) explain that without direct knowledge of the world, 'no one has a privileged access to the naming of reality, whatever that reality is'.

A clear example of constructionist therapists' adherence to the policy of respecting all points of view comes from within their own practice. Anderson and Goolishian (1992: 25–39) explain that the strategy of employing a not-knowing stance for themselves and treating the client as expert overcomes the enfeebling consequences of the traditional biomedical approach to psychotherapy by acknowledging the client's superior understanding of his or her own problem. Further, Anderson and Goolishian (1992: 28–9) explain that the not-knowing stance requires a suspension of previously held theories and interpretations. The therapist's task is to be genuinely curious and to be in the state of 'being informed' by the client. Further, the therapist, instead of being the expert about mental diseases, becomes 'an architect of the dialogical process – whose expertise is in the arena of creating a space for and facilitating a dialogical conversation. The therapist is a participant-observer and a participant facilitator of the therapeutic conversation' (Anderson and Goolishian 1992: 27). However, while social constructionism has provided an important critique of mainstream biomedical approaches, it is not without its problems.

Problems of social constructionism

Reduction of the social

Although social constructionists must be applauded for the insight that many problems are social rather than biological in origin – that is, that problems may be mislocated at the biological level – it is not beyond possibility that social constructionists themselves are also mislocating problems and unknowingly creating difficulties for the people they purportedly help.

Of course, no social constructionist denies the existence of true organic problems and diseases (e.g. epilepsy, Alzheimer's). It would be ludicrous not to acknowledge the existence of organic diseases that require 'treatment' at both the biological and the social levels, e.g. HIV/AIDS, which is a viral disease, though both its origin and its stigma may be social. It is not in or between the biological and the social levels that any social constructionists are in danger of mislocating problems.

Mislocation is more likely to occur from lack of clarity about the term 'social'. In fact, social constructionists are not always clear about this term. For example, as Danziger (1997: 410–11) points out:

> All varieties of social constructionism will see knowledge and understanding as existing within social relationships. But they do not all construct these social relationships in the same way. At one extreme are those versions which privilege macro-social structures in a way that is strongly reminiscent of the sociology of knowledge. At the other extreme are the versions which focus on the micro-social level, either concretely, by privileging everyday talk, or metaphorically, by treating all social life as a 'conversation'.

As noted earlier, it is crucial to establish the correct location of a problem, as concomitant solutions may be radically different. Those social constructionists who, with Harré (1992: 67–8), believe that society 'is not anything, not even a kind of abstract thing' and that 'it is the orchestration of individual speakings and doings', locate all social problems at the micro-social or interpersonal level. People who focus on narrative too narrowly are then mislocating those problems that are in fact societal in nature. In this way they run the risk of contributing to the difficulties of the people they are intending to help.

Consider an instance in which reauthoring therapy is successful. Epston *et al.* (1992: 97–115) relate that a woman, Rose, came to therapy because she had lost several catering jobs despite the fact that it was clear that she had talent. Her narrative included her sense of not having 'a base' inside herself and a history of physical abuse from a domineering father. In therapy, Rose and her therapist, David White, 'reauthored' Rose's life by, among other things, acknowledging that her father was indeed grossly unfair and that her distress was reasonable reaction. Further, they focused on Rose's strengths as were demonstrated in such acts as speaking out against her father's abuse and having the courage to come to therapy. As a result of therapy Rose became successful in her work and re-established contact with several members of her family from whom she had become estranged.

It is obvious that Rose's problems were not a result of brain malfunction or other organic disorder. The problem appears rather to have stemmed from distortions in past interpersonal encounters and was successfully addressed at that level. It is equally obvious, however, that Rose was, from the point of view of available therapeutic resources, very fortunate that her problem was interpersonal and solvable at that level. Most cases of unemployment do not stem from interpersonal problems but from societal problems that are unsolvable by individuals alone or in concert with therapists. High unemployment rates reflect a societal problem that forms a real barrier for many to individual life-fulfilment and a sense of well-being. The consequences of unemployment are undeniably felt interpersonally between individuals and their family and friends. If there are few or no jobs available, coupled with growing numbers of unemployed people, then the problem cannot be located or solved interpersonally but only in societal relations in which people are just as embedded as in interpersonal ones.

The 'development of new and different narratives that permit an expanded range of alternative agency for "problem" dis-solution' (Anderson and Goolishian 1992: 31) could not be a solution to a societal problem because the problem exists outside narrative in the real limitations on employment resulting from distortions in the relations of production. The problem of societal unemployment is external to the person and beyond the scope of individuals or their therapists to solve.

To mislocate a problem at the interpersonal level when in reality the problem is located at the societal level is to attribute power over a problem to an individual where there is none. To the extent that people believe that they have power over a problem they will try to exert that power. Since it is impossible for individuals to solve problems over which they have no control, at least on their own, they will fail and the fault, they will mistakenly believe, will be their own. Further, if people are convinced that the problem is in fact interpersonal, they will be discouraged from seeking a solution at the societal level.

There is no intention here to argue that societal problems are insurmountable. Their solution, however, requires a broader perspective than the interpersonal and merely discursive. Tolman (1995: 168), among others, claims that the 'helplessness of individuals is overcome . . . by the realization of their societal natures.'

We need to inquire further just what is meant by 'societal nature.' It is crucially important to remember that what is uniquely human is inextricably bound up with other human beings. Human beings are not dependent on each other just for company; they are, as well, interdependent for their very existences as humans. Even when people are alone or when people are not speaking with one another, or even if they don't know each other, human beings are interdependent. Through language, people share a system of meanings that informs their own and other's activities, which allows our activities and theirs to be intelligible. And without intelligibility, our existences would be merely organic and hardly human.

Human existence is possible because we interact with each other interpersonally. However, interpersonal interactions themselves are not sufficient to explain uniquely human behaviour, of which interdependence is the hallmark. The foundation of human interdependence is a shared system of meanings from which people draw their reasons and justifications for their actions. Meaning arises not out of simply being together, telling stories or relating to one another, but out of acting together for common purposes. It arises out of the very actions that ultimately comprise the societal arrangements that, when distorted, produce phenomena like unemployment. According to Tolman (1995: 105), meaning:

> creates for us an epistemic distance from the world. This means that our actions with respect to it are consequently mediated by meaningful reflection. We do not act with respect to the objects of our world – whether they are actual things, complex situations, values, ideas, or ourselves – reflexively or out of some other form of natural necessity. While for society there are necessities for action, these have an 'on average' character, and thus present themselves to us not as necessities but as possibilities for action.

Having an 'on average' character means that our activities, rather than being dictated by necessity, e.g. as gravity dictates that dropped objects fall to the ground, are better described as exercising rule-governed possibilities for action.

The questions of societal change are complex. They involve both alteration of the societal relations themselves and the relocation of persons within them. The relations themselves are only changed by individuals working concertedly and collectively towards ends that are plainly political in nature. Vertical relocation is obviously easier downward, from advantaged to disadvantaged positions, than the other way around. Horizontal relocations depend on many factors. It is clearly beyond the scope of this chapter to deal with the complexities of changes of and in societal relations. It is sufficient for present purposes simply to have made clear that such change is not accomplished by rhetorical means: by reauthoring or renarrating the individual's life. We are dealing here with constructions that have enormous impact on individual existences but that are well beyond discursive reconstruction in interpersonal relations or dialogue. These relations – that is, societal relations – and their modes of construction may be obscured by the social constructionists' reduction of the social to interpersonal and dialogical relations. And such reduction cannot, in the long run, serve the interests of clients in therapy.[2]

Cognitive and moral relativism

Humans are adept at participating in society, a task that would be impossible without some understanding of and confidence in the truth of key shared propositions about the world in which we live. Social constructionism's relativism and its openly implied rejection of the possibility of knowing objective reality and denial of even the possibility of truth are deeply problematic. In adopting this stance, social constructionists are crippling people's ability to judge the consequences of their actions and the actions of others, which, as we have seen, are crucially important to human interdependence.

Relativism only seems liberating. Any theory that suggests that all points of view can be respected equally appears desirable, but on closer scrutiny it becomes obvious that such a position is neither possible not desirable. Treating every point of view as valid seems liberating, in that it elevates unjustly denigrated points of view to positions of respect. However, it also has the undesirable consequence of elevating points of view that oppress us to the same level. For example, sexist or racist points of view would be as respected and valued as those points of view endorsing equality.

Further, relativism is undesirable because it contradicts the critical function that social constructionists also claim for themselves and that they succeed so well in accomplishing. As outlined above, social constructionists have explained that biomedical model practitioners may harm the very people they intend to help. Further, constructionist therapists often work with people who have suffered under the oppression of colonialist discourses (e.g. McKenzie 1997). They note that colonialism may have resulted in prosperity for some but they also note that it was (and still is) responsible for the infliction of serious crimes against others, often, with high irony, under the guise of 'helping' them.

It is in the face of these cogently and clearly argued explanations of the real contradictions inherent in the use of some 'helping' discourses and the real consequences for people suffering under the oppression of those discourses that social constructionism's relativism is most baffling. What teeth can the social constructionist critiques of traditional psychology, colonialist discourses and the biomedical model have if they also maintain that all points of view are equally valid and that it is impossible to choose between them? Further, if all points of view are equally valid, what was there to criticize in the first place?

If social constructionists are to continue to do what they do so well they cannot adhere to the relativism that they lay claim to, and with regard to therapists the same seems to be the case. As above, if all points of view are valid so is, contradictorily, the oppressive point of view of Rose's father, Rose's problematic view of herself before therapy and her re-authored view.

Further problems exist for therapeutic practice as well. The success of constructionist therapy, for instance, seems to rely on the client's conviction in the veracity, not the relativity, of the reconstructed version. When clients come to therapy they are (partially) convinced in the veracity of some problem. Through therapy a new, positive narrative is constructed. Therapy is effective not because clients come to understand the socially constructed nature of the world but because they are convinced that the reconstructed version is objectively true and that the previous, problematic version is not.

If a point of view is considered to be valid then the actions that follow from the viewpoint must also be valid. People often put their 'money where their mouth is' by acting on their points of view, but when they do so it becomes impossible to respect every point of view without seriously harming other people. A logical difficulty also arises, in that contradictory points of view would have to be considered equally valid. For example, it is not possible to respect the point of view of a racist who endorses and acts upon beliefs that, at the very least, are logically opposite to the points of view of the members of the target group and are intended to inflict serious and lasting harm on those people. Since people in society are interdependent it is, for example, impossible to respect a point of view that denies productive employment to a category of people while simultaneously pretending to enforce equality in hiring practices. It is necessary to adjudicate between points of view because, in an interdependent world, what people say and do has real consequences for themselves and others.

If relativism and treating all points of view equally are impossible, what stance is left? A still stronger sceptical position is surely not warranted: that is, one that would doubt not only the possibility of knowing the truth about external reality but also whether there is an external reality to be known. No one, surely, is quarrelling with the very existence of external reality. Gergen does not wish to suggest that no one can really be sure that Ross touched Laura's hair. We can all agree that Ross did touch Laura's hair and we can be certain that he was not off somewhere else playing golf at the time; nor was he painting Laura's toenails or anything else. The social constructionist stance is summarized by the therapists Drewery and Winslade (1997: 35), who 'do not argue that reality does not exist – only that we cannot know it directly'.

If, however, relativism is an untenable position, is there any acceptable option? Social constructionists often express views suggesting that they believe there are only two alternatives – relativism or correspondence theory – but there is a problem here. Social constructionists tend to portray correspondence theory only in its most naive and vulnerable form. In what follows, it will be shown that many reservations against correspondence theory are mistaken.[3]

Searle (1995: 175) points out that the problem arises in the mistaken expectation that truth and reality should coincide. That is, the expectation that the definition of a 'truthful' representation is that it should be a mirror of reality is incorrect. When no identical match is found between reality and representation, Searle notes that there is a temptation to believe that 'our naive notions of truth and reality have been discredited' but, he reminds us, they have not been discredited.

In explaining why truth cannot be defined as the mirror of reality, Searle writes:

> All representation, and a fortiori all truthful representation, is always under certain aspects and not others. The aspectual character of all representations derives from such facts as that representation is always always made from within a certain conceptual scheme and from a certain point of view . . . In short, it is only from a point of view that we represent reality, but ontologically objective reality does not have a point of view.
>
> (Searle 1995: 175–6)

This may seem to support the sort of relativism that leads social constructionists to endorse the position that all points of view must be treated as being equally valid. Yet there is an important difference between the 'aspectual' relativism endorsed by Searle and the relativism endorsed by social constructionists. Searle (1995: 191) writes that circularity or infinite regress is avoided because the veracity of any point of view can be checked against external reality.

For social reality, however, it is not simply a matter of checking whether 'the cat is on the mat' when someone insists that it is. For social reality, for those matters such as trust, justice, promises, as well as for discussions about the truth of past events, it may seem that there is no external reality to check: that is, no tangible 'hard' evidence. However, even though social reality is socially constructed by people through language and even though past events are irretrievable, it is not the case that 'anything goes'. People are interdependent beings whose points of view are put into action in our daily activities, and the real effects of those actions upon people and the world are the 'hard' evidence or the criteria against which we check the veracity of our points of view. If the matter under discussion is a past event and, therefore, not present to be checked, it does not mean that it is impossible to represent the event truly but only that, if it boils down to one person's word against another's, for instance, one person is not stating the truth. A person could not have been both fast asleep in bed and committing a murder. Only one version of the event is true.

Presumably, this type of correspondence test is what social constructionists carried out when they checked whether or not the biomedical approach to mental illness was as helpful for people as it professed to be. When social constructionists found that people were actually harmed rather than helped they concluded that there was a disjunction between the 'helping' narratives found in the biomedical approach and the real effects on people that occurred when those narratives were put into action.

With respect to understanding human action it is crucial to remember that the human world is characterized by an epistemic distance between subject and object (Tolman 1994: 105): that is, people share a view of the world that is mediated by the meanings in language. In understanding the behaviour of Gergen's friends Ross and Laura, this means that we can be certain that Ross meant something when he touched Laura's hair. We can be certain of that because human actions are never meaningless. Moreover, the range of possible meanings is quickly reduced by reflection on the context of practice in which the gesture was made. When this is not sufficiently conclusive, it is always possible to ask Ross what he meant by his gesture. Of course he may claim not to know or he may lie, but that does not signify that his gesture had no meaning, only that it will remain obscure to us. It is in the nature of human experience that there are many objective truths of which we have only partial knowledge. Why should those of us who deny absolutism in truth now insist upon it?

Simon (1982: 8) explains that actions 'are not things that happen to people; they are things that people do': that is, actions are to be distinguished from involuntary movements such as heart beats, tics and reflexive activities in that actions are voluntarily done, by people, for reasons that are to be found in our society's shared meanings. We can make sense of them precisely because of our interdependence: that is, because we share these meanings with others in our society.

The 'truth' about the Ross and Laura scenario seems impossible to find because the model of truth that Gergen is trying to adhere to is the one that social constructionists have, supposedly, rejected, namely naive correspondence theory. That is, social constructionists were to have abandoned the pursuit of a scientifically exact causal explanation in favour of looking at how we actually treat each other (Shotter 1989: 64). The Ross and Laura scenario is set up as a fundamentally unnatural, unhuman task: that is, no one ever tries to or needs to understand with scientific precision the causes of the behaviour of others.

There is truth to be found in any human action. However, as Searle points out, 'representation is always made from within a certain conceptual scheme and from a certain point of view.' Gergen is mistaken when he writes that there is 'no viable account of validity in interpretation' (Gergen 1988: 39), and he is suffering from the mistaken expectation that truth and reality should coincide (Searle 1995: 175). It is simply not the case that there is 'no viable account of validity in interpretation'. With respect to Ross and Laura, we are limited in what truth we can know about them. We, to use Searle's term, are deprived of a real 'aspect' from which we are trying to understand Ross's action. We do, however, know that it is true that he did touch Laura's hair and that he did so for a reason. To be able to judge the veracity of further claims about why Ross touched Laura's hair we need to know the veracity of the 'contextual indicators', despite Gergen's insistence that these indicators are useless. The indicators are not useless because their veracity is testable in the real world but, since this is a scenario that is deliberately constructed to be unlike any real human situation, there is no possibility of testing these indicators. Further, the readers are deprived of an 'aspect' (to use Searle's term) under which we are judging the action.

What are the implications for social constructionist therapies? First, social constructionist therapists must acknowledge that not all problems exist in the micro-social or interpersonal space between people. Some problems, it must be recognized, exist at the societal level of human activity and must be solved there. Second, relativism is as problematic for therapists as it is for theorists. It is logically inconsistent, impossible and undesirable that the points of view of the people with whom they work should be considered equally valid to the points of view of those who are causing them difficulty.

It must be noted, however, that there is no real evidence that social constructionists, including those engaged in therapy, ever in fact act in accordance with their relativist points of view, despite their persistent and vocal endorsements of this position. In fact, the writing of both social constructionists and therapists is often compelling and deeply moving just because of the strong stance taken in favour of one point of view against another.

Without the understanding of the 'aspectual character of truth' it would be impossible for social constructionists to make good their claim to be about the business of making psychology a moral rather than a natural science (e.g. Shotter 1989: 64). The endorsement of the 'full-scale abandonment of the concept of objective truth' (Gergen, above) would preclude the possibility of any moral striving because morality requires adjudicating between alternatives and deciding which alternative is 'really' better than the others. In explaining human behaviour it is necessary to understand the nature of socially constructed truth and to have confidence in it because, since human beings are interdependent societal beings, our beliefs and our activities (that are informed by our beliefs) have real consequences for ourselves and others.

Notes

1 The author acknowledges with gratitude the substantial contributions to this chapter in the way of comments and suggestions by Charles Tolman.

2 The argument here is simply that there is good reason to believe that strategies that are appropriate in personal relations are not necessarily appropriate in societal relations. It is not being argued that societal relations are genetically prior to personal relations. Indeed, John Macmurray (1995: Chapter 6) has argued convincingly for the priority of personal relations. This, it should be noted, does not contradict the reservations expressed in the text above.

3 The account that follows is intended mainly to show that social constructionists are mistaken on key points of their understanding of truth. It is not intended as a portrayal of the correct theory of truth, but only of one account that is easily more plausible than relativism.

References

Anderson, H. and Goolishian, H. (1992) The client is expert: a not-knowing approach therapy, in S. McNamee and K. J. Gergen (eds) *Therapy as Social Construction*. London: Sage.

Bhaskar, R. (1979) On the possibility of social scientific knowledge and the limits of naturalism, in J. Mehpham and D. H. Ruben (eds) *Issues in Marxist Philosophy, Volume III: Epistemology, Science, Ideology*. New Jersey: Humanities Press.

Danziger, K. (1997) The varieties of social constructionism, *Theory and Psychology*, 7(3): 399–416.

Drewery, W. and Winslade, J. (1997) The theoretical story of narrative therapy, in G. Monk, J. Winslade, K. Crocket and D. Epston (eds) *Narrative Therapy in Practice*. San Francisco: Jossey-Bass.

Epston, D., White, M. and Murray, K. (1992) A proposal for re-authoring therapy: Rose's revisioning of her life and a commentary, in S. McNamee and K. J. Gergen (eds) *Therapy as Social Construction*. London: Sage.

Fruggeri, L. (1992) Therapeutic process as the social construction of change, in S. McNamee and K. J. Gergen (eds) *Therapy as Social Construction*. London: Sage.

Gergen, K. J. (1988) If persons are texts, in R. L. Woolfolk, L. A. Sass and S. B. Messer (eds) *Hermeneutics and Psychological Theory: Interpretive Perspectives on Personality, Psychotherapy, and Psychopathology*. New Brunswick, NJ: Rutgers University Press.

Gergen, K. J. (1990) Therapeutic professions and the diffusion of deficit, *Journal of Mind and Behavior*, 11(3/4): 353–68.

Gergen, K. J. (1991) *The Saturated Self: Dilemmas of Identity in Contemporary Life*. New York: HarperCollins.

Harré, R. (1992) On being taken up by others, in D. N. Robinson (ed.) *Social Discourse and Moral Judgement*. San Diego: Academic Press, Harcourt Brace Jovanovich.

McKenzie, B. (1997) Health promoting conversations, in G. Monk, J. Winslade, K. Crocket and D. Epston (eds) *Narrative Therapy in Practice*. San Francisco: Jossey-Bass.

Macmurray, J. (1995) *Persons in Relation*. London: Faber and Faber (originally published in 1961).

McNamee, S. and Gergen, K. J. (eds) (1992) *Therapy as Social Construction.* London: Sage.

Parrott, W. G. (1992) Moral philosophy and social science: a critique of constructionist reason, in D. N. Robinson (ed.) *Social Discourse and Moral Judgment.* San Diego: Academic Press.

Searle, J. R. (1995) *The Construction of Social Reality.* New York: The Free Press.

Shotter, J. (1989) The myth of the mind and the mistake of psychology, in W. J. Baker, M. E. Hyland, R. van Hezewijk and S. Terwee (eds) *Recent Trends in Theoretical Psychology, Volume II.* New York: Springer-Verlag.

Shotter, J. (1992) Social constructionism: relativism, moral sources, and judgments of adequacy, in D. N. Robinson (ed.) *Social Discourse and Moral Judgment.* San Diego: Academic Press.

Simon, M. A. (1982) *Understanding Human Action: Social Explanation and the Vision of Social Science.* Albany: State University of New York Press.

Terwee, S. (1995) Deconstructing social constructionism, in I. Lubek, R. van Hezewijk, G. Pheterson and C. Tolman (eds) *Trends and Issues in Theoretical Psychology.* New York: Springer Publishing Company.

Tolman, C. W. (1994) *Psychology, Society and Subjectivity: An Introduction to German Critical Psychology.* London: Routledge.

White, M. (1995) *Re-authoring Lives: Interviews and Essays.* Adelaide, Australia: Dulwich Centre Publications.

White, M. and Epston, D. (1990) *Narrative Means to Therapeutic Ends.* New York: W.W. Norton & Company.

13 That's all very well, but what use is it?

WENDY STAINTON ROGERS
AND REX STAINTON ROGERS

Constructionist ideas are now beginning to infiltrate social policy and professional practice in areas such as law, medicine and social work. Furthermore, social constructionism now constitutes a major critical paradigm in theorizing on these fields. For example, Payne, in a highly influential textbook on social work theory, introduces it by saying, 'The major principle of this book is that *social work is a socially constructed activity*' (Payne 1991: 7; emphasis in the original). Howe goes further, arguing that 'a child of modernity, social work now finds itself in a postmodern world, uncertain whether or not there are any deep and unwavering principles which define the essence of its character and hold it together as a coherent enterprise' (Howe 1994: 513).

Howe's comment highlights a central concern for social constructionist and/or postmodern theory. While it offers a new perspective on the social world and our understanding of it, when applied to practical situations its implications are disconcerting. It is all very well for academics whose work consists of commentating on and critically analysing what goes on in the world 'out there' – commentary and critique is what they do, and, often, all they do in a professional sense. For academics uncertainty and incoherence are, if anything, markers of scholarship – ways of demonstrating erudition and intellectual sophistication. But for people whose work is largely devoted to doing practical things, uncertainty and incoherence can be a serious problem. Much social work, police work and medical practice, especially at the 'sharp end', would be impossible without the ability to act decisively when the situation demands it.

In this chapter we examine some of the dilemmas that arise when social constructionist theory is applied to professional practice. We use examples from child protection work as an illustration, both because this field of work offers a 'hard case', often involving making very difficult decisions where both action and inaction, equally, can carry heavy risks; and because it is an area of policy and praxis that been subjected to considerable social constructionist theorizing. Before we can start looking at that in any detail, in order to see what social constructionist theorizing means in relation to something like child protection, we will need to begin by examining what it is reacting against. We have called this the 'humaneering project' approach to social problems (see Stainton Rogers *et al.* 1995).

The 'humaneering project'

Under modernism, conventional social science research is conducted in pursuit of 'humaneering'. This term was first adopted by Tiffin *et al.* (1940), who defined it thus:

> The value of learning more about ourselves and human nature is obvious. Our social, political and economic theories rest ultimately upon our understanding of human nature. Upon sound knowledge of human nature depends the possibility of directing social changes, so as to make social institutions and practices better suited to human needs. As citizens, then, we need to make our beliefs about human nature as sound and rational as possible. The nineteenth century was marked by great achievements in engineering. Advances in psychology, sociology, and physiology should lead to as striking advances in 'humaneering' during the twentieth century.
>
> (Tiffin *et al.* 1940: 23–4)

This argument for the fostering of human betterment works from the assumption that by gaining a better 'understanding of human nature' it is possible to act more rationally – to respond to social problems in an informed way, doing what has been 'shown' by empirical research to be best, rather than simply 'doing what we've always done' or acting on existing prejudices and preconceptions. At the core of this agenda are three interconnected beliefs:

- That 'social problems' are naturally arising, real phenomena – that they come about as a lawful consequence of social, political, cultural, economic and/or psychological processes (or some combination of these).

- That it is possible to use established scientific method to discover how these processes operate.
- That when one has gained insight into the workings of these processes, it is possible to devise strategies to counter them, and thus resolve them, or, at least, ameliorate the damage they cause.

Research and theorization, in a formal social scientific sense, are thus seen as crucial for guiding both social policy and professional practice. Since Tiffin *et al.*, over half a century ago, formulated so clearly the human-eering project, the empirical social sciences have undergone a vast growth through addressing this agenda. This, in turn, has become a source of considerable pride to academics involved in the resultant service industry of textbook production:

> Beginning with World War II, social psychology, along with other behavioral social sciences has burgeoned on many fronts. There has been stress on empirical data collection as well as on theory, use of laboratory experimentation as well as field observation methods, concern with a wide variety of concrete social problems. It is our hope that this book – in the number of and variety of empirical methods cited, in the hypotheses and theories espoused, in the range of social problems commented upon – fully reflects this burgeoning scientific activity.
>
> (Krech *et al.* 1962: vii–viii)

The *leitmotif* which claims that empirical social science can address and powerfully inform policy over social problems is repeated in text after text, to the point where one can confidently talk of a discourse of humaneering. In the preface to a multiply re-edited text (seven editions from 1972 to 1995) called *The Social Animal*, Aronson elevates his particular empirical social science – social psychology – to quite extraordinary heights of importance:

> The purpose of this volume is unashamedly (but with some trepidation) to spell out the relevance that sociopsychological research might have to the problems besetting contemporary society . . . Implicit in all this is my belief that social psychology is extremely important – that social psychologists can play a vital role in making the world a better place. Indeed, in my more grandiose moments, I nurse the secret belief that social psychologists are in a unique position to have a profound and beneficial impact on our lives by providing an increased understanding of such important phenomena as conformity, persuasion, prejudice, love and aggression.
>
> (Aronson 1995: x–xi)

Hubris, as employed by the ancients, from Greek tragedians to the Book of Proverbs (16:18), was that which pre-echoed a fall. As Aronson was first publishing *The Social Animal*, Harré and Secord (1972) were publishing *The Explanation of Social Behaviour*. The 'climate of perturbation' (see Stainton Rogers *et al.* 1995; this term is explained below) was already disturbing the meteorology of self-congratulation:

> We begin our discussion by noting that much of experimental psychology and other empirical approaches in behavioural science are based upon three assumptions: (a) that only a mechanistic model of man will satisfy the requirements of making a science, (b) that the most scientific concept of cause is one which focuses on external stimulation and which excludes from consideration any treatment of the connection between cause and effect, and (c) that a methodology based on logical positivism is the best possible approach to a behavioural science. All three are mistaken.
>
> (Harré and Secord 1972: 5)

Child abuse as a socially constructed 'social problem'

For all that the new social constructionist and critical analytics have troubled the ontological and epistemological foundations of the humaneering project in its academic heartland for a quarter-century, challenge has taken much longer to reach the applied frontiers. Almost every mainstream textbook on the topic of child abuse is based upon the set of humaneering assumptions listed above. Just to take one example, the final paragraph of a book on prediction and prevention of child abuse written by three psychologists states: 'Our objective as professionals and academics, and as a society, must be that parents will protect their children, and refrain from abusing them. It is towards this objective, as much as towards improving professional practice, that we have in this book accumulated the best available evidence that will help us to predict and prevent the abuse of young children' (Stratton *et al.* 1988: 302).

More recently, however, this area of policy and practice has, in the UK at least, been infiltrated – to some degree – by constructionist ideas. A good example is provided by Taylor, in a review of claims being made about the incidence and prevalence of child abuse:

> No behaviour is necessarily abuse. Some sets of facts come to be labelled as cases of child abuse because they go beyond the limits of what is now considered to be acceptable conduct towards a child. These standards change over time and also vary, not only between cultures, but also between different members of the same culture. Child abuse is thus a social construction whose meaning arises from the

value structures of a social group and the ways in which these values are interpreted and negotiated in real situations.

(Taylor 1989: 46)

What is interesting is that this perspective has become sufficiently acceptable to be incorporated into a document published by the government in order to disseminate research findings to practitioners and policy-makers. A *tranche* of research projects was commissioned by the Department of Health[1] following the introduction of the England and Wales Children Act 1989. This Act fundamentally altered the legal basis of intervention to protect children who might be at risk of 'significant harm'.[2] The implementation of this new legislation was used as an opportunity to bring about far-reaching changes in practice, especially among social workers. Extensive training was organized, and a substantial body of new Regulations and Guidance[3] was issued by government. The research was designed to examine, following the change in the law, how social workers and others were going about protecting children at risk of abuse. A review of the research, *Child Protection: Messages from Research* (Department of Health 1995), was published to disseminate its findings. This report contained sentiments with a decidedly constructionist flavour. It asserted that society 'continually reconstructs' definitions of maltreatment that require intervention (according to Parton *et al.* 1997), and quotes a view expressed by Jane Gibbon that 'as a phenomenon, child maltreatment is more like pornography than whooping cough. It is a socially constructed phenomenon which reflects values and opinions of a particular culture at a particular time' (Department of Health 1995: 15).

But does it work in practice?

As Wattam (1996) has detailed, this seeming endorsement of constructionism is rather superficial in the report. First, the research makes no attempt to explore the different ways in which child abuse is defined. As she comments, 'having suggested that abuse is constructed the review then goes on to reconstruct it for practical purposes, to enable a definition which enables practice and research to get on with its job of deciding how best to intervene in this social problem' (Wattam 1996: 190).

Second, she points out that both the research itself and the review of its findings are highly constrained in how they consider the workings of the child protection system. She notes that the main concern which dominates both is about the balance between two strategies to tackle abuse:

- either providing services for children 'in need' (i.e. that support families experiencing difficulties in bringing up their children);
- or carrying out a formal investigation to see whether the child is at risk of significant harm.

'Thus', she observes, 'the nature of the concern is about how children and families are treated once they enter the system' (Wattam 1996: 194). The system itself, she observes, is never subjected to any serious challenge, and neither are the much broader issues about the social, political and environmental contexts which may be implicated in abuse, such as poverty and social exclusion. In consequence, she argues: 'This emphasis allows government to abdicate responsibility . . . A deft solution which offers no solution for the victims of child harm and injury, and a questionable solution for those suffering from a range of other social problems' (*ibid.*).

Another way in which the research is constrained, she notes, is that it is framed almost entirely within the context of the Children Act 1989. It therefore does not begin to address the complexity of the much broader legal framework within which child protection work takes place. It fails to acknowledge, let alone talk about how to tackle, the 'contradictions between criminalisation, partnership and parental involvement' (Wattam 1996: 198) which exert a considerable influence upon what happens in practice. For example, it does not look at the serious dilemmas that arise in some cases of child sexual abuse, where the pressure to prosecute abusers can create conditions which are, themselves, very distressing (and potentially harmful) to children. It is hard for policy and practice to decide what to do in such cases: allow adults who sexually assault children to go free, or put children on the witness stand and subject them to lengthy waits for the matter to be resolved, and to potentially highly confrontational cross-examination? Most notable in this regard is the absence of any consideration of children's rights. Throughout the report children are treated, Wattam asserts, as appendages – mute bodies that have abusive things done to them.

Wattam's final criticism centres on the way certain concepts are treated as unproblematic. She identifies 'mothers' as one of these, and the gender assumptions which permeate child protection work, by which it is mothers who are held responsible for caring for and protecting children. This, she points out, is particularly problematic when juxtaposed against the way in which language is used around the provision of services, which is almost always expressed in terms of 'families'. The impact is to reinforce a range of discriminatory practices towards women, which, O'Hagan and Dillenburger (1995: 10) claim, go as far as to constitute another form of abuse: 'The history of childcare work is also the history of the abuse of women perpetrated by childcare agencies . . . during the last three decades women have been hurt, humiliated, deceived, frightened, undermined, let down, coerced, endangered, impoverished and stigmatized by childcare professionals.' In other words, for all the claims to have adopted a constructionist stance that are set out in the research report, in practice it appears not to have taken its implications seriously.

There are two reasons for this, we believe. The first is that social constructionism is often not understood very well. It is sometimes treated as no more than a mild form of cultural contextualism, whereby the social processes are seen to work rather differently in different contexts, and social phenomena are understood in diverse ways, according to different perspectives. Payne (1991: 8) offers a good illustration of this watered down version of constructionism:

> We have seen that social work is complex and varies in different cultures. It is part of a complex theoretical, occupational and service network. Therefore it can only be understood in the social and cultural context of the participants. Theories about it are products of the context in which they arise, and they also influence that context, because theories affect what people do and say within social work, and that affects social attitudes towards people and their ideas and values. To understand what social work is, therefore, we have to look at its participants, its organisation and its theories about itself, and we can only understand these things if we see how they are constructed by the society which surrounds them and of which they are a part.

The rest of the chapter is devoted to *defining* these different participants, processes, contexts and so on in ways which, while acknowledging diversity, admit no difficulty over the activity of 'defining' itself. The sense is given throughout the book that while phenomena, processes and the like may be differently constituted in different contexts, there are always 'real things' there to be defined. It is the same misreading that Wattam (1996) picks up in her review of *Child Protection: Messages from Research*. It is shot through, she observes, with the 'language of practice', which assumes that there is some 'benchmark of the real' against which judgement can be made.

Adopting a constructionist approach is not just about using a somewhat different language; it is about making a radical conceptual change. Rosenau captures this well: 'These different terminologies incorporate adversarial views of the world. Learning these words and understanding their usage involve more than new ways of communicating; such intellectual activity requires re-setting the codes one normally employs in social science analysis, turning around one's thought processes' (Rosenau 1992: 8). It is this adversarial view of the world that is at the core of constructionism, and it is this, we feel, that gives so much difficulty to those in positions of authority and power. A thoroughgoing constructionism requires that *all* knowledge and *all* praxis must be subjected to critical doubt, including those which constitute current professional wisdom or government policy.

A more subtle reason why it is hard for practitioners like social workers to accept full-blown constructionism is that it asks them not just to be willing to question their expertise, but the very ethical basis of their work. The principles of social work practice are deeply infused with modernism's Enlightenment philosophy, manifested within humaneering approach it takes. Howe (1994: 518) describes social work's 'humaneering project' thus: 'The three traditional cornerstones of social work – care, control and cure – might be recognised as particular manifestations of modernity's three great projects. In its own way social work has pursued the beautiful (aesthetics), the good (ethics) and the true (science) as it attempts to bring about a pleasing quality of life and a just society.' It is hard to give up on the idea that what you are doing is 'doing good', especially when doing it can be a very hard, very thankless task, often undertaken at great personal cost. In a context like that, who would want to argue against the pursuit of goodness, beauty and truth? Yet this is precisely what a constructionist approach demands: to think the unthinkable, and open up to scrutiny all that you do and say and think, however mandated it might be by high principles and good intentions.

Under constructionism, however, notions like 'care' and 'protection' are especially in need of critical analysis, given their in-built 'feel-good' qualities, which can be highly potent in creating an illusion that all that is at stake is human betterment.

Lost children

A good illustration of how such discourses operate is provided by a review conducted by Best (1990) into the way that in the USA concern has been stirred up about the 'problem' of children who go missing from home. He painstakingly details the rhetorical devices deployed to create the impression that this is a problem of massive proportions, involving large numbers of children and resulting in horrendous consequences. Certainly emotive language is deployed to full effect, as can be seen in this example from a submission to the US House of Representatives subcommittee reviewing legislation about missing children. The claim was made that children:

> are being treated like garbage. Raped and killed, their young bodies are discarded in plastic bags, on trash trucks, and left on dumps . . . Like litter, they are thrown into lakes, rivers and streams – the tender driftwood of life. Some are found on roadsides, like empty soda and beer cans . . . or cast aside like broken furniture in dirty, empty houses or stripped, abandoned cars in wooded or swamp areas . . . Poor little wilted flowers, plucked from the vases of home and safety of parents, are, in large part, left unburied and alone in the openness of fields – and now the closed mind of our thoughts.
> (US House of Representatives 1984: 55)

Conditions are created by such rhetoric that to deny in any way that there is a problem, or to state that the problem is far from simple, or that there is another way to tell the story, is to side with the 'unfeeling' people who are turning their back on children's distress – or, worse, is to act as an apologist for paedophilia.

However, Best does just that. Adopting a constructionist approach to this issue, he argues that it is necessary to 'identify the claims-maker's *interests* in promoting a social problem; identifying the interests explains why a particular social problem emerged' (Best 1990: 11). Claims have been made that at a 'conservative estimate', across the USA some 20,000–50,000 children are abducted each year; the impression given is that the majority suffer the fate described above. Best argues that these figures are being constructed and used rhetorically; that most 'children' who go missing from home are teenagers following a fight with their parents, who mostly return within a few hours; or they are subjects of parental disputes following divorce. Only a very tiny proportion, he says, are kidnapped by persons deliberately intending to harm them.

So, he asks, what is going on? Whose interests are being served by the creation of a moral panic? Best writes in terms of competition in the 'social problems marketplace'. Not only are large numbers of people employed in child welfare work,[4] there are careers to be developed and reputations to be built. For these people, dependent, ultimately, on the public purse, it is crucial to maintain public concern. But more generally, Best suggests that spotlighting attention on this particular social problem is useful because of what it detracts attention *from*. As he comments:

> it made sense to focus on the threat deviant adults posed to children. Deviance is an important theme in American culture. We prefer to blame social problems on flawed, deviant individuals, while paying little attention to the complex workings of the social system . . . And defining threats to children in terms of child molesters, kidnappers, and other deviant adults made these fears more manageable . . . if society could bring just a few villains under control, the threats would disappear, and the future could be secured.
>
> (Best 1990: 180)

In other words, a preoccupation with the horrific attacks against innocent children which are perpetrated by perverted and sick individuals provides an excellent excuse for not having to think about other, more intractable problems. It allows people to distance themselves from any responsibility for other reasons why children may be suffering, whether these are children growing up in poverty at home, or children working as slave labour elsewhere in the world. And, as Best says, it offers the promise of 'quick-fix' solutions (as does the 'humaneering project' generally).

As we have argued elsewhere:

To embark on a crusading quest for villains is to operate within a chimeral fairy-tale world in which, once the brave knight has slain the dragon, children can all live 'happily ever after' . . . What this boils down to is a recognition that heroic 'child-saving' and villainous 'child mistreatment' are not two different kinds of action, with opposing mandates (to work for the good or bad of children). They are two alternative facets, or readings, of virtually *any* kind of conduct towards children.
(Stainton Rogers and Stainton Rogers 1992: 191)

So is constructionism helpful?

The fear many child protection practitioners have about accepting a constructionist approach is that abandoning any hope of certainty and accepting the need to question everything means being incapable of doing anything at all – this at a time when, as Parton *et al.* observe, 'child welfare practitioners and managers are feeling embattled and even under siege in a context of growing referrals and increasingly severe caseloads but where there are insufficient resources to do the job expected of them' (Parton *et al.* 1997: 1). However, we would argue that, for all its problems, this is what needs to be done.

Parton *et al.* suggest two reasons why a shift to constructionism is necessary. First, the present system is not working, at least in part because there is no moral consensus about what child abuse is, or what should be done about it. It is hardly surprising, then, that the work itself is becoming highly stressful and practitioners feel under siege – they are being expected to do the impossible, and, when they fail, are publicly pilloried for it. At the same time government is also under pressure, taken to task each time a new child abuse scandal hits the headlines. It has responded by creating an ever-more complex system of statutory regulation. It too is trying to do the impossible: devise policy against a back-cloth of irreconcilable disputes about the best strategy to adopt. Parton *et al.*'s second reason why change is needed is that the current approach, sited as it is within a positivist worldview, fails to address in any adequate way the moral issues at stake:

What is considered child abuse for the purposes of child protection policy and practice is much better characterised as a product of social negotiation between different values and beliefs, different social norms and professional knowledges and perspectives about children, child development and parenting. Far from being a medico-scientific reality, it is a phenomenon where moral reasoning and moral judgement are central.
(Parton *et al.* 1997: 67)

The point they make is that the difficulties being faced will not be solved by 'finding better checklists or new models of psychopathology' (Dingwall *et al.* 1983: 244). What is needed is a willingness to recognize that child protection is a moral and political endeavour (Parton 1985), and a preparedness to examine the implications.

How can constructionism be applied to practice?

Howe (1994) suggests four themes for doing this: pluralism, participation, power and performance.

- *Pluralism* involves accepting multiplicity, variety and conflict, and recognizing that it will not be possible to find neat or comfortable resolutions between competing interests. It also means acknowledging that no group has a monopoly of expertise or truth, or the right to determined what is valued.
- *Participation* works from the assumption that as all truths are simply 'working truths', decisions and actions should be taken inclusively, enabling the participation of all those involved or affected by them.
- Crucially, constructionism demands a sensitivity to issues of *power*, and a willingness to acknowledge how it is deployed and by whom. This includes not just the wielding of power by those with formal authority, but also the subversive use of power and forms of resistance.
- *Performance* is also about power, but looks at how it is managed, especially through institutional and bureaucratic means. This includes both professional expertise and the knowledge mongering of academics.

Parton *et al.* (1997) have made a good start at this programme of scrutiny, but are more concerned with understanding how child protection is achieved than with offering clear guidelines for practice. They are sceptical that the current system can change very much:

> The myth is to suggest that, with current resources and in the current political and economic climate, practitioners can do this [child protection work] in a fundamentally different way . . . current practice very much carries out the child protection *work* that is asked of it. The problem with much recent research and policy debates is that they fail to understand what the nature of that work is and *why* it takes the form it does.
>
> (Parton *et al.* 1997: 246)

We are more optimistic. Our agenda is a broader one than simply protecting children from risk; our concern is with promoting better childhoods. In this respect constructionism is an optimistic approach, since it appreciates that revolutions are not won with bullets and barricades, but by 'changing hearts and minds'. Nearly ten years ago one of us suggested that:

> the real power of social constructionism to point to better childhoods lies not in its ability to deconstruct our present world as a less than perfect one to grow up in, nor in any specific utopia it may open up to examination, but in the *idea of multiple realities itself* . . . That we no longer hang children, burn them as witches or brand them as vagrants is not the victory of a few reformers, it is the victory of a whole society which has overcome the constructions that made such action possible. The killings and maimings of children that our society still generates can also be consigned to the history book – by the same processes that have made possible the worlds in which we now live.
>
> (Stainton Rogers 1989: 29)

Such changes can only be made to come about by having the courage to go beyond moral crusading, and the humility to recognize that none of us has a 'hot-line' to the truth. They will be the product not of 'more research' of the kind reviewed by Browne *et al.*, with which we began, but of opening up our systems, policies and practice to scrutiny and challenge. In our view, constructionist methods are what are needed if hearts and minds are to change in ways that emancipate and well as protect children.

There are a number of ways in which this can be applied. First, the engagement by academics in constructionist critique is itself, we believe, useful, however frustrating it may be. Such work can contribute to creating a climate of change. Second, constructionist ideas and methods can be incorporated into training and education, both in a general sense (equipping those who will go on to take up jobs in practice to develop good 'crap-detectors') and specifically in relation to certain issues.

An example of this is provided by a course offered in The Open University programme *Working with Young People* (The Open University 1997). A central theme of this course is a constructionist critique by Griffin (1993), who argues that research and theorizing about the young tends to view them through a number of 'problematizing discourses'. Young people are seen as deviant (and thus in need of control), deficient (and thus in need of education) or dysfunctional (and thus in need of therapy). In the course, in order to resist this problematizing, a number of issues (for example, taking drugs, sexuality and bodily display such as piercing) are treated not under the conventional headings like 'health education' or 'trouble-making', but under the topic of *bodies*. This takes a constructionist approach, examining how young people use their bodies, and for what purposes. In this way it is hoped to challenge students' preconceptions, and make them more willing to explore alternative readings of what young people are like, and why they do the things they do.

Conclusions

We do not see some great new dawn emerging in which, overnight, practitioners in fields like social work will 'see the light' and all become fully paid up constructionists. As we have acknowledged throughout this chapter, this is much harder to do when one is faced with hard decisions in the 'real world' outside the Academy than it is for those of us working comfortably within it. But there is, at least, 'some light at the end of the tunnel'. Constructionist ideas are beginning to have an impact, and certainly (as Howe 1994 notes) they are consistent with other moves taking place, such as towards more inclusive approaches to working with parents and children, and towards what is coming to be called 'reflective practice'. Humaneering is by no means gone, but we are starting to see a preparedness to consider whether, like the feats of engineering that in the 1960s were portrayed as inherently progressive, there are not downside costs as well as benefits to its mission. Not a bad start.

Notes

1 At the time of writing, in the UK services for children, including child protection, are organized according to the three legal systems that operate: England and Wales, Northern Ireland and Scotland. In the latter two, sections in the Northern Ireland and Scottish Offices are responsible. In England and Wales it is a section of the Department of Health which is responsible for making policy in relation to child protection, and overseeing social work in this field.
2 This term assumes a legal status, being the criterion which defines whether statutory intervention can be taken to protect a child from abuse.
3 These documents are issued to local authorities, to inform them about how to go about their statutory responsibilities. Broadly, *Regulations* are mandatory. They have the same legal force as an Act of Parliament, and spell out the detail of how legislation must be applied. *Guidance* is more advisory, offering advice and guidelines for good practice.
4 It is worth noting that in the USA this is generally within private companies and is often much better paid than in the UK.

References

Aronson, E. (1995) *The Human Animal*. New York: Freeman.

Best, J. (1990) *Threatened Children: Rhetoric and Concern about Child-victims*. Chicago: University of Chicago Press.

Department of Health (1995) *Child Protection: Messages from Research*. London: HMSO.

Dingwall, R., Eekelaar, J. and Murray, T. (1983) *The Protection of Children: State Intervention and Family Life*. Oxford: Blackwell.

Gibbons, J., Conroy, S. and Bell, C. (1995) *Operating the Child Protection System*. London: HMSO.

Griffin, C. (1993) *Representations of Youth*. Cambridge: Polity Press.

Harré, R. and Secord, P. F. (1972) *The Explanation of Social Behaviour*. Oxford: Blackwell.

Howe, D. (1994) Modernity, postmodernity and social work, *British Journal of Social Work*, 24: 513–32.

Krech, D., Crutchfield, R. S. and Ballachey, F. (1962) *Individual in Society*. New York: McGraw-Hill.

O'Hagan, K. and Dillenberger, K. (1995) *The Abuse of Women within Childcare Work*. Buckingham: Open University Press.

Parton, N. (1985) *The Politics of Child Abuse*. Basingstoke: Macmillan.

Parton, N., Thorpe, D. and Wattam, C. (1997) *Child Protection: Risk and the Moral Order*. London: Macmillan.

Payne, M. (1991) *Modern Social Work Theory: A Critical Introduction*. Basingstoke: Macmillan.

Rosenau, P. M. (1992) *Post-Modernism and the Social Sciences: Insights, Inroads and Intrusions*. Princeton, NJ: Princeton University Press.

Stainton Rogers, R. (1989) The social construction of childhood, in W. Stainton Rogers *et al.* (eds) *Child Abuse and Neglect: Facing the Challenge*. London: Batsford.

Stainton Rogers, R. and Stainton Rogers, W. (1992) *Stories of Childhood: Shifting Agendas of Child Concern*. Hemel Hempstead: Harvester Wheatsheaf.

Stainton Rogers, R., Stenner, P., Gleeson, K. and Stainton Rogers, W. (1995) *Social Psychology: A Critical Agenda*. Cambridge: Polity Press.

Stratton, P., Davies, C. and Browne, K. (1988) The psychological context of predicting and preventing child abuse and neglect, in K. Browne, C. Davies and P. Stratton (eds) *Early Prediction and Prevention of Child Abuse*. Wiley: Chichester and New York: Wiley.

Taylor, S. (1989) How prevalent is it?, in W. Stainton Rogers *et al.* (eds) *Child Abuse and Neglect: Facing the Challenge*. London: Batsford.

The Open University (1997) *Working with Young People*. Milton Keynes: The Open University.

Tiffin, J., Knight, F. B. and Josey, C. C. (1940) *The Psychology of Normal People*. Boston: Heath.

US House of Representatives (1984) Title IV, *Missing Children's Assistance Act*. Hearings held by the Subcommittee on Human Resources, Committee on Education and Labor, 98th Congress, 2nd session, 9 April.

Wattam, C. (1996) The social construction of child abuse for practical purposes: a review of 'Child Protection: Messages from Research', *Child and Family Law Quarterly*, 8(3): 189–200.

Conclusion

14 Reconstructing social constructionism

DAVID J. NIGHTINGALE
AND JOHN CROMBY

[Is] it the whole truth? It's a slice of truth, a morsel, a refraction – it's a piece of the pie, certainly not the whole enchilada – and now that I'm thinking about it I don't think I could tell the whole truth about anything. That's a pretty heavy burden because we all just see the world through this little distorted piece of coke bottle. Is there such a thing as objective truth? I wonder. Don't you?

(Frolov and Schneider 1992)

In this book we have tried to do two things. First, to challenge what we see as an erroneous overreliance upon discourse and language that either implicitly or explicitly underpins much contemporary constructionist thought. Second, to begin to explore the ways in which discursive practices and human experiences are already grounded in, and structured by, embodiment, materiality and power; the various chapters in this book are all, in their different ways, engaged with this project. We also introduced what has come to be known (in psychology at least) as the realism–relativism debate. In this chapter we return to this debate with the specific aim of 'fleshing out' (a suitably 'embodied' metaphor!) and adding to our introductory critique. Our conceptual aim is to demonstrate how what we see as the theoretical inadequacies of a universal and totalizing relativism unfold, inform and intertwine with the issues at hand. We also have two practical aims. First, to provide a source of 'rebuttals to relativism', in terms of both theory and practice. Second, to offer a collection of sustainable arguments that will support the development of theory and research within a 'realist' paradigm. However, before we proceed and for reasons that will become clear, we need to define our terms.

Definitions

Defining relativism

There are many varieties of relativism – epistemic, semantic, ontological and moral – and many ways in which the distinctions between them are blurred in particular relativistic accounts (Harré and Krausz 1996). Here, as in Chapter 1, we will be concerned with the fragmentary definition of relativism offered in the 'notorious paper' (Potter 1998: ix) 'Death and furniture' (Edwards *et al.* 1995). We use the term fragmentary not to imply weak or ill-conceived (although we believe it is both) but in recognition of its rhetorical construction. As Potter notes elsewhere, their aim was 'to produce a paper which deconstructed the rhetoric of . . . [realist] arguments' (Potter 1998: 37). In this sense, the paper is not intended as a formal statement, or logically deduced defence, of relativism – even though it is often read as one. Rather, it is a systematic deconstruction of realist discourse informed by a sometimes explicit, sometimes implicit, relativistic stance. In taking this paper as our starting point we could be accused of failing to engage with the more formalized philosophical subtleties of relativism. However, within psychology at least, 'Death and furniture' is seen as an eloquent and, more importantly, influential 'performance' of relativist philosophical discourse – particularly in terms of its use as a warrant for the denial of those extra-discursive aspects of our 'reality' that we are concerned with here – and as such we believe our challenge is fair.

Having stated that 'Death and furniture' is not a formal philosophical statement of relativism, it is worth noting that it can, for the most part, be considered a form of *epistemic relativism* (Harré 1996: Chapter 3; Sokal and Bricmont 1998: Chapter 4). Epistemic relativists state that claims regarding what exist are relative to an individual, social group or culture; in other words, that the truth or falsity of a statement about the world is a function not of an external and objectively knowable reality, but of locally and historically contingent norms, values, practices and beliefs.

To summarize their arguments briefly again: Edwards *et al.* (1995: 37) believe that 'relativism is the quintessentially academic position, where all truths are to-be-established'; wherein 'the idea of Death and Furniture as things per se [or the idea of any other things] fails to resist scrutiny [as] there is no per se' (*ibid.*: 37); and consequently, that 'reality can only ever be reality-as-known, and therefore, however counter-intuitive it may seem, produced by, not prior to, inquiry' (*ibid.*: 39). In other words, there is no truth to be found outside of the language in which such 'truths' arise (that is, no extra-discursive things, processes or reality in which such truths may be grounded). Consequently, the reality we know is a product, rather than a precondition or mediator of our inquiries and activities. The truth is not out there.

We should also mention that we do not intend to pursue here the moral implications of a relativistic stance, nor will we be concerned with a more general discussion of moral relativism (or any other forms of relativism, such as semantic or ontological: Harré 1996). We recognize that morality and theoretical perspectives are intertwined, but would wish to argue that the ethical and moral difficulties that are commonly associated with a universalizing relativism cannot be resolved (or always illuminated) through appeals to the nature of reality and what we can know of it. Suffice it to say that claims have been made concerning the fundamental ways in which an all-encompassing relativism fails to offer any grounds for political or progressive activity (Burman 1990; Gill 1995; Parker 1996, 1998); which in their turn have been challenged by arguments that suggest that issues of 'practical politics' are independent of realism and relativism alike (Potter 1998: 31).

Defining realism

Realism, as we mentioned in Chapter 1, is the doctrine that the external world exists independently of our representations of it (Searle 1995). In other words, the nature of the world is somehow more than our talk regarding that world, and so what Rom Harré (1992: 157) has termed 'the Gergen extravaganza', the 'anything goes' of postmodern discourse, is incorrect. From a realist perspective, our social constructions are always already mediated in and through our embodied nature, the materiality of the world and pre-existing matrices of social and institutional power. However, we are not primarily concerned with an explicit defence of realism (of which there are as many varieties as there are of relativism), nor do we see that one is either necessary or ultimately possible (see Chapter 1). Rather, just as 'Death and furniture' offered a rhetorical critique of realism, we offer, instead, a theoretical critique of relativism.

Problems with relativism

Scepticism

[T]here is, as yet, no foolproof way to deal with . . . variation [in people's accounts] and to sift accounts which are 'literal' or 'accurate' from those which are rhetorical or merely misguided.

(Potter and Wetherell 1987: 35)

David Hume (1711–76), a Scottish philosopher and historian, is often associated with what has come to be known as 'radical scepticism', although its origins may be traced to pre-Socratic Greek philosophy. In essence, this is the belief that we have no way of obtaining reliable knowledge of an external world, since all we have available to us are our perceptions or sense data. Although we might claim that we can infer a reality to which these data might apply, we have no grounds for such an inference or any way of exploring such a postulated world (a more extreme form of scepticism is idealism, the view that the world is somehow 'created' by the mind). While radical scepticism and epistemic relativism have arisen within different (but related) philosophical debates, they none the less share a belief regarding the inaccessibility of external reality and the little (or nothing) we can claim to know of such a reality.

Some examples will clarify why we think this is highly problematic: imagine that someone were to insist that the world was really flat, or that the sun revolves around the earth, or that he was the emperor Napoleon and the moon was made out of cheese. How might we question or challenge these claims? If 'there is no *per se*' (Edwards *et al.* 1995), then we cannot either question or disprove them (in and of themselves) as there is no referent: that is, no ('external' or 'objective') things, entities or processes to which the claims might refer; hence the difficulty outlined by Potter and Wetherell in the quote that introduces this section. If we accept and pursue a relativistic solution to this lack of 'factuality' (as they have done), we might concern ourselves, within discursive psychology at least, with an analysis of the particular interactive sequences within which the statements were embedded, we might peruse the texts for rhetorical devices, linguistic strategies and truth claims, or illustrate the discourses that are being drawn upon or that operate within the text. However, we would still be wholly unable to assess the accuracy of what we had been told.

We are well aware that these are trivial examples of what are real and pressing issues, and that people's well-being – perhaps even their lives – may be dependent upon which version of reality we and they hold. However, these examples were deliberately chosen in order to present our argument in such a way as to avoid the political or moral concerns that normally attend and *obscure* these kinds of issues (for example, concerns regarding biological notions of mental illness, or the assumption that mental impairment is a consequence of disability). This should not be taken to imply that we believe that moral issues are not important, or that such a moral elision is possible or desirable with respect to real events or practices. Still less should it be read as a belief that things are ever 'simply real' or 'simply constructed'. Rather, it should be seen both as illustrative of the problems that accompany a relativistic stance, and as a recognition of the ease with which our arguments may be subverted, recuperated by relativism or simply misunderstood.

As we have already acknowledged, to demand a categorical proof regarding the factuality of statements as referents of an objective and external reality is to draw upon or presuppose a naive realist framework wherein such proofs would be possible. To this extent, we have no ultimate grounds for challenging any claims, however bizarre. However, as Sokal and Bricmont (1998: 52) state, 'the mere fact that an idea is irrefutable does not imply that there is any reason to believe it is true.' Radical scepticism may be challenged, however, on the grounds that it is a non-sustainable project (outside the academy, at least). Radical scepticism is a *universal* statement regarding the nature of the knowledge, claiming that it can never reference an external reality . . . but what would it mean to put this into practice? It would mean systematically questioning all of our everyday knowledge; that we were born, and one day will die; that we can talk with one another and be understood; that water will quench our thirst, and innumerable other aspects of our daily life that it would be both meaningless and, in practice, impossible to question *in a systematic way*. If radical scepticism does not provide a viable basis for everyday knowledge, then what possible grounds can we have for adopting it within more specialized areas of inquiry? This should not be taken to imply that knowledge is not mediated by social and historical processes (which we *do* believe), simply that the claim that it can never reference an external reality is fundamentally incorrect and cannot be sustained. Radical scepticism is not justified in its *a priori* denunciation of an external reality which our talk both refers to and is embedded within. Relativism, to the large extent that it gains support from radical scepticism, is therefore also compromised.

Self-refutation

A further, more familiar critique of relativism, is that it appears to provide the conditions for its own refutation. If all claims regarding knowledge are problematic, historically and culturally contingent and grounded in nothing other than the discursive framework within which they arise, then relativism itself may be challenged on the same grounds. Relativism, too, is nothing more than a locally convenient and historically contingent parable that has no more validity than the theories or perspectives it purportedly supersedes. The consequences of this paradox are now well documented and will not be pursued further here (Burman 1990; Gill 1995; Parker 1996, 1998). However, while we may wish to claim that relativism contains the seeds of its own de(con)struction, to pursue *this* critique is unwittingly to grant relativism an explanatory coherence it does not possess. By this we mean that it can be taken to imply that relativism is, in some senses at least, an inherently coherent and sustainable project. To utilize the 'logic of relativism', to denounce it as self-refuting, simultaneously endorses it, granting relativism a deconstructive power and analytical force we are unwilling to concede. More worryingly, such critiques are easily recuperated by relativists who claim that relativism provides 'the possibility of critique, denial, deconstruction, argument, for any kind of truth, fact, assumption, regime or philosophy – for anything at all' (Edwards *et al.* 1995: 37); an 'anything at all' that can readily subsume realist claims to the contrary as nothing more than misguided realist rhetoric (see also Davies 1998; Potter 1996, 1998).

We will now try to show why relativism's apparent coherence is illusory (see also Nightingale, forthcoming). Typically, relativistic arguments within psychology proceed as follows:

1 Knowledge is socially constructed rather than an unmediated reflection of an objectively knowable, external reality (Rorty 1979).
2 Therefore, the essentialist beliefs of mainstream psychology are incorrect; things like memories, selves, gender, race, sex and cognitive structures are produced by culture and are not the inherent characteristics/ properties of individuals.

These arguments are now well established and form the theoretical foundation of most constructionist publications, from introductory texts (Sarbin and Kitsuse 1994; Burr 1995) to erudite discussions of particular topics. However, a further relativistic claim is that we can have no knowledge regarding external reality. This is the radical scepticism of the epistemic relativist – which we have already described and critiqued – which suggests that we should concern ourselves not with a pointless and futile search for the factual, but with an exploration of the textual and linguistic ways in which we describe and construct our world. But, as Eagleton (1996: 28) notes, 'epistemological anti-realism [epistemic relativism] . . . consistently denies the possibility of describing the way the world is, and just as consistently finds itself doing so.' By this he means that, on the one hand, we have ontological claims regarding the nature of reality: people, psychological and social processes etc., are socially constructed rather than determined by their essential properties. But, on the other hand, we simultaneously have specific epistemological claims that deny the possibility of making any such ontological claims. There have been attempts to side-step this issue: for example, Potter claims that he is 'certainly not trying to answer ontological questions about what sort of things exist. The focus is upon the way people construct descriptions as factual, and how others undermine those constructions. This does not require an answer to the philosophical question of what factuality is' (Potter 1996: 6).

Although relativists may claim that they do not require philosophical answers as to the nature of factuality, their accounts presuppose and rely upon such a factuality; they rest upon particular ontological claims that their epistemology specifically denies. In other words, their claims regarding the status of knowledge (what we can know) are undermined and refuted by a reliance upon specific ontological assumptions that are, in their turn, refuted by their epistemology . . . *ad infinitum.*

So what gets constructed?

> A weakness shared by most, although not all, of these . . . arguments is that they do not lead to a constructed reality, but to a failure to get any reality constructed. On the assumptions on which the arguments are based, there is no source from which social reality could ever arise. The construction[ist] view . . . leads to massive non-determinacy of social fact; to put it more plainly, it implies that there is no social reality. I regard this as a *reductio ad absurdum* of those arguments.
>
> (Collin 1997: 21)

Another way of thinking about the discrepancy between the implicit onto-logical assumptions upon which relativism relies and its explicit epistemo-logical failure to engage with or explore such assumptions is to ask 'what gets constructed?' If 'selves, persons, psychological traits and so forth, including the very idea of individual psychological traits, are social and historical constructions, not naturally occurring objects' (Sampson 1989: 2), then what, from a relativist's perspective, are these constructions like? What properties do they come to have? The short answer, as illustrated by the quote from Collin with which we began this section, is absolutely none whatsoever. A slightly longer answer is as follows.

Constructionist views of psychological and social reality are often summarised in terms of Foucault's claim that discourses are 'practices that systematically form the objects of which they speak' (Foucault 1972: 49). How might we (mis)interpret Foucault's claim from within a purely relativ-istic framework? Edwards *et al.* claim that 'even ostensibly bottom-line instances of brute reality are demonstrably social accomplishments' (Edwards *et al.* 1995: 37), by which they seem to mean that all phenomena are fundamentally linguistic in origin. What are the consequences of this? Can it mean that things come to be the way they are because (and only because) of the ways we talk about them? If all we have is 'rhetorical practices' and our only means of analysis is the transcription and discourse analysis of texts (to search out the performative ways in which language is used, the rhetorical devices employed and the mobilization of various linguistic strategies and discourses), we are left with a groundless constructionism. Talk is then just words, divorced from the material, historical and social conditions of its origin, and the world is no more than idealist speculation (Palmer 1990). A perspective that categorically denies the extra-discursive is, as Finn Collin rightly notes, a *reductio ad absurdum* of constructionist claims.

An example should clarify the points we have raised in this and the previous section. If we accept the relativist's claim that language is the only source whereby reality gets constructed, the resultant 'constructions' (whether individuals, selves, bodies or anything else) are effectively denied. For example, to state that 'the body' is a product of discourse is to state that it is epiphenomenal to the ways in which it is talked about and, therefore, that in and of itself it has no nature or properties – it is nothing more than a 'surface for textual inscription' (Burkitt 1998: 63). As Nightingale (1999) notes, this requires a 'uniform plasticity of the body . . . [wherein] all bodies (young/old, male/female, able-bodied/impaired) must be comparably write-able, so similar as to drop out of the equation, sufficiently malleable and homogeneous that bodily discourses may write over or through them as though they were not there.' This means that our lived experiences as embodied beings and our sensuous physical nature are forever denied.

Methodology

Although the methodologies utilized within relativistic inquiry are not necessarily problematic in and of themselves, the theories that inform these methodologies (and the assumptions that are subsequently drawn from them) often give rise to difficulties that further illustrate the issues we outlined above. For example, in seminars and debates we have seen relativists being questioned about the issue of power and its seeming absence from their analyses. Typically, they are asked: 'How can a micro-analysis of a particular transcript or interactive sequence ever hope to reference notions of institutional or societal power that are immanent to our understanding of the texts as social artefacts, but are not specifically referenced by the talk?' Faced with such questions, their strategy has been to pick up the transcript, peer at it in a confused and studious manner (perhaps turn it over and peer at it again) and declare 'No, sorry, can't see any power here.' Their now familiar point is to demonstrate their claim that we cannot transcend the text, we can only examine the data themselves – a banally empirical claim (Parker and Burman 1993: 160–6) – so as to identify the various linguistic strategies, rhetorical devices and so on that are being deployed. Of course, 'discourses', 'interpretative repertoires' and the like are no more self-evidently present in a transcript than is power, as novices to the practice of discourse analysis will confirm. Moreover, the written transcript here serves the same kind of function for relativists as those tables which realists like to thump in order to demonstrate their physical existence. The transcript, which is already a reductive, interpreted abstraction taken from a real inter-active sequence, is here rhetorically invoked as though it was in itself a warrant for the relativist position.

Elsewhere, Potter states that 'the full Jefferson Pilsner [a transcription system] . . . can throw up all kinds of reality construction business going on in talk' (Potter 1998: 36). While it is true that there are instances when we should be explicitly concerned with notions of 'reality construction' – in analyses of courtrooms and trials (where reality and truth are actively contested), within analyses of multiply authored texts and news reports (where the truth is being actively constructed) – to argue that this method is universally applicable to all analyses of language and talk is highly problematic. Cromby and Standen summarise these problems as follows:

> If what people say is shaped not only by the functional demands of the situation in which they currently find themselves but also by extra-discursive features of their embodiment and untranscribable elements of their personal histories, then it is possible that there are circumstances in which a functional discursive analysis of the static and disembedded transcript of a conversation would be so partial as to be inadequate, even invalid.
>
> (Cromby and Standen 1997)

They identify a number of circumstances within which the 'functional aspects of discourse are not highlighted because, simply put, the aims of the participants, the discursive achievements which they want to bring off, are not wholly apparent or present in the transcript which the analyst examines' (*ibid.*). These include circumstances wherein preceding events (either personal or social) exert a 'massive' but unspoken influence upon the transcript, and when the aims of the conversation do not extend any further than the simple maintenance of the conversation itself. 'In everyday language these moments when the functional aims of talk are non-existent, minor or subsidiary are usually described as "gossip" or "chat" (by highlighting these aspects of experience we also, conversely, draw attention to a masculinist, instrumentalist bias in discourse analysis and its assumption that all talk is goal directed)' (*ibid.*). In short, a discourse analysis explicitly grounded in relativism can be seen as a useful tool in certain circumstances, but is a method that will ultimately fail to describe or explain anything other than the locally contingent aims of particular instances of talk. It is a useful method in *certain circumstances*, but even within these circumstances can never offer more than a partial, textually contingent analysis of the particular functional aims of a particular piece of talk.

The preceding sections demonstrate what we see as some of the major theoretical, methodological and practical difficulties, errors and incoherent assumptions of relativism, which lead us to conclude that it is far from being the 'quintessentially academic position' that Edwards *et al.* claim. In contrast, the following sections seek to challenge what we see as some of the erroneous assumptions regarding realism that have been rhetorically deployed to (explicitly) denounce and misrepresent realist claims, assumptions which are then erroneously drawn upon to buttress relativistic claims further.

Misconceptions of realism

The god's eye view, 'bottom lines' and the 'simply real'

> Invocations of Furniture and Death are the stock in trade not, in prac-
> tice, of 'naïve realists', who, being universally recognised as persons
> made of straw, are unable to indulge, but of those sophisticated realists
> or moderate relativists for whom there has to be a bottom line, beyond
> which they refuse to go.
>
> (Edwards *et al.* 1995: 26)

A disconcerting trend in many defences of relativism is the nonchalant
introduction, often despite claims to the contrary, of naive and simplistic
stories regarding realism; specifically that realists are claiming a *knowable*,
bottom-line reality. While realism, in the context of this book and its
various chapters, presupposes some form of external reality it does not
presume that this reality is either directly perceptible or ultimately knowable. There is, as Hilary Putnam (1991: 109) rightly claims, no 'god's eye
view'; we do not have, nor will we ever have, any means whereby we might
transcend our earthly bonds and glance down upon the 'wonders of creation', nor would such a non-human view make much sense if we could
achieve it. However, while this is often cited as a knock-down argument by
relativists (see Chapter 1), it need not imply that we abandon all hope of
engaging with a world outside of language and discourse. As Niels Bohr
(1934: 53) noted, 'an independent reality in the ordinary physical sense can
be ascribed neither to the phenomena nor to the agencies of observation' –
and this from a physicist writing over sixty years ago.

Furthermore, these misrepresentations of realism are used in two contradictory ways: first, to demonstrate what are, supposedly, the fundamental
problems of realism; second, as explanatory devices *within* justifications of
relativism. For example, 'It is not obvious exactly where the line should be
drawn, between the objectively and the constructedly real, between rocks
and quarks, furniture and fascism. A principled questioning of *all truths
as claims* is the only assurance; whatever is simply real, if that means anything, will surely survive scrutiny' (Edwards *et al.* 1995: 26). It seems likely
that in this example the 'simply real', and its juxtaposition with 'if that
means anything', was contrived so that we might concede that there simply
is no real(ity) to be had. However, as we have already argued, the idea that
we can always be (radically) sceptical of every aspect of reality cannot be
maintained. Furthermore, the distinction that Edwards *et al.* draw between
the 'objectively and the constructedly' real does disservice to realists and
relativists alike, in that it merely replicates – rather than engages with – the
various dichotomies with which constructionist accounts are concerned:
realism/relativism, idealism/materialism, subjective/objective and so on. In
other words, they reference an external reality (the simply or objectively

real), but as a consequence of their commitment to relativism are rendered mute as to its nature.

Trickery and the textual ladder

> It is a kind of trickery when writers introduce reality in the form of specific descriptions of it, and then kick away the textual ladder and ask us to consider the thus-described reality as out-there.
>
> (Edwards et al. 1995: 31)

We would agree. An objective representation of reality or a 'specific description of it' (either deprived of its 'textual ladder' or with its rungs intact) is clearly not evidence that an 'out-there' reality exists independently of our engagement with it. However, as should be obvious by now, we would not wish to claim that it was. As noted above, to talk of an 'out-there' reality is to draw upon naive representations of realism; of an external and objective reality that is forever beyond the grasp of both relativists and realists alike.

While a number of the chapters within this book are specifically concerned with how the real may be incorporated into our social constructionist analyses, we include two final examples here. Both are concerned with issues of embodiment, and both demonstrate the inadequacies of a purely linguistic or textual analysis. The first reiterates the specific limitations of both relativism and a wholly linguistic or discursive analysis; the second explores the ways in which the incorporation of the extra-discursive may enhance and enrich our accounts of psychological and social reality (see also Nightingale 1999).

Considering the real

Post traumatic stress disorder

In a seminar at Bolton Institute, Yvonne McEwen described her concerns with the notion of post traumatic stress disorder (PTSD), arguing that its 'professional practices' serve to create victims of trauma rather than providing resolutions to the problems they may have incurred through their involvement in a crisis or other traumatic event (McEwan 1998). A section of the talk (which is necessarily decontextualized here) concerned Yvonne's role as a trauma officer at the time of the Lockerbie disaster. On 21 December 1998, Pan Am flight 103 from London Heathrow to John F. Kennedy Airport, New York, exploded in mid-air and crashed on to the Scottish town of Lockerbie killing 259 passengers and eleven people on the ground. Yvonne described how, nine months after the incident, she became involved with the case of a senior emergency services officer who had developed various problems since the incident. He was agitated, experienced night sweats and was becoming withdrawn. Prior to her meeting with him he had seen his doctor, who diagnosed depression and referred him to a psychologist. The psychologist, being unable to help, referred him to a psychiatrist, who arranged for him to have regular visits from a community psychiatric nurse. By this time, the man had become extremely disillusioned with the medical profession. The common diagnosis he had received was that of PTSD. However, despite this diagnosis and the various medical interventions suggested by it, his agitation had increased, his night sweats had worsened and he had become increasingly frustrated and withdrawn.

As critical psychologists (whether realist or relativist) we are probably tempted to intervene at this point, to interrupt the narrative, to challenge the seemingly oppressive, medicalized discourses of mental distress that appear to have informed these events. And we would be right to do so. When Yvonne got involved she visited him at his home and noticed that he had a tremor:

Yvonne: Greg, how long have you had that tremor?
Greg: Oh, probably about nine months now.
Yvonne: Did your doctor do a blood test?
Greg: No.

It eventually transpired that Greg had a 'thyroid condition', which when treated resolved the problems that numerous medical personnel had ascribed to PTSD. Yvonne's concern was with the ways in which the discourses of PTSD were so uncritically drawn upon by medical personnel to position Greg as a victim of trauma – he had been involved with the Lockerbie disaster, therefore he must be traumatized. The ways in which various forms of discursive or critical psychology could have intervened are obvious. The conversation analysts could have looked at the particular interactive sequences (or transcripts) of Greg's various meetings with the professionals. Those concerned with a more structural analysis could have explored the genealogy of PTSD and the ways in which the concept operated within current institutions and practices to define, oppress and marginalize. While we would agree that these forms of analysis are useful, and central to *any form* of constructionism, they would have been of no practical assistance *in this particular case*. Their failure would not have occurred because notions of PTSD, mental illness, depression, anxiety and withdrawal are not fundamentally social in origin; but because discursive reality is grounded in extra-discursive factors, which in this instance were crucial.

While the above demonstrates the ever present limitations of a purely linguistic account, what follows demonstrates how we might begin to weave other areas of (extra-discursive) knowledge into our constructionist accounts.

Neurology and the social construction of practical reason

But now I had before my eyes the coolest, least emotional, intelligent human being one might imagine, and yet his practical reason was so impaired that it produced, in the wanderings of daily life, a succession of mistakes, a perpetual violation of what would be considered socially appropriate and personally advantageous. He had an entirely healthy mind until a neurological disease ravaged a specific sector of his brain and, from one day to the next, caused this profound defect in decision making.

(Damasio 1994: xi–xii)

Antonio Damasio claims that our ability to make decisions (of even the simplest variety) involves a complex series of neurological processes. Specifically, he suggests that our ability to reach a decision depends not just on our rational or 'cognitive processes' but on our 'ability to experience feelings' (Damasio 1994: xii). In the case study above he shows that the patient's neurological insult damaged an area of the brain which usually functions to integrate our conscious thought processes with our feelings ('feelings' being the continual baseline sense of our own bodies that our nervous system provides us with, and that provides the raw neurophysiological material by which we experience emotions). He notes that subsequent to this damage, but not prior to it, his patient became unable to make even the simplest of decisions and once spent several hours attempting to decide which appointment (on two consecutive days some months hence) he should choose. Damasio queried him regarding his difficulties, and was informed that the problem was extremely complex and could not easily be resolved as there were so many variables to take into account. When Damasio suggested that it might be better to 'just pick one', the patient admitted that this 'obvious' solution had simply not occurred to him.

That neurological damage may change people in complex ways will probably not be questioned by many. Particular claims that specific areas of the brain are instrumentally involved with the nature of our behaviour and experiences are clearly more problematic. While we could easily deconstruct Damasio's account – attending to its linguistic construction and the various discursive resources that he inevitably calls upon, and in so doing produce alternative social, psychological and discursive accounts of these events – we ask you instead momentarily to suspend your disbelief. If we accept Damasio's claim that damage to an area of his patient's brain responsible for the integration of feelings and emotions with conscious thought severely impedes the operation of 'practical reason' (a claim which can, of course, be empirically verified), what might we make of this from a constructionist perspective? As mentioned, we could dismiss it in the ways we describe above. However, we believe that this example illustrates some of the ways in which we might begin to incorporate, rather than deny; wherein we might develop an account of our embodied being that transcends the either/or conceptions with which we are currently plagued.

The key point here is Damasio's (1994: xii) statement that the ability to make practical decisions depends upon the 'ability to experience feelings'. It is important to note that this is a phenomenological claim, a claim that our feelings are bound up with our lived experiences: they cannot simply be reduced to a particular area of the brain or neurological structure, however much they might be crucially dependent upon such a mechanism. Let us consider Damasio's account alongside constructionist analyses, which demonstrate that our emotions are mediated in and through the cultural and historical domain within which we reside (Harré 1987). We would, of course, need to recognize that what it means to make a practical decision is clearly also culturally and historically mediated. But having done so, we might then begin to draw together two domains of knowledge which are usually seen as oppositional. If practical decision-making (of which our understandings are social) depends upon our ability to experience feelings, and the ways in which we experience our feelings are mediated (or constructed) by our particular cultural and historical location, then variations in the ways that people make practical decisions are inextricably and necessarily bound up with both socio-cultural transformations *and* neurological processes. In this sense, rather than considering neurology as diametrically opposed to social constructionism (as essentialistic, biologistic etc.), the realist orientation we propose here suggests that neurological evidence can act to warrant our constructionist claims.

To put this another way, we might examine the ways in which practical decision-making is both socially constructed *and* neurological. In this sense, then, discourse analysis (or other constructionist methodologies) can both inform and be informed by neurological evidence concerning the relationship between our embodied experience (feelings and emotions), our lived skills and capacities (practical decision-making) and our neurophysiological nature. Our point is that such an analysis (potentially at least) provides a richer and more compelling narrative that would allow us to transcend the simply linguistic, the 'autistically self-enclosed . . . prison, in which there exist no doors leading out' (Freeman 1993: 223).

(And finally) Words fail us at this point

Analysis of discourse is like riding a bicycle compared to conducting experiments or analysing survey data which resemble baking cakes from a recipe . . . Just as with bike riding, it is not easy to convey the analytic process in abstract. Words fail us at this point.

(Potter and Wetherell 1987: 168)

As we stated in the introduction, the purpose of this chapter is to offer a series of 'rebuttals to relativism'; to demonstrate the fundamental ways in which we feel that relativism, as a theoretical perspective within which to ground social constructionism or broader notions of critical psychology, is both incoherent and fundamentally mistaken in its assumptions. However, arguments as to the nature of reality have a long history which we do not imagine will stop here. This final section demonstrates what we see as the consequences of adopting relativism. If our previous arguments have not convinced you, then let us demonstrate the necessarily narrow and impoverished nature of the psychology that results from a relativistic denial of our extra-discursive reality.

'Words fail us', 'I'm lost for words', 'I can't put it into words' express a trite but common sentiment; that the experiential aspects of our lives, which we often attempt to express, cannot always be captured or rendered meaningful (or meaningful enough) in language. Those sensuous aspects of experience – from riding a bicycle to a passionate first kiss, from the feel of the wind in our hair to the misery of a bad cold – that these can be talked about is not in question, that all there is to know about them can (always) be captured in language, or explained as a performative function of language, or that language somehow 'caused' the experience, are considerably more problematic claims to make. 'I didn't put that very well', 'You know what I mean' reference those occasions when we know that our language has failed us in some important way or another.

An example may clarify the points we wish to make. When my (David's) daughter was about three years old, I came home from work one day and as I opened the door she ran up the hall to greet me. As I bent down to pick her up she buried her face in my neck and sniffed. 'You smell nice,' she said. 'What do I smell like?' She pulled away from me and stood there for a few moments, frowning and looking puzzled. Suddenly, her face lit up and she declared triumphantly, 'You smell like a daddy!' That this was a social experience (thoroughly embedded with cultural and historical ways of being a parent and being a child) is not in doubt, nor would we wish to privilege the extra-discursive in this account, or claim that the experience may be reduced to it. However, a (discursive) psychology wherein 'words can never fail' is mute with respect to either their explanation or description.

Of course, it could be argued that a three-year-old's grasp of language is not sufficiently developed for her to deal with the all the subtle complexities of adult social interaction, and that our use of this example as evidence for an extra-discursive, experiential component of human existence is for us to 'overdetermine' her experience (as a young child) through the lens of our own experience (as socially 'developed' adults). In other words, it could be suggested that we are applying *our* discursive resources to account for what seems to us to be an expression of confusion regarding her experiences. However, we do not believe this is the case. There are many aspects of our own experience and histories (as both children and adults) that in their experiential living could be neither captured nor expressed as we might have wished: for example, the birth of our children, in our intimacies with others, and being present at the death of a parent after a long and painful illness. Our inability to express the extra-discursive aspects of these experiences is not a failure of our expressive abilities, it is a failure of language. Our lives are more than we can say.

Another way to approach this issue is to consider the often high cultural value we place upon the arts, specifically literature, and particularly poetry. Poetry's worth does not lie in its ability to *construct* realities (although its plausibility and technical competence may be judged in those terms) but is more often judged with respect to its capacity to transcend the normal, mundane and everyday aspects *of* such realities. It is not that it creates new experiences or realities of which we can vicariously partake (by providing discursive resources upon which we can draw, although clearly this does occur); but that, somehow, it captures those experiences and in its expression allows us to frame the experiential aspects of our lives in more comprehensive, 'truthful' or expressive ways – to put into words what we could not. The skill of great poets lies in their ability to 'disclose or reveal' (Freeman 1993: 223), not merely to perform.

Conclusion

> Emphasis must be moved away from abstract epistemological considerations of discursive knowledge and re-centred around an analysis of the processes that underpin these knowledging activities. In other words, constructionists must focus upon the development of a 'realist' ontology of the generative processes of the life world as opposed to an epistemological relativism regarding the necessarily contestable outcomes of such processes.
>
> (Nightingale, forthcoming)

In this chapter we have challenged and attempted to rebut the excesses of extreme relativism that pervade many areas of contemporary constructionist thought. This should not be taken as a condemnation of social constructionism, for as we have stated we are committed to a constructionist analysis of the human condition. However, it *is* a condemnation of those versions of constructionism that steadfastly refuse to engage with anything other than talk. While there are understandable reasons why many constructionists have so far failed (or refused) to theorize and take account of those extra-discursive aspects of our reality, we believe that the shortcomings of this position now render it untenable.

Bringing in the extra-discursive requires us to ditch the commitment to an all-encompassing relativism that underpins much contemporary constructionist work. We do not deny that relativism has served as a useful deconstructive tool, with which social constructionists and other critical psychologists have been able to challenge and undermine the oppression and marginalization consequent upon the 'truth claims' of mainstream psychology. But we have tried to show that its incoherences and inherent limitations renders it highly problematic as a framework within which we might pursue the *future* development of social constructionism or critical psychology.

While we agree that the nature of our being is such that we are always embedded within historical and cultural processes, our embodied and material nature cannot be dismissed or explained away as a simple consequence of those processes, as merely epiphenomenal to language. In this sense, relativism fails. Its systematic denial of the conditions that underpin and mediate the production of the knowledge it programmatically deconstructs renders it mute as to the nature of those conditions. In our view, the task we now face is that of integrating the extra-discursive, material and embodied aspects of our being into our constructionist frameworks – not to replace or supersede them, but to enhance them. As Potter (1998: 38) states (and admittedly in a somewhat different context from this one), 'get real!'

Acknowledgement

We would like to thank Dee Dempsey Nightingale, Rachel Fyson, Danny Goodley, Sharen Keim, Matthew King, Moshe Landsman and John Morss for their help in the preparation of this chapter.

References

Bohr, N. (1934) *Atomic Theory and the Description of Nature.* Cambridge: Cambridge University Press.

Burkitt, I. (1998) Bodies of knowledge: beyond Cartesian views of persons, selves and mind, *Journal for the Theory of Social Behaviour,* 28(1): 63–82.

Burman, E. (1990) Deconstructing social psychology, in I. Parker and J. Shotter (eds) *Deconstructing Social Psychology.* London: Routledge.

Burr, V. (1995) *An Introduction to Social Constructionism.* London: Sage.

Collin, F. (1997) *Social Reality.* London: Routledge.

Cromby, J. and Standen, P. (1997) The map is not the territory: discourse, bodies, selves, *Proceedings of the British Psychological Society,* 5(1): 42.

Damasio, A. R. (1994) *Descartes' Error: Emotion, Reason and the Human Brain.* London: Picador.

Davies, B. (1998) Psychology's subject: a commentary on the relativism/realism debate, in I. Parker (ed.) *Social Constructionism, Discourse and Realism.* London: Sage.

Eagleton, T. (1996) *The Illusions of Postmodernism*. Oxford: Blackwell.

Edwards, D., Ashmore, M. and Potter, J. (1995) Death and furniture: the rhetoric, politics and theology of bottom line arguments against relativism, *History of the Human Sciences*, 8(2): 25–49.

Foucault, M. (1972) *The Archaeology of Knowledge*. London: Tavistock.

Freeman, M. (1993) *Rewriting the Self: History, Memory, Narrative*. London: Routledge.

Frolov, D. and Schneider, A. (1992) Crime and punishment. Episode 10, Series 4 of *Northern Exposure* (television programme). Produced by Joshua Brand and John Falsey.

Gill, R. (1995) Relativism, reflexivity and politics: interrogating discourse analysis from a feminist perspective, in S. Wilkinson and C. Kitzinger (eds) *Feminism and Discourse: Psychological Perspectives*. London: Sage.

Harré, R. (ed.) (1987) *The Social Construction of Emotions*. Oxford: Blackwell.

Harré, R. (1992) What is real in psychology: a plea for persons, *Theory and Psychology*, 2(2): 153–8.

Harré, R. and Krausz, M. (1996) *Varities of Relativism*. Oxford: Blackwell.

McEwan, Y. (1998) Has trauma care become a travesty? Paper presented at the Critical Psychology Seminar Series, Bolton Institute, 26 November.

Nightingale, D. J. (1999) Bodies: reading the body, in I. Parker and the Bolton Discourse Network (eds) *Critical Textwork*. Buckingham: Open University Press.

Nightingale, D. J. (forthcoming) (Re)Theorising constructionism, in W. Maiers, B. Bayer, B. Duarte Esgalhado, R. Jorna and E. Schraube (eds) *Challenges to Theoretical Psychology*. York: Captus Press.

Palmer, B. D. (1990). *Descent into Discourse: The Reification of Language and the Writing of Social History*. Philadelphia: Temple University Press.

Parker, I. (1996) Against Wittgenstein: materialist reflections on language in psychology, *Theory and Psychology*, 6(3): 363–84.

Parker, I. (1998) Against postmodernism: psychology in cultural context, *Theory and Psychology*, 8(5): 601–28.

Parker, I. and Burman, E. (1993) Against discursive imperialism, empiricism and constructionism: thirty-two problems with discourse analysis, in E. Burman and I. Parker (eds) *Discourse Analytic Research: Repertoires and Readings of Texts in Action*. London: Routledge.

Potter, J. (1996) *Representing Reality: Discourse, Rhetoric and Social Construction*. London: Sage.

Potter, J. (1998) Fragments in the realization of relativism, in I. Parker (ed.) *Social Constructionism, Discourse and Realism*. London: Sage.

Potter, J. and Wetherell, M. (1987) *Discourse and Social Psychology: Beyond Attitudes and Behaviour*. London: Sage.

Putnam, H. (1991) *Representation and Reality*. Cambridge, MA: MIT Press.

Rorty, R. (1979) *Philosophy and the Mirror of Nature*. Princeton, NJ: Princeton University Press.

Sampson, E. E. (1989) The deconstruction of the self, in J. Shotter and K. Gergen (eds) *Texts of Identity*. London: Sage.

Sarbin, T. R. and Kitsuse, J. I. (eds) (1994) *Constructing the Social*. London: Sage.

Searle, J. (1995) *The Construction of Social Reality*. London: Penguin.

Sokal, A. and Bricmont, J. (1998) *Intellectual Impostures*. London: Profile Books.

Glossary

Cartesian dualism. René Descartes's (1596–1650) famous assertion – *cogito ergo sum* (I think, therefore I am) – lies at the heart of his 'method of doubt', wherein he challenged the validity of anything other than the simple fact that he was a thinking being. The legacy of this approach is Cartesian dualism, where mind and consciousness (*res cogitans*) are separated from everything else – the material world, the body, the brain (*res extensa*).

Critical psychology is a term that covers a range of perspectives that challenge (are critical of) the theories and practices of mainstream psychology, from approaches that aim to give voice to those oppressed by psychology to those that seek to undermine and destabilize the disciplinary practices of mainstream approaches.

Critical realism is a perspective that recognizes that knowledge is not and can never be an objective, unmediated reflection of external reality. However (in contrast to relativism), it stresses that 'real' processes and structures (economic, social, neurological etc.) underpin and generate observable and experienceable phenomena. See Chapter 3.

Deconstruction(ism) arose within literary theory and is concerned with the exploration or unravelling of the often 'hidden' internal contradictions, assumptions and repressed meanings of a text, discourse or practice. By revealing these repressed meanings, deconstructive analyses function to destabilize, subvert and resist dominant forms of knowledge.

A discourse is a set of images, written texts, beliefs, metaphors (and anything else that can be 'read' for meaning) that shape, inform or construct a particular practice or 'phenomenon'. Within contemporary social constructionism there are two broad understandings of this term: (a) that discourses are 'practices that systematically form the objects of which they speak' (Michel Foucault), in other words, that discourses create or determine the nature of reality; and (b) that discourses are social and cultural resources that people can draw upon to warrant or explain their activities and the activities of others.

Discourse analysis is an umbrella term for the various ways in which we can analyse discourses. Such analyses depend, however, upon our definition of 'discourse'. Those forms of analysis that draw upon Foucault's conception of discourse are concerned with a historical (or genealogical) analysis of the development of particular forms of knowledge and the ways in which such knowledges construct our reality. Those who see discourses as cultural or social resources are often concerned with particular interactive sequences – with the performative and functional aspects of people's talk.

Discursive psychology is a term used to categorize social constructionist or critical psychological approaches that are concerned with the analysis of language and discourse.

Embodiment (within the context of this book) means to be within a body. We have used the term to indicate that we see bodies as central to our concerns as psychologists, not as a biological vessel within which a separate 'person' resides but as a fundamental component of personhood. To be a person is always to be an embodied person.

Empiricism is the belief that valid knowledge can be obtained only through experience. Within (mainstream) psychology this takes the form of an adherence to objective and scientific observation and experimentation.

Epistemology is the branch of philosophy concerned with the theory of knowledge. Typical epistemological questions are: What is knowledge and where does it come from? What are the limits of our knowledge? What validity do our knowledge claims have?

Essentialism is the belief that the nature of objects (including people) is determined by their internal properties or essences. Much mainstream psychology is essentialistic. For example, notions such as personality, cognitive structures and processes, and the self are all discussed as though they are the objective and inherent properties of individuals.

Ethnomethodology literally means 'people's methods'. Coined by the socio-logist Harold Garfinkel, it is a term that draws our attention to the ways in which people construct the world (as opposed to the world being con-structed by social structures). It is often referenced within social construc-tionism, as one of Garfinkel's concerns was with the role of language in the everyday construction and maintenance of reality.

Grammar is a term used by Wittgenstein in his analysis of the role of lan-guage in the constitution of reality. It differs from the everyday definition of the term in that Wittgenstein was concerned not with the abstract rules that govern the use of language, but with language-in-use, i.e. the practical ways in which we employ language in everyday talk. Such an investigation, he suggests, allows us to investigate the organization or evolutionary structure of our concepts – the fundamental ways in which we construct our world.

Idealism is the belief that the world is (somehow) created by (or only exists within) the mind. In other words, material objects (including people) exist as nothing more than thoughts or objects of perception.

Intentionality (within phenomenology) refers to the consciousness/world relation and stresses that one is always linked to the other. Consciousness is always consciousness of something: we are frightened *of* something, think-ing *about* something, yearning *for* something.

Materialism is the philosophical belief that everything that exists either is 'matter' or depends upon matter for its existence.

Materiality (within this book) references the ways in which our experiences are always grounded in various material aspects of both ourselves (biology, neurology, physiology etc.) and the world.

Ontology is the study of the fundamental nature of reality.

Perspectivism (see also *relativism*) is the view that the external world is interpreted through alternative systems of beliefs and concepts and that there is no means of establishing that one view is necessarily any 'better' than another.

Phenomenology is a philosophical perspective developed by Edmund Husserl that seeks to overcome the objective/subjective (or idealism/materialism) dualism. It draws attention to the ways in which our conscious relation to the world is neither subjective (merely of the mind) nor a simple conse-quence of objective reality. See *intentionality*.

Positivism is the belief that the world as it is given to observation (experi-mentation, perception etc.) is the way that the world actually is. In particular, that questions that cannot be answered by scientific methods must remain forever unanswered.

Postmodernism (*after* modernism) can be defined in many ways but is most often used to denote the cultural expression of a postmodern age wherein such notions as truth, objectivity, reason and other grand narratives have been superseded by notions of diversity, instability, fragmentation and indeterminacy.

Post-structuralism is often presented as though it was synonymous with *post-modernism*. However, while the recent history of postmodernism may be traced through architecture and art more generally, post-structuralism has its roots in literary theory. It arose as a challenge to linguistic claims regarding the meaning of signs (words) and demonstrated that such meanings are not fixed or stable, but are always changing and contestable.

Power: see Chapter 1 for an extended discussion of this term.

Praxis is a term derived from the writings of Karl Marx. It denies the separation of theory and practice, emphasizing instead that ideas emerge in real situations, both informing them and being informed by them. Therefore, critical activity is simultaneously practical activity.

Realism is the belief that reality exists independently of our representations of it. While realists are often concerned with ontological questions as to the nature of reality, debates concerning realism and relativism often 'spill over' into epistemological debates regarding the status of particular beliefs or knowledge. It should be noted, however, that ontological realism (claims regarding the nature of the world) need not imply epistemological realism (that we can have objective knowledge of the world). See also *critical realism* and Chapters 1 and 14.

Reductionism is the belief that complex phenomena may be explained by reference to or as a consequence of less complex processes or phenomena: for example, that human behaviour may be explained as driven by genetics (sociobiology), by schedules of reinforcement (behaviourism) or by thoughts and cognitions (cognitive psychology).

Reflexivity is a term used: (a) to describe the ways in which a theory may be turned back upon itself and its practices; and (b) to explore the ways in which a researcher's involvement with a particular study influences, act upon and informs such research.

Relativism is a bad thing (see Chapters 1 and 14). But, more seriously, relativism is the belief that there are no grounds for postulating or investigating a reality independent of the knower; that there is no ultimate truth and, therefore, no ground for presuming that any one truth claim is 'better' than any other. There are many forms of relativism, including ontological relativism, epistemic (or epistemological) relativism and moral relativism. See also Chapters 1 and 14.

Social constructionism is an umbrella term that describes a set of approaches within contemporary psychology that are opposed to the empiricism and positivism of mainstream psychology. Broadly, social constructionists are concerned with the ways in which social and psychological reality are actively constructed (rather than pre-existing) phenomena.

Solipsism is an extreme form of *idealism* wherein the only presumed reality is the consciousness of one individual. If I were a solipsist there could be no others, as everything (people, the world, material reality etc.) is the sole product of my mind.

Subjectivity is used within social constructionism to refer to people's experiences of identity and the self. It is explored not as the property of an individual psyche, but as a product of particular social and cultural arrangements or local interactions.

Symbolic interactionism developed from the work of George H. Mead and is concerned with the self–society relationship as a product of symbolic communication between social actors. Symbolic interactionists tend to see society not as external to individuals, but as emerging from the numerous interactions of social actors.

Text: see *discourse*.

Umwelt is a term that refers to those aspects of our world that we can explore through our senses (or extensions of our senses, such as telescopes, scanning electron microscopes, Geiger counters). It references an external world but it is a world that we can only ever know in limited ways.

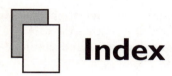

Index

CRITICAL TEXTWORK
AN INTRODUCTION TO VARIETIES OF DISCOURSE AND ANALYSIS

Ian Parker and the Bolton Discourse Network

- What is a text?
- Can discourse analysis help our understanding even when a text is not spoken or written?
- How can we use discourse analytic approaches for different varieties of text?

This clearly-written and innovative introduction to discourse analysis for the uninitiated takes a broad view, building on a range of studies carried out on different kinds of text. The chapters work through examples of analysis on many texts that are beyond the range of spoken and written material usually tackled by discourse researchers.

Methodological issues of reading and representation are explored in critical descriptions of how we might read such things as advertising, bodies, comics, film, letters, organizations, sign languages and other language systems. The book illustrates ways in which discourse may be studied wherever there is meaning, and it accessibly introduces the principles of discourse research to conversations, interviews, newspaper articles and fiction, providing an overview of existing research on these kinds of texts.

Critical Textwork is a comprehensive introductory text for students of discourse across the social sciences, including psychology, critical studies, sociology and human geography. It looks at the organization of language and examines ways of reading texts to excavate and illuminate signs in cultural life.

Contents
Foreword – Introduction: varieties of discourse and analysis – Interviews: meaning in groups – Letters: embracing letter writing within discourse analysis – Fiction: five run round together – clearing a discursive space for children's literature – Lessons: philosophy for children – Comics: strip semiotics – Advertising: critical analysis of images – Television: signs on the box – Film: a surface for writing social life – Cities: resident readers and others – Organizations: breaking the body of the text – Gardens: planning and presentation – Sign language: space, community and identity – Bodies: reading the body – Ethnography: reading across culture – Silence: absence and context – Action: self-advocacy and change – Index.

240pp   0 335 20204 7 (pbk)   0 335 20205 5 (hbk)

APPLIED DISCOURSE ANALYSIS
SOCIAL AND PSYCHOLOGICAL INTERVENTIONS

Carla Willig (ed.)

- What is 'applied discourse analysis'?
- How can discourse analysis inform social and psychological interventions?
- What are the advantages and disadvantages of these applications?

Discourse analysis has become increasingly popular as a research tool in psychology and as a subject taught on undergraduate courses. However, discourse analysts have been reluctant to move beyond deconstruction and to make recommendations for practice in the social world. This book seeks to identify ways in which discourse analytic research can inform recommendations for social and psychological practice. It presents six detailed discussions of discourse analytic studies, each of which engages with a contemporary social practice: reproductive technologies, police-suspect interviewing, stress self-help literature, sex education, clinical diagnoses of 'schizophrenia' and cigarette smoking. These six chapters map out a continuum of orientations to application, ranging from a clear commitment to specific interventions to a position of cautious engagement. The book concludes with a summary and evaluation of the ways in which discourse analysis may be used to reconcile the spirit of deconstruction with a commitment to practical application.

Contents
Foreword – Introduction: making a difference – Stress as regimen: critical readings of self-help literature – 'It's your opportunity to be truthful': disbelief, mundane reasoning and the investigation of crime – An analysis of the discursive positions of women smokers: implications for practical interventions – Deconstructing and reconstructing: producing a reading on 'human reproductive technologies' – Discourse analysis and sex education – Tablet talk and depot discourse: discourse analysis and psychiatric medication – Conclusion: opportunities and limitations of 'applied discourse analysis' – Glossary – Index.

176pp   0 335 20226 8 (pbk)   0 335 20227 6 (hbk)